Flip the System US

This powerful and honest book uncovers how we can flip the system, building a more democratic, equitable, and cohesive society where teacher expertise drives solutions to education challenges. Editor Michael Soskil brings together a team of diverse voices to highlight solutions, spark positive change, and show us the path forward towards a more civil and more peaceful America. In each chapter, inspiring educators describe how we can create lasting and meaningful change by elevating teacher expertise; educating the whole child; increasing teacher morale; and fighting for all of our children to have equitable opportunity and quality schools.

Michael Soskil is an author, an international keynote speaker, and has spent the past 22 years in various teaching roles. He is a Pennsylvania Teacher of the Year, a recipient of the US Presidential Award for Excellence in Math and Science Teaching, and in 2016 was announced as one of the top ten teachers in the world and a finalist for the Global Teacher Prize.

Flip the System: Changing Education from the Ground Up
Jelmer Evers, René Kneyber

Flip the System UK: A Teachers' Manifesto
Lucy Rycroft-Smith, Jean-Louis Dutaut

Flip the System Australia: What Matters in Education
Deborah M. Netolicky, Jon Andrews, Cameron Paterson

Flip the System US

How Teachers Can Transform Education
and Save Democracy

Edited by
Michael Soskil

Routledge
Taylor & Francis Group

NEW YORK AND LONDON

First published 2021
by Routledge
52 Vanderbilt Avenue, New York, NY 10017

and by Routledge
2 Park Square, Milton Park, Abingdon, Oxon OX14 4RN

Routledge is an imprint of the Taylor & Francis Group, an informa business

Library of Congress Cataloging-in-Publication Data
Names: Soskil, Michael, editor.
Title: Flip the system US : how teachers can transform education and save democracy / edited by Michael Soskil.
Identifiers: LCCN 2020034002 | ISBN 9780367374563 (paperback) | ISBN 9780367374570 (hardback) | ISBN 9780429354601 (ebook)
Subjects: LCSH: Educational change–United States. | Democracy and education–United States. | Educational equalization–United States. | Teachers–Professional relationships–United States. | Teachers–In-service training–United States.
Classification: LCC LA217.2 .F59 2021 | DDC 370.973–dc23
LC record available at https://lccn.loc.gov/2020034002

ISBN: 978-0-367-37457-0 (hbk)
ISBN: 978-0-367-37456-3 (pbk)
ISBN: 978-0-429-35460-1 (ebk)

Typeset in Sabon
by Taylor & Francis Books

Contents

Illustrations

Figures

Tables

About the Editor

Michael Soskil is an author, an international keynote speaker, and has spent the past 22 years in various teaching roles. He is a Pennsylvania Teacher of the Year, has received the Presidential Award for Excellence in Math and Science Teaching, and in 2016 was announced as one of the top-10 teachers in the world and a finalist for the Global Teacher Prize.

The book that Michael co-authored, *Teaching in the Fourth Industrial Revolution: Standing at the Precipice*, has received international acclaim and has been translated into multiple languages. Articles that he has written have appeared in the *Washington Post, Education Week, Education Post*, and various other publications.

In addition to teaching, writing, and speaking, Michael is Vice-President of the Pennsylvania Teachers Advisory Committee, a non-profit organization that is working to ensure every decision that impacts students is informed by teacher expertise. He lives in northeastern Pennsylvania with his wife Lori, an award-winning high school science teacher, and two children who inspire him on a regular basis. See www.michaelsoskil.com

Acknowledgements

As I write this, millions of teachers across the United States and around the world are rising to meet the challenge of continuing education during a global pandemic. They are innovating ways to build human connection in a time of distancing and isolation. They are researching and learning how to use new resources. They are networking, sharing, and supporting each other. Most importantly, they are doing what they do best: caring for and protecting their students.

Teachers are heroes. This has never been more apparent than during this crisis, and I have never been prouder to have chosen this profession. To every teacher who helped me during my time as a student, every colleague who has pushed me to be better for my students, every educator who has helped my own children develop into the exceptional people they are, each of the thousands of conference attendees I've gotten to meet and learn from the past few years, and all of the other teachers who are dedicated to ensuring the next generation has a successful, democratic future—I thank you. This book is for you.

A few of those teachers deserve individual recognition, as this book wouldn't have been possible without them. I am blessed to get to witness the love and dedication that my wife, Lori, shows for her students on a daily basis. The inspiration she provides me as a teacher, along with her incredible support, have made it possible for me to dive into projects like this. Often, when I think about how our education system would be better if it were driven by the expertise of teachers, it is her voice that I imagine needing to be elevated.

Special thanks go to Mairi Cooper, Jinni Forcucci, and Jelmer Evers. From the moment I began considering this project, Mairi has been there to support me, help me organize my thoughts, and provide critical feedback. Jinni was instrumental in helping develop the focus and many of the main ideas in this book, and in pushing me to make sure student voices were represented. None of this would have happened if Jelmer hadn't suggested I edit an American version of Flip the System a few years ago, encouraged me on several occasions to get started, and provided me any help I needed after I agreed.

Several others also made important contributions. I'd like to thank Cameron Paterson, Deborah Netolicky, and the other editors of past Flip the System books, who supplied invaluable advice through this process. Marilyn Pryle was always willing to read and give editing suggestions on my writing, and I am grateful for her insightfulness. My publisher, Lauren Davis, has been amazingly helpful in guiding me through this undertaking and in offering suggestions. I am appreciative of the mentorship that Shanna Peeples has provided over the past few years and the effort she spent developing my capacity to do this kind of work. David Edwards and Armand Doucet were generous with both their time and assistance from the beginning. Jennifer Williams, Koen Timmers, Katherine Hernandez, Matt Miller, Brian McDaniel, Dyane Smokorowski, Alex Harper, Eric Crouch, Miriam Mason, Naomi Volain, and Yasodai Selvakumaran all motivated me with the excitement they expressed for the project and ideas they shared at different times.

My children, Abigail and Michael, have my thanks and deserve a mention, as they were willing to put up with me rambling on about ideas that were bouncing around my head for the past year, as well as being willing to share their own school experiences to give me an important student perspective.

Of course, this work would have been impossible if not for the exceptional contributions of the chapter authors. Each of them added their unique perspective, shared their expertise, and helped shape my thinking in profound ways. I am a better educator, a better advocate, a better writer, a better editor, and a better person because of their willingness to participate.

Finally, I want to thank all of those who are fighting for more democratic systems—in education, in government, and in our economies. All of these systems need to be flipped. All must be driven by the experiences of those closest to the practical implications of policy decisions. I hope this book gives you hope, gives you ideas to continue your work, and lets you know that there are many others by your side. As Helen Keller said, "Alone we can do so little; together we can do so much."

Michael Soskil
Newfoundland, Pennsylvania

Introduction

Michael Soskil

Moments of consequence often happen when we least expect them. I was at a conference, drinking a large Peppermint Patty mocha by a fireplace in Hershey, Pennsylvania, when Mairi Cooper first approached me about helping create an organization that would elevate teacher expertise. We had never met before. At that time, in 2016, Mairi was serving as Pennsylvania's Teacher of the Year, and I had just been announced as a Top 10 Finalist for the Global Teacher Prize. Before I had finished my coffee, she convinced me to join her. I was excited to help create structure for teachers to inform the decisions that impact our students.

Many stakeholders in the American education system have genuine motives in trying to provide a quality, equitable education for all children. However, a lack of teacher input informing policy decisions has led to unforeseen negative impact on our students and an undervaluing of teachers as professionals. Expressed simply, those making the most important decisions that affect the children in our schools don't know what they don't know. The rigid hierarchical education systems at the federal, state, and local levels rarely demand that teacher expertise makes it to the level of policy makers. Decisions made without intimate knowledge of the lived experiences of those who will be impacted, like the context and narrative that teachers can provide, are doomed to suffer from unintended consequences.

It was shortly after the fireplace conversation in Hershey that I met Jelmer Evers at the Global Education and Skills Forum in Dubai. He shared his vision of "Flipping the System," (completely unrelated to "flipped classrooms" where teachers assign videos for students to watch outside class) This model, detailed in the book he edited with René Kneyber (Evers & Kneyber, 2016), called for a flattened educational hierarchy and renewed teacher professionalism. (Figure 0.1) I instantly understood how a flipped American education system would bridge the divide between decision makers and classroom practitioners.

Much has changed since those two formative conversations in 2016. In fact, the world is changing at a faster pace than ever before in human

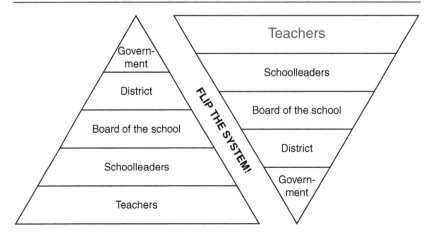

Figure 0.1 Original "Flip the System" Model

history. The book that Jelmer and I co-authored with four other Global Teacher Prize finalists in 2018, *Teaching in the Fourth Industrial Revolution: Standing at the Precipice*, showed how the exponential growth of technological innovation is transforming our human interactions and impacting our schools (Doucet, et al., 2018). In that book I made the case that the keys to building a cohesive and prosperous society in this time of upheaval were:

- finding a balance between technology and humanity in schools;
- focusing on the uniquely human ability of teachers to show and teach empathy; and
- using technology as a tool for closing equity gaps rather than widening them (Soskil, 2018).

We are woefully deficient in meeting those ideals in our schools, in our nation, and worldwide. Social media is creating ideological bubbles among voters, spreading false information at unprecedented rates, and being wielded as a weapon by schoolchildren and politicians. In an example of Orwellian doublethink, "personalized learning" that has computers choosing academic content for students is rising in prominence at the expense of true personalized learning—driven by student interest, relationships, and human interaction with a teacher. Top-down evaluation systems are forcing teachers, increasingly demoralized by a lack of autonomy and agency, to focus on easily obtained and quantified data rather than empathy, humanity, and student wellbeing. We want our children and our citizens to learn to think for themselves, but increasingly allow technology companies that harvest our data to influence our choices or make them for us.

A democracy cannot function well and serve the needs of the people without educated, engaged citizens. Throughout its history, the prosperity of the United States and the health of the country's education system have been linked. As suffrage expanded from a small group of white, male property owners in the late 18th century to include a broader constituency, so too did our education system expand to include children of every race, creed, and economic background. The expansion of liberty, knowledge, and economic opportunity created by these reforms fueled the country's rise as a global superpower.

At this pivotal moment in our history when personal liberties, respect for intellectualism, and economic opportunity are threatened by an erosion of democratic norms, we must examine our education system by asking both if public education is supporting democracy, and if our democracy is supporting public education.

This book is borne out of the necessity to improve both sides of this relationship. Politicians increasingly use campaign tactics that spread false information and prey on the emotional insecurities of voters. At the same time, lawmakers denigrate and disparage teachers who are trying to develop critical thinking and rational thought that would make these campaign tactics less effective. For decades, federal and state education policy has been driven by what is politically and economically advantageous to those in power rather than by what strengthens our society. At the school level, many mission statements include language about creating engaged and active citizens, but then refuse to allow input from the teachers and students in classrooms when making decisions. Engaged citizens cannot be developed in places where democracy is absent.

The call of the contributors in this book to "flip the system" is inherently a call to restore the United States education system to its roots as the foundation of American democracy. Teachers serve where educational policy and practice meet the plethora of lived experiences of our nation's children. The expertise that is contained within the teaching profession must be central in both the daily decisions made in schools and the policies that shape the system itself. Teachers are uniquely positioned to understand both the individual and collective needs of our students.

While our public schools cannot alone fix all of our societal ills, schools and the communities they serve have always been intimately intertwined. The health of the community has a profound impact on the quality of the school, and the success of the school is a determining factor in the wellbeing of the community. Since the United States is composed of thousands of diverse communities around the country, the symbiotic relationship between communities and public schools is the foundation upon which the health of our nation resides. Indisputably, a public education system that does not equitably serve the needs of all communities or does not serve the holistic needs of all children is a threat to national welfare. Just as a patient with a healthy pancreas, liver, kidneys, and lungs, but a failing heart is not healthy, America is not healthy if some of our communities, schools, and neighbors are suffering from poverty, violence, lack of opportunity, or systematic marginalization.

If schools are the heart of our communities, then teachers are the heart of our schools. When you ask successful individuals about their time in school that prepared them for success, they don't talk about great textbooks, technology that was available, or well-designed curricula. It is the narrative of teachers that they remember and recount. They share stories of teachers who helped them through difficult times, teachers who inspired them to love learning, and teachers who helped them see their value. Schools can only be successful if the teachers in them are able to do these things. The quality of a school cannot surpass the quality of the teachers who are directly interacting with children inside.

But our teaching profession is in crisis. Revitalizing our public schools must begin from the inside out by strengthening support and respect for our teachers. Few of our talented youngsters are choosing to teach because it is not seen as a desirable career. Individuals, companies, and organizations outside our schools have too often used their financial and political influence to denigrate teachers and marginalize teacher associations for their own benefit. In our current political system that is driven by super PACs, dark money campaign donations, and lobbyists, those on a teacher's salary are at a serious disadvantage compared to billionaires, hedge fund managers, and behemoth for-profit corporations.

Many who do decide to become teachers leave within the first five years because of crippling student loans or the crushing emotional toll caused by a lack of adequate resources. Others are frustrated by the disconnect between the demands of the system and the reason they choose the profession. These teachers intended to develop the unique talents of their students and prepare the next generation for their complex future. Instead, they learned that the system places far more value on testing, data collection, and covering curricular content. These factors are also causing veteran teachers to leave the profession before retirement. Just as our students are struggling with historic levels of anxiety, depression, and self-harm, too many of our teachers are dealing with mental health issues. It is unrealistic to expect our educators to nurture students when they are not well themselves.

None of these issues are inherently American, and there is no reason why we cannot find the will to overcome them. In the United States, we know how to do public education well. Many of our communities are served by excellent public schools—among the best performing in the world. Yet, we choose not to provide the benefits of quality public education to all. While some communities are afforded beautiful school buildings, fairly compensated and qualified teachers, rich arts and humanities programs, and safe schools, others are not. Children in economically depressed communities are faced with partially condemned schools contaminated by asbestos and mold, unqualified teachers, a curriculum stripped down to "core" academic subjects and learning environments that feel like prisons. Potential is evenly distributed among children in the United States, but opportunity is not.

It is not shocking that a system wrought with such inequity has failed to produce the societal outcomes to which we aspire. America is more polarized than at any time in recent history, our democracy is strained, and there is a massive disparity between the health of our affluent communities, and that of our poorer urban and rural communities. A tiny number of wealthy individuals have consolidated more money and political power than the most disadvantaged 50% of the country combined.

I have long held that whatever the question, education is the answer. Yet, if we are to believe that education is a solution, we must also acknowledge that flaws in our education system were a factor in creating some of the problems in our democratic society.

This book strives to look critically at our shortcomings, but also focus on current and possible solutions. It is not comprehensive, as no one book could examine every one of the complexities that face our education system or our democracy. Each contributor brings her/his unique, diverse perspective. Not all agree on some of the topics in the book—nor would I want them to. Problems in a democracy are complex and messy, and our conversations on how to solve them need to be equally nuanced. My hope is that each chapter provides the basis for an important conversation that needs to take place and a spark for positive change that will move us closer to both a more democratic education system and a country with renewed faith in democratic values.

Each of the five sections delves into a different aspect of how education and democracy need to support each other. The first looks at how the two interact, and the role of our schools in a healthy democratic society. The second section examines how we can build a more equitable system, because democracy cannot thrive when inequity and marginalization limit the opportunity of some members. In the third section, the chapters give us insight into the mental health crisis in our schools and provide solutions so that all of our children are holistically well and able to participate in our democracy. Section four looks at the structural changes and professional responsibilities that must be transformed to produce teacher agency at the local, state, and national level. Finally, the fifth section shows how the system can support teachers so that they can best fulfill their roles as practitioners and professionals.

Evers and Kneyber showed us how the traditional top-down hierarchy must be flipped. Afterward, teachers in the UK and Australia edited books examining how this could be accomplished in those countries (Rycroft-Smith & Dutaut, 2018; Netolicky et al., 2019). Now, for the sake of our country, we must start working toward a flipped American public education system.

We can no longer tell teachers what to do, how to do it, and when it needs to be completed without accounting for the unique needs in their classrooms and communities. This prevents the most important information—the experiences of children in classrooms—from reaching those developing policies. Governments, superintendents, school leaders, teachers, parents, and students have to see the others as partners in the process of educating the community rather than rungs in a bureaucratic ladder. A rejuvenated and respected teaching profession with a reclaimed identity as the foundation of American democracy must be prioritized. Instead of vertical accountability, we need structures for lateral decision making and oversight.

Building these structures and the capacity of teachers within them is exactly what Mairi and I continue to work toward with others on the Pennsylvania Teachers Advisory Committee—the organization catalyzed by the fireplace discussion in Hershey. My hope is that this book sparks more educators to have conversations like the one we had: about creating organizations to connect teachers to policy makers, about starting grassroots movements within unions and communities to advocate for student and teacher needs, about changing teaching practices to engender civic activism, about fighting for more equitable opportunities for marginalized communities, about demanding education that meets the holistic needs of all children, about networking to support and empower each other.

I am an optimist, and I have always believed in the power of teachers to affect positive change in their communities, in our nation, and in the world. This book emanates from that optimism and provides us a path forward to a more democratic, more cohesive, more equitable, more civil, more prosperous, more peaceful America. Education is the answer. Teachers will save our democracy if we flip the system.

References

Doucet, A., Evers, J., Guerra, E., Lopez, N., Soskil, M., & Timmers, K. (2018). *Teaching in the Fourth Industrial Revolution Standing at the Precipice*. New York: Routledge.

Evers, J., & Kneyber, R. (Eds.). (2016). *Flip the System: Changing Education from the Ground Up*. New York: Routledge.

Netolicky, D., Andrews, J., & Paterson, C. (Eds.). (2019). *Flip the System Australia: What Matters in Education*. New York: Routledge.

Rycroft-Smith, L., & Dutaut, J. L. (Eds.). (2018). *Flip the System UK: A Teachers' Manifesto*. New York: Routledge.

Soskil, M. (2018). Education in a Time of Unprecedented Change. In A. Doucet, J. Evers, E. Guerra, N. Lopez, M. Soskil, & K. Timmers, *Teaching in the Fourth Industrial Revolution Standing at the Precipice*. New York: Routledge.

Part I

Public Education as the Foundation of Democratic Society

An educated electorate is critical to a successful democracy. There is, of course, a difference between being "knowledgeable" and being "educated." The former involved knowing facts and information, while the latter is much more comprehensive. True education includes comprehension of how knowledge intersects with our understanding of ourselves, the context in which our learning occurs, the perspectives of others around us, and how information can be applied to situations outside school. Healthy democracy demands an educated populace, not just a knowledgeable one.

In the decentralized United States education system, state and local jurisdictions have a great deal of influence over curriculum decisions, policies, and the role of teachers. This is important because public schools are, and will continue to be, intimately intertwined culturally and financially with our communities. Decision making is most effective when decisions are driven by those who are impacted most.

A challenge that we have is coordinating those state and local education systems to educate for societal health in their states and communities, but also for our American society. Are there universal values on which education should rest? What is the purpose of education in a democracy? What skills and competencies should our students learn in order to be informed and engaged citizens? How do we do this in our schools and classrooms?

These are some of the questions the authors in Part I will try to answer.

In Chapter 1, **Dennis Shirley** explains how an evolution from old educational practices to new imperatives for educational change can produce a flipped system with integrity that can better serve our democracy.

Next, **Estella Owoimaha-Church** (Chapter 2) provides insight into how we can engender civic activism by sharing the results of a student focus group and allowing teenagers to explain what teaching practices are effective—and what makes them disengage.

Gert Biesta (Chapter 3) then provides a detailed examination of the purpose of education in a democracy, explaining that a balance is needed between preparing students for the work they will do after graduation, helping them find themselves as individuals, and assisting them in understanding their place in our society.

In Chapter 4, Michael Soskil delves into the need for our schools and classrooms to reflect the democratic norms we are trying to develop by sharing examples from his own classroom and a school that is based in a democratic philosophy.

Chapter 1

An American Education System with Integrity

Dennis Shirley

This chapter provides a vision for American education in which evidence, teacher expertise, global context, and knowledge of the unique needs and situations of students fuel the system and coincide with a stronger teaching profession. The author asserts that an education system grounded in these new imperatives of educational change and renewed teacher professionalism is critical to transform education and improve democracy in the United States. By overturning an overly bureaucratic and unresponsive system that limits students' potential and replacing it with a system that is flexible and inclusive of diverse perspectives and opinions, we can shape a future of which we can be proud.

What would it mean to "flip" the American educational system, and to do so in a way that doesn't inadvertently exacerbate previously existing problems, but actually moves us forward in a fundamentally new and better direction? Looking back on decades of reform, it's hard not to conclude that in spite of honorable intentions and herculean efforts, at the ground level of our schools and classrooms many reforms have reinforced a traditional grammar of schooling in which emphasis has been placed upon teacher-centered instruction, rigorously sequenced curricula, and elaborate assessments. The effort to streamline teaching and learning and to guide the whole constellation of potential practices in the direction of tests has had many arguments on its behalf and is perfectly attuned for those who place a premium on accountability.

For those with other ends in mind however—such as the preparation of critical and self-directed thinkers who view the strengthening of democracy as not just one option among many, but as an essential task of public schools in an age of democratic decline—a different kind of education is needed. This would be a system designed from the ground up to prepare students to examine multiple perspectives on complex matters, to provide opportunities for spirited debate in the search of the unencumbered truth, and to be willing to do the hard work of compromise and negotiation in the interests of advancing the public good. Such an education cannot be achieved, however, when prominent advocacy groups like the National

Council on Education and the Economy (NCEE) use all of their considerable clout to try to get Americans to focus on "surpassing Shanghai" on international large-scale assessments (Tucker, 2011). The greatest value of such rhetoric is that it lays bare the authoritarian premises of so many recent reforms for all to see.

The odd paradox of our time is that at the very moment when so many of the world's peoples have been brought into continual contact with one another and when one technological breakthrough after another demonstrates the limitless potential of the human imagination, our schools appear on many levels to be entrenched in practices that have no foundation either in research or in demonstrable efficacy. Given the nature of contemporary political polarization, it is perhaps not surprising that when many reformers seek to improve education, they try to circumvent politics altogether—often by using new technologies in innovative ways. When I have discussed the "Flip the System" series with teachers in the U.S., for example, their immediate assumption has been that books such as this one address first and foremost the "flipped classroom," in which instruction is provided by on-line resources that students view at home, and in which they then work on problems or have their homework checked in class the next day.

The purpose of this volume, however, is not solely instructional in scope. We are serious about wanting to flip the entire school system. We are not only asking just what can be done at the micro-level of individual classrooms by teachers, but rather what also can be done at the meso-level of their schools or the macro-level of their districts or states to improve our schools and to strengthen our democracy. We know that without addressing the larger organizational framework of schools, practice will revert back to what is familiar. We need to have the courage to be honest and to admit that while there is a great deal of potential for democratic participation in American public education, there also have been powerful counteracting forces in place for many years now. These have steered our schools in other directions and away from their true moral purposes.

What would be necessary to "flip the system" in this more capacious sense? In what follows, I propose five different ways that we could envision the evolution of our schools in a way that could transform education and improve American democracy. The overall argument is that educators need a recovery of professional integrity, from the Latin *integritas* meaning "whole." When we let one part of a system grow to a disproportionate influence—be it an unwieldy bureaucracy, a testing apparatus, or a particularly popular classroom management system—it is easy for educators to lose sight of an overall focus on why schools actually exist. Schools have been created to promote students' *learning* and their overall personal and social development. This in turn requires their enculturation into norms of civic participation and joint problem-solving that give them the skills and the disposition to persist in tackling the epochal problems of our time. "Flipping the system" here means getting back to that original definition of education—*educare* in Latin—meaning a "leading out of," in the sense of facilitating students to lead from a vantage point of their own emergent sense of agency and identity. It means overturning a bureaucratic and unresponsive system in which our students' potential is limited because our schools do not know how to build upon their interests or are not able to convey to them why the social issues characterizing our time require their engagement and assistance.

If education is to be for the practice of freedom in this broad sense, then the intention here cannot to provide a blueprint, but rather to open up new spaces for public and professional deliberation about a preferred future. These spaces have to be invitational and flexible, in which all of the opinions of all of the members of our diverse communities are welcomed. The following chapters of this book will explore in depth different facets of what such a flipped system could look like. For now, let us examine five concrete "imperatives," or actions we must undertake—to achieve such a transformation.[1]

From the Ideological to the Evidentiary Imperative

In retrospect, one of the great tragedies about the past decades of school reform in the U.S. has been that insistence about improving learning outcomes precluded a discussion about what outcomes we might most wish for our young people and why. It would be going too far to say that the rise of new accountability systems *caused* the dramatic increase in anxiety and depression among our young people in the past decades, but there is no question that it is *correlated* with it. An *ideology* of narrowed emphasis upon academic results has made it difficult for educators and the public to look at more holistic *evidence* of how our students are doing.

As research increasingly documents that not all is well with our young people, however, policy makers and school leaders at various levels have recognized that they need to respond. Even the Organisation for Economic Co-operation and Development (OECD) in Paris ultimately reversed its long-standing fixation on the tested achievement of 15-year-olds in mathematics, reading, and science to include well-being measures in 2016. Meanwhile, a tsunami of professional development offerings, individual classroom interventions, and curricular units have entered into the school improvement marketplace. The Collaborative for Academic, Social, and Emotional Learning (CASEL) has been the hub for these activities in the U.S.

On the whole, the new emphasis on gathering all kinds of evidence about our students, including their personal and social well-being, should form a foundational component of "flipping the system" in the U.S. While there inevitably will be missteps here and there, we now have a wealth of evidence that those schools that are integrating meditation, yoga, and other exercises to calm the body and quiet the mind are experiencing positive outcomes. Nor are these kinds of practices just for students; we are finding that teachers and administrators benefit from them also.

As we work to "flip the system" to accommodate the diverse needs of our students in response to evidence of their well-being, however, we should be cautious in two regards. First, if well-being solely is introduced into schools to pacify students and to improve classroom management approaches that deprive them of opportunities to exercise any agency, we will not be changing the system but rather reinforcing it. In some cases, meditation, for example, has become co-opted into the pre-existing practices in schools in ways that have no research base and raise ethical concerns. At Brooklyn Urban Garden School in New York, students are graded on how well they appear to meditate, and their grades are entered into their report cards (Kaleem, 2015). Class scorecards of meditation rankings are posted in the school's hallways, and those classes with the best results are given trophies that are placed in public display cases. Such practices appear to be implemented exclusively for purposes of satisfying a pre-existent ideology of social control rather than to promote student well-being. This is not integrity, but an abrogation of it.

Second, we should be cautious that the legitimate concern for student well-being does not turn into a stupefying quest to try to make our students happy all of the time. It's a good thing, not a bad one, when students express anger with respect to violations of social justice in our society. Righteous indignation about the inability of policy makers to cope with climate change has sparked a global movement of the young who are not satisfied with bland reassurances that everything will be taken care of in good time. When we say that we want integrity and know that integrity means "whole," we have to address those parts of education that are unpleasant, not just those that are agreeable and fun. This means that while we should gather evidence about our students' well-being, we should also study those pressing issues that students are upset about and that they are willing to work long and hard to address. Otherwise, we are not changing the system, but simply are replacing one kind of one-sided education with another.

From the Imperial to the Interpretive Imperative

In public schools in the U.S., a curious phenomenon has unfolded in the past 20 years. When the No Child Left Behind Act of 2001 was legislated, teachers at the most heavily tested grades (3–8) began adjusting their instruction and their curricular units to those areas that were emphasized on their state examinations. When teachers struggled with lifting their students' results, school and district leaders responded pragmatically, cutting out recess and reducing time for the performing and visual arts that were not tested. Third grade teachers didn't like carrying all of the weight for their students' outcomes, so backward planning was used to help to prepare students for the tests, first in second grade, then in first grade, and finally in kindergarten. The "academicization" of early childhood was complete.

Many of these curricular transformations were carried out quietly in schools, without much public deliberation or debate. Students had little opportunity to shape these reforms and simply had to adjust. Dissidents could be silenced with an equity argument that results were paramount in a dog-eat-dog society. There was an *imperial imperative*, it seemed, to push test preparation into every crevice of the school system. And I mean *every* crevice. When my colleagues at Boston College and I applied for a prestigious Teachers for a New Era grant from major foundations in the U.S. a decade and a half ago, our funders wanted to know how we were preparing to teach numeracy in *every* school discipline, as a precondition for funding.

There is another way to think about curriculum, however, which is that every discipline has its own internal integrity. Biology, history, foreign languages, music and art, all have content and sequences that are proper to their constitution of knowledge. While interdisciplinary learning is valuable, it should never be forced. When it is imposed, we usually are experiencing an imperial imposition of a "strong" discipline upon a relatively weaker, "colonized" subject.

What could be the resolution to such distortions, that rob our students of the rich intellectual adventure that could be in waiting for them if we were to give them a measure of choice to explore all kinds of heterodox subjects in school? At the very least, every school should provide students with opportunities to access a full range of disciplinary subjects. Arbitrarily deciding that the arts, or foreign languages, or physical education are expendable does symbolic violence to the growing child's curiosity and legitimate aspirations to excel across a range of disciplines. So too does every child have the right to play—which, incidentally, is identified as a fundamental human right in the United Nations' Convention on the Rights of the Child (2009).

More fundamentally, however, schools need to provide settings in which students have opportunities to shape their reflective judgment on matters large and small so that this free exploration of their interests and talents becomes a foundational component of their everyday lives. One of the lost opportunities of recent decades has had to do with the blossoming research in the area of area of what is called "meaning and purpose" studies. Young people seek guidance in a quest for meaning and purpose in their lives, but they cannot find this in schools that are over-structured and that preclude rigorous inquiry into such matters. It does not help us in the U.S. that, unlike schools in many other countries, disciplines such as philosophy and religion form the "null" curriculum of content areas that by and large simply are not taught. Here is where our pragmatic orientation fails us, for we know that young people who can acquire a sense of meaning and purpose in their lives experience a host of positive outcomes, on everything from academic achievement to prosocial attitudes to resiliency in the face of personal tragedy or other kinds of setbacks.

The *interpretive imperative* is of particular importance for education in times of democratic decline. One of the more horrific developments of the most recent years has had to do with skyrocketing rates of bullying among the young, which have ascribed by many to contemporary political polarization. When the highest political leaders in any country routinely demonize their opponents and reduce their positions to caricatures, one cannot anticipate our students to be immune to such developments. Democratic education, however, requires minimal thresholds of civility and the capacity to entertain another's point of view as part of a shared quest for the public good. These skills and aptitudes can and must be taught in public schools.

What is needed in order to do so? An emerging body of research literature (Jacobs, Lamb, & Philipp, 2010), primarily focused on elementary mathematics instruction, is documenting what teachers *notice* in their classrooms about their students' learning. This "noticing research" has found that while some teachers are able to interpret their students' mathematical problem-solving in robust ways that make sense of "strategy details in a variety of ways," most teachers provided only "limited evidence of interpretation of children's understandings" or a complete "lack of evidence of interpretation" (p. 171). What is most promising about this research, however, is not the problems identified, but rather the finding that teachers' noticing capacities and their skills at interpretation can be scaffolded provided they are given the proper professional development and support.

Whether we are dealing with social matters like bullying in our schools or the intricacies of teaching fractions in upper elementary school classrooms, imperial mandates from on high, either scolding bullies, or admonishing teachers do not get us very far. Instead, we need greater capacity and will in our busy schools and systems to be able to notice what is going on before our very eyes. We need scaffolded support to be able to interpret it accurately, in a community of like-minded educators, and then to take direct action to improve teaching and learning.

From Prescription to Professionalism

There is nothing inherently wrong with a fair amount of prescriptive activities for both students and teachers in schools. Even if it is unpleasant for students to learn about such matters as the Atlantic slave trade and the Holocaust, for example, we should require them to, simply because it is impossible to be an informed citizen without knowing what occurred in the past and how it could be prevented again in the future. Even if teachers would rather not deal with the additional burdens entailed in learning new technological tools or updating their disciplinary knowledge base, so too, should it be required of all of us to keep up with the most recent developments in our disciplines.

There are some kinds of foundational knowledge for our students and professional responsibilities for educators that are required of everyone, then, no matter what their individual idiosyncratic preferences might be. Our understanding of participation in a shared destiny compels us to ascribe to one another certain minimal forms of behavior: We stop at red lights and drive through green ones. If all goes well, this task allocation allows our society, or any society, to minimize conflict and to maximize our collective well-being.

If prescription in our schools goes too far, however, it becomes impossible to attain the kinds of deeper learning that are characteristic of high-quality education. Research has documented that students who come from homes with low socio-economic status are subjected disproportionately to highly prescribed teaching strategies, often transmitted by beginning teachers. Yet virtually all of the exemplary teachers described by Jal Mehta and Sarah Fine in their study entitled *In Search of Deeper Learning* (Meh ta & Fine, 2019) had been teaching for at least ten years. These teachers gave their students complex cognitive challenges that catalyzed their engagement. They had a broad repertoire of strategies that they adapted to each class to facilitate their students' participation. They abstained from banter that took them away from the curricular demands that students needed to master. These teachers were consummate professionals, with the hard-won expertise to raise academic press while providing students with the support they needed to excel.

Understanding the *professional imperative* to uplift the learning of *all* of our students is essential for democratic education. It may surprise some that it is not just conservative autocrats who can fall prey to the lures of prescription. Seven schools recently studied by Edward Fergus, Pedro Noguera, and Margary Martin that focused on the education of Black and Latino boys placed so much emphasis on culturally responsive pedagogies that their teachers neglected high-impact strategies the students needed to overcome their difficulties with academic achievement, such as reading comprehension. The researchers questioned whether students' achievement "can be improved with this one-sided instructional program" (Fergus, Noguera, & Martin, 2014, p. 94). Teachers in these schools needed experience with a diverse repertoire of teaching approaches and the freedom to choose amongst them. Culturally responsive pedagogies were good, but incomplete. Students need their teachers to bring all of the resources of the profession together in the right way to flourish.

How can we do this? The first step is to strengthen the teaching profession in the U.S. We now have a large body of research on what an empowered teaching profession looks like in countries like Canada, Finland,

Germany, and Singapore (Darling-Hammond et al., 2017; Hargreaves & Shirley, 2012; Shirley, 2017). Educators in these systems have high levels of professional autonomy, but they understand this autonomy in a collective sense of responsibility to their peers and to the system. Precious little time is lost on infighting amongst teachers and administrators. While salaries might only be average by international comparisons, public confidence in the profession is high, and professional development support is generous. There is testing, but nothing like the levels of external intrusion and surveillance we experience in the U.S. These countries provide us with exemplars of the *professional imperative* in action.

From the Insular to the Global Imperative

In 1992 a hitherto obscure political scientist named Francis Fukuyama wrote what was to become a block-busting bestseller entitled *The End of History and the Last Man* (Fukuyama, 1992). Following the collapse of the Berlin Wall in 1989 and then the entire Iron Curtain, Fukuyuma argued that humanity was ending a long period of struggle with tyrannies of the fascist or communist bent, and all were gradually evolving towards liberal parliamentarian governments with market economies. At the time, as he freely admits today, he did not entertain "the possibility of a modern liberal democracy decaying or going backward" (Fukuyama, 2018, p. xiii).

It was a fatal mistake, as Fukuyama conceded in *Identity: The Demand for Dignity and the Politics of Resentment.* "A number of countries that had seemed to be successful liberal democracies during the 1990s slid backward toward more authoritarian government," he wrote (Fukuyama, 2018, p. 5). Instead, a new kind of nationalism, often directed against immigrants and refugees, surged to electoral success around the world. This can be understood as an *insular imperative* as native populations band together to protect their nation against what they perceive as dangerous outsiders who are conspiring not only against their well-being, but also against their very survival as a people.

Why is it that precisely at a time when our global economies and ecologies are more and more part of a shared system, that what appears to be a counter-intuitive movement towards building walls and erecting trade barriers is attractive for so many people in so many countries? Is it because of soaring income inequality? Or is the cause a mismatch between artificial intelligence destroying jobs for some kinds of workers while creating employment for others, with different skills? What role does racism play, or the apparent difficulties that liberal democracies have in defending their populations against random terrorist attacks?

Whatever the causes of our current "democratic recession" (Diamond, 2015, p. 141), educators have a role to play in responding to it. But how? From the U.S. to India to Brazil to Germany, we've entered a new age of nationalism that is testing our abilities to collaborate across borders. Nationalism is working its way into school textbooks and the equivalence of McCarthy-era loyalty tests are being brought back with a vengeance. Since educational systems are beholden to individual nation-states, educators are finding themselves placed in vulnerable situations, in which their jobs and their very financial security is at stake.

How to respond, then? At least part of the answer involves understanding the hitherto underestimated threat of different aspects of globalization. Economic globalization has devastated local industries that have sustained families for generations and replaced a stable working class with a vulnerable "precariat" suffering from slashed wages and reduced buying power. Technological globalization means that while individual users of social media and the Internet can experience levels of instant access to information even the wealthiest plutocrats could only have dreamed of just thirty years ago, their private lives are subject to levels of surveillance previous generations were able to avoid. Finally, the shift of economic and technological modes of production and consumption means that we increasingly have "governance without governments" (Dale, 1999, p. 4). This means that local and national governments cannot keep up with the pace of change. They are considered inefficient, and potentially corrupt, by the very populations that should protect and serve. The consequence is a hollowing out of the political center and a shift of power to non-state actors like corporations on the one hand and their affiliated non-profit organizations on the other. In response, desperate populations register their protests at the ballot box or on the streets, often without clear solutions of their own to the problems that plague them, but have gone unaddressed for years.

What can schools do about all of these issues? "Flipping the system" would mean that educators would need to become far more attentive to students' perceptions of the world they are entering, and more proactive about providing curricula that address their concerns. A recent Gallup poll (Saad, 2019) showed a 20-point spread on climate change, with only 47% of Americans over 65 years old greatly concerned about it, and 67% of young Americans greatly worried. In September 2019 hundreds of thousands of U.S. students participated in an international strike for action on climate change. Nor were the students alone. An NPR/Ipsos poll (Kamenetz, 2019) earlier that year showed that even though 80% of parents want climate change to be taught as a school subject, and 86% of teachers would like to teach about it, less than half of teachers currently are doing so.

Grasping the need to develop a *global imperative* to flip school systems to address issues like climate change that their students view as urgent matters of public concern is an essential test of the integrity of our school systems. This is not a matter of party affiliation; two-thirds of Republicans surveyed in the U.S. agree that climate change should be taught in schools (among Democrats the percentage is 90%). It is rather an issue of having a flexible professional culture that can adapt rapidly to deal with topics that must be addressed by a rising generation.

Strategically, it may be wiser in our current times not so much to teach *against* the rising tide of nationalism as *for* the enculturation of our students to a collective understanding of a common human destiny for which we all must share responsibility. One of the more exciting cross-curricular ways in which this work is being undertaken now is through the teaching of the Sustainable Developmental Goals (SDGs) of the United Nations. These are 17 ambitious targets for urgent agendas such as the elimination of poverty, the provision of health care, and guarantees of free, high quality public education around the world by 2030. Educators from many different nations have been working to create curricular frameworks for teaching the SDGs and these are being piloted by "ambassadors" and "advocates" in their schools (for more information, go to www.teachsdgs.org). Here is a clear example of a bottom-up, teacher and student led transformation of schools with a rigorous, globally-oriented curriculum.

From the Instrumental to the Existential Imperative

It is natural for the public to have high expectations of schools to prepare young people to enter the workforce, and it is entirely understandable that the young themselves want to learn disciplines in schools that will help them to gain financial independence in the years to come. There is nothing inherently wrong with acknowledging that education always must have some kind of practical outcome, even for the most theoretically inclined students, of whom by definition there are not many. This concern for objective, real-world skills recently led to the high priority given to the study of informational text in the Common Core State Standards, as well as to school reform movements like the Pathways to Prosperity Network, sponsored by Jobs for the Future (www.jff.org). It also has prompted philanthropies and government agencies like the National Science Foundation to provide millions of dollars of funding for new courses in computer coding in public schools, and in general to rush support to fields like science, technology, engineering, and mathematics.

Much of this new sense of urgency about practical outcomes for education is long overdue. Increasing job market polarization—in which those with the right skill sets and dispositions experience soaring incomes, and those without them are thrown into a bottomless pit of low-wage work with no health care or other benefits—has been prevalent in the American workplace since the 1970s, and shows no signs of stopping (Cass, 2018; Piketty, 2014). Even the prospects of college graduates have turned increasingly grim, with over half of them now working at jobs that require no higher education whatsoever (Ford, 2015).

At the same time, however, these economic difficulties do not mean that it is right or appropriate to deprive the young of a rich and balanced curriculum simply because of uncertain economic prospects. We have no research evidence that introducing elementary school students to informational text rather than thrilling fiction or incantatory poetry improves their motivation to read. Children pass through their own stages of development and are not simply raw material to be prepared for their roles as future workers. If educators want our students to flourish as whole human beings, we have to make sure that we are always treating them as such.

This means that, in addition to addressing economic considerations, "flipping the system" entails enabling our schools to do a better job with supporting the formation of our young people's identities and their quests for meaning and purpose. Much has been made of the rise of "identity politics" in recent decades, with some viewing this phenomenon as an essential prelude to genuine social recognition and others deploring what is viewed as an excessive preoccupation with the self or a group (Appiah, 2018; Michaels, 2006). Wherever one might lie on the spectrum of advocates to antagonists of the new preoccupation with identity—and for many this is a sliding scale—we should all be able to agree that it is best for our students, our schools, and our society when we create conditions in which all can participate as whole human beings on terms of free and mutual interaction.

Identity is a *psychosocial* process, meaning that the cultivation of the individual personality and a sense of belonging in a social group are shared projects of the young. Positive youth development in schools needs to provide support for individuals to become their authentic selves, and at the same time, should help the young to find membership in an entity and a purpose larger than themselves. Especially when the young experience their group identity as stigmatized because of their race, gender, or gender orientation, for example, schools have a responsibility for social affirmation. This does not need to be done in a blandly celebratory way, but also can entail elements of critique and debate, as for example when educators using Hip-Hop in their classes ask students to explore ways in which lyrics are sexist or otherwise exclusionary (Alim & Paris, 2017).

Coda

Note what flipping the system as defined by these five imperatives of educational change does *not* entail. It does *not* mean overthrowing the traditional, decentralized organization of American schools and replacing them with either an unregulated marketplace model of competition or a nationally centralized system on the model of France or Japan. It does *not* mean viewing teachers as expendable because so much information now is available on the Internet that real live human beings are no longer needed to guide the young to maturity. It does *not* mean a never-ending campaign to promote our students' self-esteem on the one hand, or to turn them into robotic regurgitators of disconnected and ultimately meaningless snippets of information, on the other.

Flipping the system, as outlined here, has five components:

1   Take up an *evidentiary imperative* to study all kinds of data about how our students are faring, including their well-being, but also going beyond it.
2   Explore an *interpretive imperative* that gives educators the space and support to notice how their students are learning so that they can better accommodate their interests and needs.
3   Enact a *professional imperative* that will provide U.S. educators with the same level of trust and public confidence enjoyed by their colleagues in high-achieving countries like Finland, South Korea, Singapore, and Canada.
4   Recognize a *global imperative* that overcomes our local parochialism to achieve a shared destiny worthy of the rising generations to come.
5   Embrace an *existential imperative* that will provide our young with opportunities to find their own sense of meaning and purpose in their lives, both as singular individuals and as members of social groups which provide them with a sense of belonging and inclusion.

This is in no way intended to be an exhaustive list (those tend to be exhausting!) Like signposts on a mountain trails, these five imperatives are pointers that can and should be mixed with your own repertoire of preferred practices. Together, we can collaborate with one another to "flip the system" of our schools in ways that produce genuine improvements and that will shape a desired future we all can be proud of.

Note
1   For a fuller elaboration of these arguments, see Shirley (2017).

References
Alim, H.M., & Paris, D. (2017) What is culturally sustaining pedagogy and why does it matter? In: Paris, D., & Alim, H.M. (Eds.), *Culturally sustaining pedagogies: Teaching and learning for justice in a changing world*. New York: Teachers College Press, 1–21.
Appiah, K.A. (2018) *The lies that bind: Rethinking identity*. New York: Liveright.
Cass, O. (2018) *The once and future worker: A vision for the renewal of work in America*. New York: Encounter.
Dale, R. (1999) Specifying globalization effects on national policy: Focus on the mechanisms. *Journal of Education Policy*, 14(1), 1–17.
Darling-Hammond, L, Burns, D., Campbell, C., Goodwin, A.L., Hammerness, K., Low, E.L., McIntyre, A., Sato, M., & Zeichner, K. (2017) *Empowered educators:*

How high-performing systems shape teaching quality around the world. San Francisco, CA: Jossey-Bass.

Diamond, L. (2015) Facing up to the democratic recession. *Journal of Democracy*, 26 (1), 141–155.

Fergus, E., Noguera, P., & Martin, M. (2014) *Schooling for resilience: Improving the life trajectory of Black and Latino boys.* Cambridge, MA: Harvard Education Press.

Ford, M. (2015) *Rise of the robots: Technology and the threat of a jobless future.* New York: Basic Books.

Fukuyama, F. (1992) *The end of history and the last man.* New York: Free Press.

Fukuyama, F. (2018) *Identity: The demand for dignity and the politics of resentment.* New York: Farrar, Straus, and Giroux.

Hargreaves, A., & Shirley, D. (2012) *The global fourth way: The quest for educational excellence.* Thousand Oaks, CA: Corwin.

Jacobs, V. R., Lamb, L. L. C., & Philipp, R. A. (2010) Professional noticing of children's mathematical thinking. *Journal for Research in Mathematics Education*, 41 (2), 169–202.

Kaleem, J. (2015) Reading, writing, required silence: How meditation is changing schools and students. Retrieved from www.huffpost.com/entry/schools-meditation-quiet-time_n_7544582?guccounter=1&guce_referrer=aHR0cHM6Ly93d3cuZ29vZ2xl LmNvbS88&guce_referrer_sig=AQAAAAEg3LmGu9U-rkmIUi2l92syyeAZNMCsBs8z kIgWfRLgc81LgnO_3ztRYCp9oalU-MxDuXHxgScXNWkFG0nP0K1HJ-nqW0RVML8 Z8LMQdoSRZxbQEyzYHhh3Z8-vigUlXpEMyWgJ_nllv4z28U6aqAGX1QrtTi9sYHm b249fzjrb.

Kamenetz, A. (2019) Most teachers don't teach climate change; 4 in 5 parents wish they did. Retrieved from www.npr.org/2019/04/22/714262267/most-teachers-dont-teach-climate-change-4-in-5-parents-wish-they-did.

Lamb, V.R., Lamb, L.L.C, & Philipp, R.A. (2010) Professional noticing of children's mathematical thinking. *Journal for Research in Mathematics Education* 41(2), 169–202.

OECD (2017) *PISA 2015 results (Volume IIII): Students' well-being.* Paris: OECD.

Mehta, J., & Fine, S. (2019) *In search of deeper learning: The quest to remake the American high school.* Cambridge, MA: Harvard University Press.

Michaels, W. B. (2006) *The trouble with diversity: How we learned to love identity and ignore inequality.* New York: Picador.

Piketty, T. (2014) *Capital in the twenty-first century.* Cambridge, MA: Harvard University Press.

Saad, L. (2019) Americans as concerned as ever about global warming. Retrieved from https://news.gallup.com/poll/248027/americans-concerned-ever-global-warming.aspx.

Shirley, D. (2017) *The new imperatives of educational change: Achievement with integrity.* New York: Routledge.

Tucker, M. (2011) *Surpassing Shanghai: An agenda for American education built on the world's leading systems.* Cambridge, MA: Harvard Education Press.

United Nations (2009) *Convention on the Rights of the Child.* New York: United Nations.

Chapter 2

Engendering Civic Engagement among Learners

A Los Angeles Student Focus Group

Estella Owoimaha-Church

Introduction

Education is a manifestation of democracy and educators are its shepherds. The environments in which we serve are microcosms of our society as a whole, including issues beyond the school walls. As educators, our duty is to ensure students have equitable access to spaces where knowledge can be constructed. No matter where or when learners enter, school should serve as a conduit to freedom. To serve a diverse and pluralistic United States, students must practice shaping their learning spaces so that, as future citizens, they will shape society in a way that allows everyone to hold space and participate in the democratic process.

In my experience, when students are given time and space to exercise choice, learning becomes experiential. My priority as an educator is not content delivery, but to create brave spaces that allow learners to explore, grow, and fail safely, understanding that peers and mentors are supportive components to the process. Teachers are often told curriculum should engage students in a way that enables application beyond the classroom. These applications are often only imagined. Imagining what is possible is simply not enough.

As a steward of democracy, I facilitate learning experiences guided by student passions and desires by crafting courses based on direct input from learners. The classroom environment is shaped by who occupies the space, and it serves as a reflection of who they are and who they hope to become. Moreover, as an educator, civic participation is showing up to class to teach; each day I serve is a form of direct-action. In this way, I am able to model civic engagement for my students.

While our expertise as educators should drive instruction and education policy, we should also welcome regular feedback from students to guide decisions. In order to write this chapter, I did just this; engaged students in a focus conversation to learn what motivates young people to engage civically.

Summary of the Literature Review

A review of the literature revealed six elements crucial in motivating youth to engage civically. These elements (Figure 2.1) are not required in any particular order. In fact, they are fluid and should occur as frequently as possible. For one, content and spaces should be culturally relevant. Curriculum must lend itself to real-world applications beyond the classroom. In addition, learners need to build relationships with mentors as well as community members within the community. Learners must develop a strong sense of self in regard to ethnic, racial, and gender identity. Lastly, students must be given multiple and regular opportunities to develop social awareness and build up consciousness.

Focus Group

In a democratized learning environment, students are equal partners in developing curriculum, projects, and more. If we expect our students to learn to be good citizens as adults, we must allow them to practice citizenship skills while at school. To ensure learning spaces remain student-centered dialogue and educators should remain grounded in praxis.[1] Educators

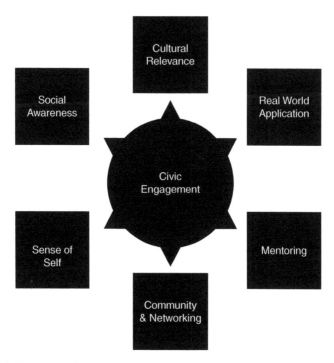

Figure 2.1 Elements of Student Civic Engagement

should seek a feedback loop between teacher and learner. With this in mind, a focus group was conducted with young people around civic engagement. Eight diverse secondary students were asked questions related to civic engagement and their inspiration to take action within their community. Table 2.1 details demographic information of focus group participants.

All teens attend school at a Title I secondary institution, live in working-class communities, and receive free lunch. At least four students are identified as gifted, taking at least half of their courses in honors or Advanced Placement programs. In addition, two students participate in college preparation programming both during and beyond the school day. Each student has struggled with emotional disturbance, anxiety, or mental illness. One student has been diagnosed with Autism Spectrum Disorder (ASD). Focus group participants are current members of their theatre arts club at school; more than half of them have been members for four years. They share a deep passion for theatre arts and love for one another. Above all, each of them has a unique story to tell.

The goals of the focus group were to understand (1) how youth viewed their role in civic engagement and (2) what role, if any, they felt their teachers or formal education plays in encouraging community action. The conversation spanned two hours. Afterwards, participants had an opportunity to submit written responses. The conversation evolved organically as new questions arose. As a facilitator, I did not comment on students' responses except when clarification was needed. While a focus group is anecdotal in nature, the results might enable teachers to make contextually informed decisions by establishing students as equal partners in education.

Table 2.2 provides a snapshot of students' impressions. The table is separated into two columns; column one lists themes that arose during the discussion, while column two lists paraphrasing of students' responses. Students were asked about their understanding of civic engagement and activism, to define both terms, and explain the differences in their own words. Then, students were asked a series of questions related to their perceived preparedness to take action on global issues of concern. The line of questioning evolved organically and ranged from issues to their intrinsic motivation to take action. Participants were asked if their plans to engage civically were sufficient and how they might gain skills they feel are lacking. Lastly, students were asked what has helped prepare them, what might help prepare them, and what they need from educators in order to be more prepared.

Before beginning the focus conversation, I had a preconceived notion about how youth viewed civic engagement, especially in regard to the use of social media. I assumed social media would be considered a prime tool of engagement for their generation. However, when asked, students pushed back on this notion citing social media as an insufficient form of political engagement and simply a means of building awareness. Students also asserted that online actions are superficial forms of civic engagement that lack

Table 2.1 Focus Group Demographics

Student	Gender	Age	Grade	Race	Ethnicity	Religion	Grade Point Average	Other
S1	Female	18	12th	Asian	Indian-Ukrainian	Hindu	3.0	
S2	Male	17	12th	Hispanic	Chinese-Mexican	N/A	3.0	
S3	Transgender Male	18	12th	Asian	Indian-Ukrainian	Agnostic	4.2	English is second language
S4	Female	17	12th	Hispanic	Mexican-Salvadorian	N/A	3.0	Severe visual impairment
S5	Female	17	12th	Hispanic	Mexican-Salvadorian	Atheist	3.0	
S6	Non-binary	18	12th	Hispanic	Peruvian	Atheist	3.7	
S7	Male	17	11th	Black	African-American	Christian	2.7	Diagnosed with Autism
S8	Female	16	12th	Black	African-American	Christian	3.5	

Note: N/A denotes information that was not available or not applicable. Grade Point Averages are based on a four-point scale.

Table 2.2 Snapshot of Los Angeles Youth Focus Group

Themes	*Student Responses*
Definition of civic engagement and activism	• Lines between civic engagement and activism were blurry; no real distinction was made between the two terms • All students believe true engagement and activism must be tangible and take place in the community • Students believe that the action taken must benefit all community members • Generation Z seems to be fond of using social media as a tool or strategy for activism and civic engagement • However, students also believe social media is never sufficient and is mere performative activism
Prepared to take action	• Students feel like they are more aware of local and global issues because of projects that have taken place in classes • Some students felt they needed to better understand self in order to be more prepared
Inspiration to take action	• Students believe that while there are several important local and global issues to tackle, climate change is the most pressing issue; they are terrified and feel as though its more important than planning for college or careers after high school • Climate change is one issue they are all motivated to act on immediately, followed by racial and social justice issues • Often find inspiration in artists from various mediums • Are not often inspired by elected or political figures
Plans to engage	• Students seek to engage while still in high school but feel they are lacking some tools in order to stay engaged beyond graduation from secondary school • Hope to support someone in the future as a mentor
How school or educators can help	• Student believed that all educators and administrators should encourage civic action among students, even if—especially if—it disrupts the regular school day or function • Students believe all educators should spend time within the class day teaching about or exploring important topics such as climate change, racial injustice, LGBTQ+ visibility, police brutality, and more • Students feel that educators should model civic engagement and activism by taking stances on issues and sharing experiences with students in the classroom • Learners wish for more projects that have real-world application and allow them to take action on issues with the guidance of a teacher • Students seek for more mentor relationships with their teachers • Students feel relationship building with students is key in inspiring action or change among learners • Help connect learners to other youth with similar concerns or plans

Source: own recording, E. Owoimaha-Church, Los Angeles Youth Focus Group, September 11, 2019 depth and empathy. They expressed that actual civic engagement or action requires physical proximity to the community.

The focus group garnered concrete suggestions for educators. To begin, students shared that they often feel overwhelmed by the number of issues around the globe; they feel helpless and are paralyzed by their emotions or personal traumas. Sometimes they are made to feel incapable of affecting change within their community. That burden worsens when they fully empathize with peers around the globe. On one hand, students are grateful to learn new things and believe hard truths about the world should be taught. On the other hand, as they continue to grow and empathize with others, it becomes more painful to learn these truths. Students offered specific feedback regarding (1) learning environments, (2) curriculum and classroom strategies, and (3) student–teacher relationships.[2]

Learning Environments

The physical space our students meet in should not be an afterthought. Students shared that the posters on the walls do matter and the ways in which the room is arranged—whether conducive to collaboration or not—can affect whether they feel safe or welcome in a space. For example, one student cited a poster in theatre class that reads, "None of us are well until we are all well" as being an inspirational reminder to be tolerant, empathetic, and considerate of others. Another student cited a poster in the same room that reads, "You are on Tongva land," explaining it reminds him of history that is absent from textbooks.

According to participants, educators must set boundaries that create safe spaces where diverse ideas can be expressed. All learners should feel protected but at the same time responsible for maintaining a hate-free environment. One student shared that he appreciates when teachers correct students who use derogatory language in class. He believes when teachers leverage these teachable moments, the whole class benefits by developing a deeper understanding of issues related to race, gender, and identity. All participants agreed that calling a student out and openly shaming or ostracizing was detrimental in facilitating healthy spaces for learning. Instead, young people want to understand the history, meaning, or context of certain words would be more beneficial.

Curriculum and Classroom Strategies

Views on curriculum and projects were discussed as well. One participant shared that he and his peers enjoy when the class discussions go off-topic for the sake of cultivating dialogue on current issues. Others agreed and added that in these moments they are especially inspired when teachers share personal narratives and information from beyond the curriculum. Moreover, students argue that educators should create projects that not only have real-world applications but that allow learners to feel successful upon its conclusion; when they feel successful after completing such projects, they are inspired to continue working beyond the classroom on an issue. One student shared that her perspectives on many issues have grown more compassionate to the needs of others because she felt a sense of accomplishment.

Students would also like to encourage teachers to not shy away from major global events in the classroom—issues of climate, poverty, war, and other injustices. Students assert that this might help in motivating youth to do more but also deepen tolerance and empathy within students towards one another. As educators teach these topics, youth find it equally important to share positive examples of youth around the world who have taken successful actions. They believe these models provide needed inspiration for civic engagement.

Student–Teacher Relationship

Participants conveyed that educators have to take time to engage with students by deepening relationships. They expressed that they seek teachers with whom they believe they can serve as mentors. It is imperative for teachers to earn the trust of students in order to deepen relationships, deepen learning, and facilitate engagement in the classroom.

As teacher and student relationships grow, students say they feel emboldened to create action plans around issues they are passionate about. The aid of a teacher as a mentor through this process is important. Because this may be difficult to do for every single child in a teacher's charge, the focus group students suggest leaning on outside organizations, community leaders, and other support staff to serve in the capacity of mentor as well.

The last two recommendations from the group were to listen and praise. Students say all stakeholders across their educational careers must *listen* to youths' concerns. They wish to be recognized as "thought-partners" on their campuses, in class, and within the community; more than anything, they want to *feel* heard. Moreover, they seek external acknowledgment and praise as they grow, even in the case where change is slow or incremental. One student stated she is often discouraged to act whenever she notices peers designated as gifted receive praise but she is ignored. This particular student sees herself as academically average. Young people with low academic self-concepts are asking to be seen in a positive light for what they have to contribute rather than being seen for their skills deficit.

Conclusion

> The web of interrelated neoliberal economic, political, social, and education policies that favour the wealthy and disempower the poor in the United States today appears normalized as the natural state of things, and overwhelming as if it were intractable.
>
> (Goodman & Cocca, 2014, p. 211)

This web of injustice is evident to young people, whether in an ideal learning environment or not. Even when youth lack the nomenclature to name their oppression, it is felt deeply. Young people who have been given access to educational spaces where civic engagement is a learning outcome will, undoubtedly, stand equipped to diagnose injustice. They will be able to move their learning beyond the walls of the classroom and into their communities in order to challenge power structures. As we aid young people in escaping this complex web of injustice, marked by neoliberal policies and oppression, we must be cautious about how we employ language in this effort.

Consider the use of the word "empower." To say we "empower students" implies educators somehow endow young people with power as if they never had it to begin with. If we understand that their power exists regardless of us, we are in a better position to foster or cultivate innate power. Students and teachers become partners and can identify skills that already lie within. In this way, we begin to reposition marginalized youth as change-agents without our communities (Rhoades, 2015).

It is also imperative that educators remain reflective and mindful of personal shortcomings. Transformation—true, systemic change—depends heavily on our ability to reflect and take appropriate actions based on those reflections. This cycle of praxis depends on our ability to remain engaged in effective dialogue (Freire, 1972). We must be comfortable with being wrong and apologizing to young people whenever necessary. If we recognize young people as active partners in our learning spaces, then we see them as equals. Moreover, among other educators, we must set aside our ego to make room for collaboration and civic engagement across the profession. In other words, we must model the collaborative behavior we hope to inspire among young leaders. I find myself apologizing to students on a regular basis; I misspoke, taught something wrong, or botched an assessment. My shortcomings as an educator do not make for a short list, but I remain in reflection and seek support from the young people I serve in order to continue growing as an educator.

Authenticity is a crucial element when deepening intrinsic motivation among young people. In my experience, students with identified special needs perform exceptionally well when faced with challenges presented through authentic learning experiences such as project-based learning or service-learning opportunities. These learning experiences give students the chance to engage in real-life problem solving related to their community (Lee et al., 2007).

How do we engender civic engagement among the next generation? Further examination of intergenerational mentor relationships might yield additional findings. Based on the focus conversation and literature, a high-impact benefit of building intergenerational mentorships with students lies in the opportunity to model collaboration and dialogue. These are nuanced relationships that help build a foundation upon which collective understanding is built.

These relationships are just as impactful for educators as they are for students. My practice continues to evolve as I learn from young people. Their input informs my reflection, and therefore, my practice. For example, when I needed further insight on issues related to gender identity, expression, and sexual orientation it was queer students who engaged me in dialogue. Collectively, we were able to take action on campus.

To that end, education cannot truly serve as a democracy unless it serves all. Education must be driven by teacher input. In a flipped system, teacher expertise met with student input converges to meet the needs of the diverse populations we serve. Positive student–teacher relationships are a necessity in deriving insights that will enable educators to reshape a system that is holistic and equitable for all—as our democracy should be.

Education would benefit from a reframing of civic engagement as a fluid process through which the act of democratizing learning spaces becomes an act of praxis (reflection, action, and transformation). If education is the practice of freedom, then it is also the bearer of democracy. Our youth, responsible for shaping democracy through civic engagement, must be protected at all costs. It is our responsibility to provide them with the tools and leverage necessary to shape the future.

As we continue to engage in flipping the system and preserving democracy, take a moment to celebrate young citizens working to keep democracy alive in our communities:

- Brianna Fruean and the Pacific Climate Warriors.
- Raheejah Flowers and the youth of Black Lives Matter.
- Greta Thunberg and Student Climate Action Strikes.
- David Hogg and the other young leaders of March for Our Lives.
- Every student I have had the pleasure of serving.
- Every student who will allow me the opportunity to serve alongside them.

Notes

1 Praxis is a concept discussed in *Pedagogy of the Oppressed*. Reflection and action lead to transformation (Freire, 1972).
2 There was correlation between all six elements of student civic engagement described in Summary of the Literature Review and focus group findings.

References

Freire, P. (1972). *Pedagogy of the Oppressed*. London: Penguin Books.
Goodman, S., & Cocca, C. (2014). "Spaces of Action": Teaching Critical Literacy for Community Empowerment in the Age of Neoliberalism. *English Teaching: Practice and Critique*, 13(3), 210–226.

Lee, S.-Y., Olszewski-Kubilius, P., Donahue, R., & Weimbolt, K. (2007). The Effects of a Service-Learning Program on the Development of Civic Attitudes and Behaviors among Academically Talented Adolescents. *Journal for the Education of the Gifted*, 31(2), 165–197.

Rhoades, M. (2015). LGBTQ Youth + Video Artivism: Arts-Based Critical Civic Praxis. *A Journal of Issues and Research*, 53(4), 317–329.

Chapter 3

Regaining the Democratic Heart of Education

Gert Biesta

All about Learning?

I have stopped counting times I've read or heard people saying that education is "all about learning," that schools are "places for learning," that classrooms are "learning communities," that the work of teachers is to "facilitate student's learning" and that all of us should become "lifelong learners." If education is all about learning, and if such learning should go on throughout our lives, we'd better close the schools, because the lessons we learn on the street are much more powerful than what schools can ever achieve. From the point of learning it is nothing less than a scandal that young children in Pakistan and Bangladesh are perfectly capable of stitching together designer clothes and Nike shoes, whereas schooled children from the Western world would have no clue where to begin with such tasks. Similarly, whereas modern neuroscience claims it is only after the frontal lobes have sufficiently developed that we can expect a sense of responsibility from young people, just a century ago children as young as eight years old would work full days in the mines with a great sense of responsibility, even under appalling working conditions.

The dominance of the language of learning in education, a phenomenon to which I have referred to as the "learnification" of educational discourse and practice (see, for example, Biesta, 2009, 2010), continues to surprise me. This is not because learning and education have nothing to do with each other (albeit that I think that there is more to education than learning because there is more to life than learning). Rather it is because the language of learning is not precise enough and not sufficient enough as an educational language. The point of education is never that young people only learn; it is that they learn *something*, that they learn it *for a reason*, and that they learn it *from someone*. What the language of learning hides is that, unlike learning, education always raises the question *what* children should learn, *why* they should learn it, and *through what kind of relationships* they might learn it. Education, unlike learning, always raises questions about *content*, about *purpose* and about *relationships*.

This doesn't mean that when the education discourse is a learning discourse, content, purpose, and relationships are absent. But, the language of learning has contributed significantly to the emergence of a rather meagre educational "diet," in which the sole focus of education has become that of producing measurable "learning outcomes" in a small number of curricular areas. This is partly the result of an ongoing rhetorical reference to the alleged "basics" of education, without engaging in a meaningful discussion about what those basics are supposed to be.[1] It is partly the result of an obsession with effectiveness amongst educational researchers and policy makers, forgetting that effective education is never automatically or necessarily *good* education (see Biesta, 2016). There is also the problematic impact of the global education measurement industry, which has not just contributed to a new "common sense" about what allegedly counts in education—measurable learning outcomes—but which has also spurred countries into a battle for the top position in the PISA rankings, rather than focusing on the question of what good education in their specific context and setting might be.

This situation is not good for students, who are pressured into "performing" in a small number of curricular areas. It is not good for teachers, who are pressured into making sure that their students "perform." It is not good for education itself, increasingly a production machine in which only certain outcomes count and the questions of what it requires to "produce" such outcomes, why certain outcomes matter and others not, and whether we should even focus on outcomes, are no longer seen as relevant. This is a sad situation, particularly when students succumb under pressure to perform in cultures where failure is not tolerated. It is a sad situation, particularly when teachers' job security depends on their ability to pressure their students towards performance. And, it is a sad situation in light of a proud history in which education was intrinsically connected to the democratic project of equality—the equal right to a meaningful education for everyone, rather than the trivial right to compete in the global performance rat race.

Rebooting the System: The Priority of Purpose

What seems to have been forgotten in the frenzied quest for effectiveness, outcomes and "performance," is that everything hangs on the question what education is actually *for*—the question of the point and purpose of education. This question has been hijacked by the simplistic (and hence seductive) answers of the global education measurement industry (Biesta, 2015; D'Agnese, 2017). The question as to what education is *for* will remain a political question (Kliebard, 2004; Apple, 2018) with no easy answers. We will always find a range of competing views and values, at least when we engage with this question in a democratic way. Acknowledging all this is particularly important to counter suggestions that the question of the purpose of education is merely *technical*, able to be resolved if we just have more data, more research, more measurement, and so on. While this may generate interesting information, it can never resolve the issue for us.

This is not to suggest, however, that the discussion about the point and purpose of education is entirely open and that education can be kicked around in any possible direction (although this is how it may sometimes feel like that from the perspective of those "at the chalkface"). I have found it useful—as have many others—to distinguish between three legitimate domains of purpose that all education should consider. Schools, colleges and universities have an important role to play in providing children and young people with the knowledge and skills that makes it possible for them to act effectively in the world. This is the work of *qualification*—different from the work of obtaining qualifications or certifications. While qualification is an important task of education, it is not its be all and end all. Education also has an important role to play in providing children and young people with orientation: with finding their way around in an increasingly complex world. This is the educational work of *socialization*, where we introduce our students into traditions and practice, and invite them to find their own place within them—be it professional traditions and practices, social and cultural traditions and practices, religious and non-religious traditions and practices, scientific and artistic traditions and practices, and so on. The ambition here should never be "strong" socialization, that is, just forcing children and young people into particular ways of being and doing. It is, rather, to provide them meaningful orientation and a sense of direction.

Qualification is a fairly uncontested domain of educational purpose, although there are both difficult questions about which knowledge and skills should be on the agenda and about what it means for students to "obtain" such knowledge and skills. I would argue that just being able to reproduce knowledge or performing a skill without understanding of what it is one knows or masters, is meaningless if not dangerous. The work of socialization is more contentious, because our world is complex. Because providing orientation always entails selection, we are faced with difficult choices even before we begin to ascertain how we might invite our students to find their way in our complex world (which, again, requires understanding, plus the capacity for "navigation" and wise judgement).

Both with regard to qualification and socialization, contemporary societies have many expectations towards education. One way to describe the contemporary crisis in education is that these expectations have entirely focused on a narrow view of qualification and a restrictive view of socialization—to the detriment of everything that should make the work of qualification and socialization exciting and meaningful, rather than dull, repetitive, and punitive for students and teachers. Although society has legitimate expectations towards education, I wish to argue that education is not only a function of society, to put it in sociological terms. In more everyday language, education is not just a shop that should give customers what they ask for. Education must make sure young people are not only *objects* of what other people think they should learn, be, and become. Instead, education should ensure that children can be *subjects* in their own right, that they can lead their own life—and lead it well. This is the third domain of educational purpose, *subjectification*. It is in this domain that the question of democracy emerges and, as I will argue, has its proper "home."[2]

Education, Freedom, and Democracy

The question of freedom has a long history in educational thought. Yet for a long time, education was mainly available to those who were already free—the free men in the city state of Athens, for example, who through education (in Greek: *paideia*) gained the opportunity to work on their own perfection. This opportunity was not available for women, not for slaves and not for the artisans—they were supposed to do work, rather than be(come) educated. It is only in modern times that the freedom of all human beings became a concern for education, *not* as something that needed to be constrained or suppressed through cultivation, socialization and moralization, but as a value in its own right and, in more contemporary language, as a fundamental human right. The idea that the freedom of each individual matters is connected to what we might term the three "R's" of modern times: the R of the Renaissance which increasingly put humans in the center of attention; the R of the Reformation which argued that everyone has the right to read the Bible; and the R of the revolutions that emerged in the western world throughout the 18th and early 19th century.

Jean-Jacques Rousseau, in *Emile, or On Education*, argued in 1762 for the importance of freedom and acknowledged that educators have important work to do in relation to the freedom of children. Rousseau fully understood that the child's emerging freedom runs the risk of being overpowered by everything that comes to it from the "outside," through all the expectations, demands, pressures, and temptations that society generates. That is why educators must create a degree of distance between society and the child; a kind of free space in which the child can meet the world rather than be completely overtaken by the world. The work of educators is not to hide the world from the child, but to create a "sphere" from which the world can be encountered in such a way that the child can achieve a degree of "sovereignty" (we might also say independence or autonomy) vis-à-vis the "outside" world. This task is perhaps even more urgent today than it was in Rousseau's time, as the outside world is constantly coming into the lives of young people, particularly through digital technology.

Rousseau also pointed out that there is not just the ongoing challenge to keep standing in light of everything that comes from the outside; but that there are also forces emerging from the "inside"—Rousseau called them the "passions"—that run the risk of overtaking the child. In addition to the challenge of coming into a relationship with the world outside rather than being determined by it, there is therefore also the challenge to come into a relationship with the world "inside" rather than being determined by it. In relation to both challenges there is important work to be done by educators in order to allow the "I" of the student to emerge and enter the world.

As educators we can never produce the "I" of the student. The whole point of being an "I," to use an awkward but nonetheless accurate expression, is that it's the work of the "I" and of no one else. What we can do is approach the student as "I"—or better: address the "I" of the student—and encourage our students to be an "I" and not walk away from this challenge. German educational thinker Dietrich Benner (2015) introduced the beautiful phrase "Aufforderung zur Selbsttätigkeit" for this educational work, which can be translated as "summoning" or, "encouraging" young people to "self-action"—and the emphasis here lies on "self" not on "action." It is of crucial importance to see that subjectification, as a "modality" of what educators do vis-à-vis their students rather than a process, is *not* about encouraging our students to be themselves, but encouraging them to be *a* self. More precisely, it is encouraging them not to forget that they can be *a* self, which can be quite difficult.

Marking the difference between "be yourself" and "be a self" is important because many of us, particularly in neo-liberal capitalist societies, are constantly being told that we can and should be ourselves and, more specifically, that we can be anyone we want to be (if we have sufficient money and resources). The question of identity—which is the question of being yourself—is a relevant question, particularly in those situations where some identities are still not being allowed to exist. Finding one's identity and expressing it fully can never be the be-all and end-all of education, just as it also cannot be the be-all and end-all of life. To put it bluntly: if all human beings would only strive to achieve their own "pure" identity as individuals or groups, we would, particularly in the over-populated world in which we live, soon be heading for war. After all, pure identity can only exist without the presence, let alone the interference of others with other identities. As soon as we acknowledge that we have to live our lives in a world that we share with others, we have to acknowledge that there are limitations to what and how we might be. These limits come from other people who are keen to achieve their own place in the world. They also come from the physical and natural world, as evidenced by the current environmental crisis.

As educators we are keen that children will find their own freedom, and that the new generation will want to step into the world and find sovereignty within it. We work with the hope that children will be interested in more than themselves and pursuing their own desires. We work with the hope that they will move "beyond" the infantile way of being in the world. As educators we also work with the hope that, in finding their sovereignty, they will not renounce the world and push it away. We work with the hope that they will move "beyond" the "teenage reflex," so to speak. Although these may be necessary phases we all need to go through to achieve sovereignty, we hope that children will eventually manage to stay in a relationship with what and who is other—finding room for themselves without forgetting that others need to find room as well, and that this will require an ongoing negotiation and give-and-take. We work with the hope that the new generation will manage to come into a grown-up relationship with their own desires and the world around them.

This is not just an educational theme or educational ambition. It is precisely here that the "concern" of education, if it is interested in the grown-up freedom of the child and not the infantile "just-doing-what-you-want-to-do," meets the "concern" of democracy. The "project" of democracy—which is fragile and precarious, but nonetheless crucial—is not about the war for pure identity, but about the ongoing, difficult "give and take" that seeks to make sure that there can be equal freedom—real freedom, grown-up freedom, democratic freedom—for everyone. This freedom means being-in-relation rather than being-in-isolation. If the school can be a place—a "sphere"—where we provide the new generation with time and space to meet themselves, meet the world, and work on this difficult challenge of trying to exist in and with the world in a grown-up way, it will fulfil its educational task and at the very same time contribute to the ongoing, never-ending work of democracy.

Notes

1 I tend to think that a country in which everyone can read, write and count perfectly but where no one has a sense of democracy has really not taken care of its basics.
2 Elsewhere, see for example Biesta (2017, ch. 1), I have explained in more detail the reasons for using this slightly awkward term. One important distinction is between being an object of other people's wishes and desires and being a subject of one's own life. One can also think in terms of grammar where the subject of a sentence is the one who acts, who "does" the action.

References

Apple, M.W. (2018). *Ideology and the curriculum.* 4th edition. New York: Routledge.
Benner, D. (2015). *Allgemeine Pädagogik. 8. Auflage.* Weinheim: Juventa.
Biesta, G.J.J. (2009). Good education in an age of measurement: On the need to reconnect with the question of purpose in education. *Educational Assessment, Evaluation and Accountability* 21(1), 33–46.
Biesta, G.J.J. (2010). *Good education in an age of measurement: Ethics, politics, democracy.* Boulder, CO: Paradigm Publishers.
Biesta, G.J.J. (2015). Resisting the seduction of the global education measurement industry: Notes on the social psychology of PISA. *Ethics and Education* 10(3), 348–360.

Biesta, G.J.J. (2016). Improving education through research? From effectiveness, causality and technology, to purpose, complexity and culture. *Policy Futures in Education* 14(2), 194–210.

Biesta, G.J.J. (2017). *The rediscovery of teaching*. New York: Routledge.

D'Agnese, V. (2017). *Reclaiming education in an age of PISA. Challenging OECD's educational order*. New York: Routledge.

Kliebard, H.M. (2004). *The struggle over the American curriculum: 1893–1953*. 3rd edition. New York: Routledge.

Chapter 4

Teaching for Democracy

The Role of Student Autonomy and Agency

Michael Soskil

The last thing I expected was for Daniel [1] to ask me if he could continue working at home. For years, before ending up in my 5th grade class, he had been a "reluctant learner." He rarely found his time in school relevant or motivating, and despite being very intelligent and interested in many of the things he found outside school, his work in classes rarely reflected his ability. On good days he would daydream through math and reading lessons, and on bad days he would allow his frustration to boil over or act disruptively. For Daniel, school was not a place of joy, but rather a place that he had to endure.

I could relate to Daniel. My elementary report cards were riddled with comments that expressed my teachers' disappointment in my lack of effort or interest. Like Daniel, I loved to learn but had no interest in learning from passages in whatever reading series we were using, or from "real world" problems in my math textbook that had no relationship to the real world. Now that I am an educator and have learned to speak "teacher" I can truly appreciate the frustration and disappointment that is hidden between the lines of those report card comments. Remembering my own experiences motivates me to provide a different learning environment for my own pupils.

Many teachers know that issues of motivation, as in Daniel's and my examples above, are common with our students. When students don't care about learning, they don't learn. If school is not directly relevant to them (at the moment they are experiencing it, not in some perceived relevance years in the distance), they disengage.

It is telling that the lack of engagement in our schools echoes the lack of engagement in our democracy. Less than half of secondary school students (48%) feel that what they are learning in class helps them outside of school, and only 52% enjoy coming to school most of the time (Youth Truth, 2017). When it comes to civic participation, only about half (53%) of Americans who were eligible to vote participated in the 2018 midterm elections did so—and that number is considerably lower when you look at Americans under the age of 65 (U.S. Census Bureau, 2019). When Burden et al. (2013) examined reasons why Americans choose not to vote, they found two of the main reasons included a lack of education and apathy caused by a belief that voting didn't matter. People were unsure of how to participate and believed that voting was irrelevant—not a meaningful way to bring about societal change.

Public education can contribute to the solution to both of these problems. Understanding of Civics, how to complete voter registration, and explicit instruction on voting procedures can be taught. In fact, former United States Supreme Court Justice David Souter (2012) warned that there is no larger problem in the U.S. than "the pervasive civic ignorance of the Constitution of the United States and the structure of government." He went on to say, "If something is not done to improve the level of civic knowledge, [an authoritarian despot seizing power] is what you should worry about." Civic understanding is as critical to the wellbeing of a democracy as participation. If our schools are to meet their purpose in providing the foundation for a healthy democracy, we must find ways to teach civics directly and engage students as democratic citizens inside and outside the classroom.

I have found that many school mission statements include language about developing this citizenship. However, in addition to the lack of civics education referenced by Justice Souter, too many of our practices in schools ignore this commitment. Schools often give "Good Citizen" awards based on who is most obedient to the rules of the school. Grades themselves are too frequently used as a means to ensure and measure compliance rather than the ability to apply knowledge. In many schools, children have little say in what they learn, how they learn it, the culture and norms of the learning environment, and how learning is applied to social issues outside the school. We cannot expect our children to graduate at the age of 18 as engaged citizens after being trained to unquestioningly obey authority for 13 years. Our students will not develop the skills they need to participate in our democracy if they are not allowed to be democratic citizens of their own schools or classrooms.

The experiences of students in schools should reflect the democratic values we hope to see outside of them. Our democratic society is dependent on a balance between two ideals that we consider fundamentally American: Liberty and Equality. While entire books have been written on the definition of and relationship between these two concepts, for the purposes of this chapter I will simplify and generalize the terms.[2] As much as I enjoy a deep philosophical discussion, our focus here is really on matters of classroom application.

Liberty can be understood as individual freedom and the ability to act as one pleases. This is, of course, one of the foundations of American democracy. Thomas Jefferson's listing of "Life, Liberty, and the Pursuit of Happiness" in the Declaration of Independence is perhaps one of the most well-known phrases in our country's history.

Yet, we do not and cannot have absolute liberty. If everyone were to have the ability to do anything they please, inevitably the liberties of other people would be infringed upon. There must be restrictions on our individual autonomy in order for society to function. We have come to generally understand that liberty should extend as broadly as it can, so long as it does not violate the rights of others.

Equality (not to be confused with "equity," which is discussed in depth in future chapters by Josh Parker, Jinni Forcucci, Kristin Nichols, Karli Sunnergren, T. Jameson Brewer, Amanda U. Potterton, and others) can be understood as everybody being treated the same. This, too, is a foundational concept for the United States. This country was built on a belief that nobody is above the law, and that each of us should have equal agency in choosing our leaders and shaping the decisions of our government.[3]

Once again, though, absolute equality is neither possible, nor desirable. In an extreme scenario in which absolute equality were the goal, individual liberties would have to be disregarded to ensure every person had exactly the same wealth and opportunity. The government would have to become authoritarian to enforce such extreme measures.

Healthy democracy resides in the equilibrium between these two concepts, and many of our political discussions stem from disagreements over where this point lies. Likewise, promoting democracy in our classrooms must emanate from a balance between liberty and equality. If we are too authoritarian and overly focused on making sure that everyone gets the same curriculum, the same assessments, the same instruction, and the same experience, then we have strayed too far toward extreme equality. In such a situation, students are unlikely to find relevance or motivation, much like Daniel above. If, on the other hand, we are too focused on providing students absolute freedom by giving them complete control over all decisions regarding learning, behavioral norms, and curriculum, they are likely to suffer poor academic outcomes due to lack of leadership.

Culture is determined by leadership—in classrooms, in schools, and in democracies. True leadership is not telling others what to do, but rather in inspiring them and empowering them to become leaders themselves. This is our charge as teachers. We need to find the balance between liberty and equality so that our students can develop as learners, as leaders, and as citizens.

During Daniel's 5th grade year, I had decided to provide my students with more control over classroom decisions. Rules were voted on by students after a managed discussion about what students wanted to accomplish during the year and what norms would be important to uphold. We decided to revisit these guidelines frequently to make sure they were working. While many learning activities were determined by the required curriculum, I found ways to give students more freedom over how they demonstrated their learning, and what materials they used to learn. If they finished the work that was required, I allowed them to pursue their own passions and use technology to share their new knowledge with the world.

Many of my students struggled to understand this newfound freedom at first. Even by late elementary school, most students had become accustomed to being told what to learn, where to learn it, when to learn it, and how to learn it. Autonomy can be scary for those who aren't used to it. Teachers can relate to this. Many of us who have used a mandated scripted curriculum feel anxiety when offered the opportunity to be creative again in our practice.

Over time, students began to thrive with the autonomy they were given. Some took months to realize the joy of exploring their passions and sharing them with others. Others found inspiration more quickly. Daniel didn't need much time at all. He started his own blog within the first few weeks of the year and the fires of purpose and creativity took hold inside him.

Daniel loved marine animals and started sharing his love with others on his blog. His first post was passionate and informative. But he was used to writing without proofreading, spell checking, or really taking much time at all to make sure he was expressing himself well. Some of the comments on his initial post were positive, but others told him that his lack of punctuation and bad grammar made his post hard to understand. Others expressed disappointment at the poor spelling.

Daniel was determined to do better, not because I told him to, but because he was invested. He spent time during school doing more research and writing his second post. He not only poured his heart into his writing, but spell checked every word and made sure every sentence had punctuation and a capital letter. Unlike the comments from teachers before who had pointed out his writing deficiencies on assignments, the feedback he got from those who read his blog mattered to him and motivated him to improve. When the school day ended and his new post was still not finished, Daniel did something totally unexpected.

He asked me, "Mr. Soskil, can I finish this, and maybe write some other blog posts at home?"

He wasn't the only one. The agency and autonomy I had given my students translated into motivation. Learning had relevance. Students not only improved as readers, writers, mathematicians, and historians; they learned to love learning. They also began to realize the power they held to use their learning as a tool for good. Many of my students wrote persuasive pieces that year on issues they cared about in order to advocate for change they wished to see in the world, and a few started or participated in initiatives outside school to improve the community. They were becoming the engaged citizens to which our school mission statement referred.

For Daniel, the highlight of his year came later in the school year when he received a request from a group of students in another state. They lived near a beach and came across a dead crustacean that they couldn't identify. Their teachers and parents couldn't help them, and they were now searching the internet with no success. They told Daniel that his blog posts convinced them that he was the expert they needed to solve their mystery. While many adults had failed, Daniel instantly recognized their picture as a Mantis Shrimp. Being consulted as an expert and being able to help others allowed him to see just how empowering learning could be.

Educating in a way that provides for a healthy democratic society must go beyond civics and engagement. Our shortcomings in those areas are apparent, but we also are seeing great failings in the ability to communicate. The art of compromise has been lost as hyper-partisanship and polarization have taken root. Watching 10 minutes of any prime-time cable "news" show exemplifies this. The problems that our society faces are more complex than ever. To solve them, we will need to have respectful and nuanced conversations with those who disagree. This is a skill that can be taught in our schools.

Prerequisites for this type of communication are empathy and humility. Without empathy, we cannot understand those with different perspectives. Without humility, we cannot understand how to learn from our mistakes. Designing the learning environment to promote these traits is vital. Fortunately, increasing the autonomy and agency our students have in their education provides us this opportunity.

Sean Bellamy (2018) describes this type of environment as providing students with the ability to take "nurtured risk"—the ability to make mistakes and learn from them under the guidance of adults who are conscious and mindful of each student's unique needs.

Thirty years ago, Sean sat in a garden with fourteen teenagers and two other staff members from a school that was slated to close. Determined to find a way to help those students pass their exams after their school ceased to exist, they started a discussion of what an ideal school would be. Instead of assuming the adults in the conversation knew best, everyone in the discussion contributed as equals. Soon after that discussion, the group decided to make that ideal school a reality.

The Sands School was born out of a philosophy that teenagers can and will make good decisions about their education when given the opportunity and surrounded by others who support them. Sean, like the other staff members at the school, believed that teenagers are better positioned to take chances and learn from failures than adults because they are naturally wired to be less risk averse. In the school, all decisions are made collaboratively by pupils and staff together. Each member of the school gets one vote, regardless of age or position. Whether deciding to change the paint color of a classroom, to suspend a student who has broken the rules, or to fire a teacher, the democratic process is used to make decisions.

The combination of autonomy and democratic responsibility has helped students at the Sands School develop into civically minded problem solvers. Only when children are given choice can they truly understand the consequences of those choices. To see failure as a learning opportunity, one must be given the opportunity to fail and to learn from it. Right now, there is significant focus being paid to find ways to bring the problem-solving process into school curricula, but at Sands, problem solving is built into the ethos. [4]

This book is based on the premise that a healthy democracy is dependent on a flipped education system. Instead of a strict hierarchy based on mandates and compliance, each rung in the traditional ladder of authority should ask those below (i.e. the federal government asking states, states asking districts, district administrators asking principals, principals asking teachers), "What do you need to be successful?" It makes sense that this system needs to be flipped all the way down to students. Teachers must ask students the same question and give them enough leeway to be able to answer it.

The structure of the Sands School is grounded in this philosophy, that all those in a school should be equally accountable partners. We've heard so much in the past two decades about the "21st-century skills" of communication, collaboration, creativity, and critical thinking. These can best be developed by creating conditions of nurtured risk that allow students to learn from their mistakes. While Sands is a private school in England, there are lessons that we can learn and strategies that we can adapt to our own situations. By giving children both increased autonomy and accountability in our schools, we can help them develop the humility and empathy they need to be good democratic citizens.

During a time at the Sands School when students were disrupting classes by entering late, a meeting was called to look at possible solutions. The cause of many of these disruptions was determined to be trips to a neighboring convenience market by students and staff. To solve the problem, a rule was instituted by vote that prohibited anyone from the school to visit the market during school hours. After this meeting, many of those who had just voted to institute this rule found themselves headed to the very market they had banned in order to grab a snack. The irony was not lost on them.

The next day, a second meeting was called. Understanding that learners learn better and teachers teach better when they are not hungry, the new rule was revisited. Collaboratively, it was decided that the market was not the problem. The issue was with classes being disrupted. A change was made and voted upon that allowed school members to visit the market, but also allowed those disrupting classes after they started to be excluded from them. The new rule created a situation where students had to be more respectful of their teachers' and classmates' time.

Sean points out the advantages of this type of democratic autonomy for developing critical thinkers and problem solvers. When a decision is found to not work, or to be ineffective, it can be changed. This stands in contrast to policies made by managers in schools who are disconnected from the implementation of those decisions. In many cases where policy comes from above in a hierarchy, students (and teachers) who are affected by poor decisions have no choice but to conform. In that situation students lose a learning opportunity and often become disenfranchised with school.

Even in more traditional classroom and school settings, the most important aspects of the Sands School culture can be replicated. It all starts by engaging with each person in the school as an individual personality. We must move away from systems based in conformity and obedience, instead developing cultures in which children walk through our classroom door with a sense of choice.

"It's a gravitational model," says Sean. "How do you create a lesson that has a strong enough gravitational field to hold each young person's personality in it? The facts are just the planets and moons orbiting around the lesson. That kind of gravitational force isn't created by fear, rejection, conformity, or obligation. It's created by fascination, interest, humor, and passion. If you can get students to feel engaged before they walk in the door because they know you are interested in them as people, and what you offer them has this gravitational force, you've got it."

Benjamin Franklin once famously said in response to a question about what type of government was created by the U.S. Constitution, we have "A republic ... if you can keep it." His implication was that the American democratic republic would require constant diligence from the populace to remain healthy. He was warning us that we must be intentional about protecting democratic values and norms.

Public education is where this work starts. In the previous chapter, Gert Biesta reminds us that *socialization*, to "introduce our students into traditions and practice, and invite them to find their own place within them," is a core function of education in a democracy. As educators, one of our roles is to provide opportunities for students to not only learn about civics and representative government, but to allow them to experience democracy in their education. This is how they understand their own place within our society. This is how they find relevance, both in school and outside its walls.

Sooner than we may realize, our students will assume the mantle of leadership from the generations before them. Many will graduate at the age of 18 with equal opportunity as every other voter to shape our nation. It must be our mission to help them understand the gravity of this responsibility, and to prepare them to lead wisely. This critical moment in our history requires us to flip our education system all the way down to our students. If we find the balance of liberty and equality in our classrooms, provide children agency and autonomy in their education, and support them with a culture of nurtured risk, we will lay the groundwork for a stronger, healthier, more democratic United States.

Notes

1 The student's name has been changed for privacy.
2 Within the following generalizations, I want to acknowledge that the history of the United States is riddled with contradictions and marginalization of certain communities. As I write about liberty and equality, it is important to note that those words have not always been applied to all.
3 Again, I want to recognize that equal agency in choosing representatives or creating laws, while mentioned in founding documents of the United States, has not been the reality for many in this country throughout our history.
4 Information about the Sands School, events that took place at the school, and quotes from Sean Bellamy were learned from either a personal interview conducted through Zoom Meeting on September 17, 2017 or Episode 2 of the Education for a Better World podcast, of which I am a host, that aired on December 12, 2018 and can be found at https://soundcloud.com/michael-soskil/episode-2-democratic-education-with-sean-bellamy

References

Bellamy, S. (Guest), Smokorowski, D., & Soskil, M. (Hosts). (2018, December 12). Democratic Education with Sean Bellamy. Education for a Better World podcast. Retrieved from www.ed4betterworld.com/episodes/episode-2-democratic-education-with-sean-bellamy.
Burden, B. C., Canon, D. T., Mayer, K. R., & Moynihan, D. P. (2013). Election Laws, Mobilization, and Turnout: The Unanticipated Consequences of Election Reform. *American Journal of Political Science*, 58(1), 95–109. doi:10.1111/ajps.12063.
Souter, D. (2012, September). The Danger of America's "Pervasive Civic Ignorance." PBS NewsHour. Retrieved from www.youtube.com/watch?v=rWcVtWennr0.
U.S. Census Bureau. (2019, July 16). Behind the 2018 U.S. Midterm Election Turnout. Retrieved from www.census.gov/library/stories/2019/04/behind-2018-united-states-midterm-election-turnout.html.
Youth Truth. (2017). Learning from Student Voice: Are Students Engaged? Retrieved from http://youthtruthsurvey.org/wp-content/uploads/2017/12/YouthTruth-Learning-from-Student-Voice-Student-Engagement.pdf.

Part II

An Equitable System for All

A democratic society cannot thrive when systemic inequity and marginalization limit the opportunity of some members. If some communities have access to excellent, comprehensive public schools that prepare them for civic engagement and participatory democracy, while other communities are starved of safe schools, the arts, necessary resources, quality teachers, and other critical aspects of a quality education, our democratic system cannot serve its purpose. We are at our best when all students have equal freedom to realize their potential.

The challenge of making this a reality is complicated by a lack of shared American experience. Right now, the life experiences of those in cities, those in the suburbs, and those in rural areas are becoming increasingly divergent. In 2017, while working with the Organisation for Economic Co-operation and Development in Paris, Michael Soskil was told: "We are finding that the experience of the average American living in a rural area right now has more in common with someone living in rural Romania than someone living in New York City."

Even among those living in close geographic proximity, social media and cable news have allowed us to create ideological bubbles that prevent us from understanding others' points of view. Pluralism and respectful debate have too often been replaced by polarization and bullying. How can we move past our own limited perceptions, shaped by experiences in our local communities and those we interact with online, to create a system that protects opportunity for all—including those who don't have the same experiences that we do? How can we build a system that does not reflect and impose the values of the majority on those in the minority?

Teachers have a vital role to play in working toward a more equitable system that answers these questions. No group of people have greater ability to understand the collective experiences and needs of vast numbers of students. No group is better positioned to understand the intersection of community and school. Nobody else serves at the point where policy and practice meet as intimately. Teachers are uniquely able to use their experiences and professional knowledge to improve and shape education.

Part II lays out a vision of how we can work toward an educational system that has equitable outcomes and opportunity for all. The chapters help define the role of teachers within that system.

In Chapter 5, **Josh Parker** explores the qualities of both inequitable and equitable systems and provides guidelines on how we can design a flipped education system that promotes freedom for all.

In Chapter 6, **Jinni Forcucci** and two of her students, **Kristen Nichols** and **Karli Sunnergren,** give powerful insight into ways privilege impacts the experiences of students and how we can each examine our perspective.

Next, **Andy Hargreaves** (Chapter 7) looks at the upheaval caused by the coronavirus pandemic, the ways that class shapes opportunity in the United States, and the lessons that we can learn from the inequities that have been exposed.

Lindsey Jensen builds off this in Chapter 8 to examine the divergent experiences between rural, suburban, and urban communities and how we can close the opportunity gap faced by children in rural areas.

Lastly, **T. Jameson Brewer** and **Amanda U. Potterton** (Chapter 9) expose how some of the same market-based, privatization approaches being touted as solutions to educational equity issues are actually eroding education as a public good and driving equity gaps wider.

Chapter 5

Systems that Promote Equitable Outcomes

Josh Parker

After watching Benji, a powerful documentary, a few years ago I had trouble sleeping. Toward the end of the film, an all-too-familiar story of a young African American male athlete killed by gunfire, a statistic was shared that kept me up all night.

Long after the credits rolled, I could not shake the number that was casually mentioned as the story was nearing its conclusion. It was not 17, the age of the basketball phenom when he was murdered. It was not his jersey number, 25, which went on to be worn both in remembrance by NBA players and by future Simeon Career Academy basketball stars at his high school until it was retired. It was a three-digit number that dumbfounded me. 669.

In 1984, the year Ben "Benji" Wilson was slain, he was one of 669 people to be murdered in his home city of Chicago.

As I tossed and turned trying to fall asleep, I unsuccessfully tried to imagine living in a city where murder was so commonplace. I thought back to when I was the same age as Benji Wilson at the time his life was taken. My graduating class in high school was less than half of the 669 people slaughtered in his city that year. I grew up in the suburbs of Washington, DC, a city that was smaller, but similar to Chicago in a lot of ways. Like Chicago, there were rampant homicides that occurred as well. According to CDC statistics (Weil & Escobar, 1991), 482 people were murdered in Washington the year before I moved to Prince George's county, less than a thirty-minute drive away.

W. Edwards Deming has been attributed with saying, "Every system is perfectly designed to get the results it does" (W. Edwards Deming Institute, 2020). As I thought about the documentary and this quote, I kept coming back to the same thought: people in inner cities continue to be killed at alarming rates. At the time I was living in a suburb of Baltimore, another city where murders were far too commonplace. I will never forget how I felt coming to the realization that the homicide crisis that has been plaguing us for more than three decades was not an accident or an unlucky occurrence. In that moment I came to understand something that is even more jarring than the notion of lives being taken, violently, over and over again.

These murders were both a product of individual bad decisions and perpetuated by a system. These murders were not just committed. They were the product of a design. They were engineered. Color-coded. Class-based.

The nation's capital is nicknamed "Chocolate City" due to its majority black population. In the year that Washington had 482 homicides, the neighboring community of Montgomery County had twenty-five. Nearby Howard County had five (Gross, 2017).

Both of those communities were majority white and affluent.

The reasons for the concentration of certain races in certain geographic areas has its roots in slavery, but also has deep connections to the segregation that came afterward. Locations that were concentrated with people of color were deemed to be the least desirable places to live. The practice of redlining made sure they were the only areas where brown and black families could get loans to buy or build a house (Camera, 2015).

Redlining and other prevalent real estate and city planning practices ensured that in the late 20th century, over 100 years after the Emancipation Proclamation, we had de facto segregation of historically marginalized people within inner cities across the United States. This was not just common, it was codified. The system was aligned to produce specific outcomes, and it was very successful. Yet, in order to keep this residential and racial segregation in place there was one more sub-system that had to play a pivotal role—our public schools.

The shocking number of people killed in majority minoritized cities throughout this country is paralleled by the number of students failing, and who have been failed by the schools that populate these same cities (Camera, 2015). This, too, is by design. As an African American male educator, I have experienced this system from every angle. I have been a student who has been fairly and unfairly treated. I have been a teacher, who has been both damaged and supported. I have been a member of the central office, where I have seen destructive and transformational leadership.

My participation in the school system has been impacted by the body that I live in and the words that come out of it. I have been told to not stand so close to people, "because of my height." I have been confronted by multiple people in a public staff meeting for asking a question that penetrates beyond surface reasoning. I have been the teacher that gets "those kids" because I can "handle them."

If you are black and male in the current education system, you will be damaged. If we can unpack the characteristics of the system, we can change this. I implore you to analyze what you read, examine your role in the system, and strive to understand how your locus of influence intersects with the work that must be done to create an equitable, flipped system. For all students. All teachers. All of society.

The Features of Inequitable School Systems

> I hear education systems are failing, but I believe they're succeeding at what they're built to do.
>
> —London (2013)

Defining a system is akin to describing the game of basketball. Is basketball the act of two teams alternating shot attempts at a ten-foot goal, or is basketball rules and regulations that allow the action to take place? It is both. That analogy is where we can start to understand the idea of systems.

A system is the product of people, actions and materials around a set of policies, practices and procedures that ritualizes the way the people act within a set area. It is both people and policies. This is important because any time someone points to a system as being too big or too powerful to stop they have reduced a system to its intangible aspects. We must understand, however, that a system consists of humans that bring their experiences, perspectives, biases, and learning to the decisions they make.

People run systems.

Therefore, a first characteristic of systems that encourage inequitable outcomes is a separation of people of influence from the policies, practices, and procedures they enact. Policies, practices and procedures come from people. People have beliefs which inform the rules and regulations they create. Therefore, when the people of a system describe it as "the way it has always been done," without acknowledging their ability to change it, they willfully ignore their role in perpetuating the damaging parts of it. Unaccountable people produce unaccounted for results.

A second characteristic of systems that encourage inequitable outcomes is sociopolitical blindness. Consider all of the functions of a system: transportation, observation, evaluation, assessment, and school demographics. In this non-exhaustive list, issues of race, class, and power are implicated. For instance, who gets assigned to which school? What students have access to advanced course offerings? The answers often fall along color and class lines. Systems that encourage inequity may acknowledge these disparities but will not invite a sociopolitical critique into the discussion. Instead, they might present data as organically stemming from the region. They may also explain it as "big bang" data, that these disparities sprang from some ill-defined history and just continued to form and grow. This is insufficient. We know the history and if we fail to acknowledge the roots of the tree of injustice, we will only hack at the branches. The tree will still grow and flourish.

A third characteristic of systems that encourage inequity is a preoccupation with fixing people over fixing injustice. Paul C. Gorski, in his article entitled "Avoiding Racial Equity Detours," speaks to this principle:

> Effective equity efforts focus not on fixing students of color, but on eliminating racist conditions. If we find ourselves, in the name of equity,

adopting initiatives meant to improve educational outcomes by adjusting mindsets or cultures in students of color, it's time to reconsider our efforts.

(Gorski, 2019)

This characteristic is particularly insidious and sometimes hard to root out because it is often camouflaged in concepts like personal accountability and blaming the backgrounds that historically marginalized students come from. Of course, students will ultimately have to decide to complete work and apply themselves, but often the assignments they receive and the support to which they have access to are of low quality. When we critique the choices of students without critiquing their options, we create a system based on a child's inherent ability to overcome obstacles. That is a system where inequitable outcomes are to be expected.

The characteristics above are a non-exhaustive list but begin to give us a foundational understanding of the ways systems establish and maintain inequity. If we understand what makes systems promote inequitable outcomes, we have a pathway to articulating how school systems can promote equity.

The Features of Equitable School Systems

> The reality is that any social system (including an organization or a country or a family) is the way it is because the people in that system (at least those individuals and factions with the most leverage) want it that way.
> —Heifetz, Grashow, and Linsky (2009)

Features of equitable school systems include the inverse of the above. Most importantly, systems that promote equitable outcomes do just that—produce outcomes where students of color are not persistently achieving below their white peers. To that end, these systems connect people to policy, interpret functions through a sociopolitical lens, and seek to rectify unjust options rather than the people who have to engage with them.

These systems reveal the people that are "behind the curtain" as it pertains to issues of teacher and administrative placement, curricular choices, and other systemic functions that contribute to the academic success of all students—but especially students of color. In contrast to the features of a system that encourages *inequitable* outcomes, this system connects people to the practices they enact.

Furthermore, they connect issues of race, power and class to the decisions made. The people in these systems do not simply highlight disproportionality, they speak about the origins of it and then evaluate the policies, procedures, and practices that are implemented through two pervasive questions:

- Do policies, procedures, and practices contribute to inequitable student outcomes relative to race and class?
- How should the people who produce these policies, practices and procedures adjust them to avoid predictable and persistent elements of disproportionality according to race and class?

Finally, instead of putting the bulk of focus on what students are, or are not, doing relative to their achievement, equitable systems evaluate the conditions and contexts where students learn. Then, they seek to upgrade those conditions and contexts. From curriculum resources to human resources, equitable systems always prioritize focus on the environment before students, faculty and staff within that environment.

Why the Shape of a System Matters

> The more people participate in the process of their own education, the more the people participate in the process of defining what kind of production to produce, and for what and why, the more people participate in the development of their selves. The more the people become themselves, the better the democracy.
>
> —Horton, Freire, Bell, Gaventa, and Peters (1990)

Systems that encourage equitable outcomes for all students are both fair to the students of that system and a pillar to our democracy. If students are not engaged in education that empowers them to consume, critique, and evaluate, then their ability to participate in civil society is diminished. Instead of having power over the creation and enforcement of laws, laws of the country will instead possess a power over them. If we fail to provide systems that support all students to have equal ownership of our society, we will be graduating them into a de facto oligarchy. Our democracy is threatened when the education of those who should benefit from it is compromised.

Making a school system work for all children supports a democracy that should work for all citizens. Healthy democracy cannot exist without true equity, and true equity cannot exist without comparable educational outcomes. We cannot realize this ideal without flattening hierarchies and allowing decisions to be informed by the lived experiences of students and teachers. We have to flip our system.

How We Create an Equitable Flipped System

1 We acknowledge that the current education system contributes to other systems of inequality in our society. In America, we do not have to go looking for racism. We don't need to argue whether it exists. It is a pervasive characteristic of the systems we have built. To flip the system,

we must acknowledge that it impacts our students and our society and that we each play a role in either eliminating it or perpetuating it. There is no middle ground. Our cognizance must then lead us to understand the role education systems play in advancing inequality. Once we own these truths, we must count up the costs. How much will it cost us to fight for what we know to be right? How much will it cost to continue to perpetuate systems that oppress students of color? How expensive is our passive resistance to them? Then, we have to ante up.

2   **We require those who run our systems to be accountable to the communities they serve.** An unaccountable person who holds influence over other people and systems is dangerous. No matter the character of such an individual, if they are not connected to the communities they serve, there is a low possibility of a profound commitment to the community's survival. Historically marginalized people don't suffer from lack of ability—they suffer from lack of visibility. They are best seen when their lived experiences are intimately understood by the leaders of systems.

3   **We give agency and autonomy in the system to those who are impacted by it.** Oppression always flows in one direction—from the top of an organization to the bottom. Liberation always flows in multiple, mutually reinforcing directions: from leaders to followers, from followers to each other, from followers to leaders. In a true system of liberation, it may be hard to distinguish leaders from followers as all have a vested interest in each other's liberation. This type of dynamic is a flipped system, a flattened hierarchy with decision-making driven by those at the intersection of policy and implementation. Teachers, students and communities must be key decision-makers, not just stakeholders, if a system is to be just.

4   **We design a system for both short term *and* long-term transformation.** Systems that contribute to equitable outcomes are important now *and* later. The struggle for African Americans did not just materialize in the 1960s with the Civil Rights Movement. It began as soon as we arrived. Through slave rebellions, abolitionist speeches and more—African Americans focused on generations to come as well as immediate actions to better their condition in life. So it must be as we flip our system to work for all students. All options and solutions should be considered because when we change what happens now—we invariably change what is possible later.

5   **We commit to this as our highest priority.** This work cannot happen without the strongest possible commitment to see it materialize in our lifetimes. We can no longer focus on intent; we must identify current injustices and seek to change them. The work of flipping the system is about impact. Therefore, we must organize ourselves around this

commitment—across differences and despite the bitter battles of our history. In a unified way, we must proclaim that our children's futures are our futures. Each of us, as educators, as community members, as Americans, and as fellow humans must take ownership over the impact, we have to create a more equitable school system and a more just society. We cannot expect others to flip the system for us—it is our responsibility to demand and create the change we wish to see. This might mean running for office, advocating for particular bills or policies, informing people about the impact of race, power, and class on student outcomes, or any number of other direct actions. If it is to be, it is up to "we."

Life-Saving Systems

> There is no neutral education. Education is either for domestication or for freedom.
>
> —Joao Coutinho (as quoted by Pippin & College, 2017)

I will end where I began. On the streets of several cities throughout this country, too many young men of color are simply trying to survive. We can change this reality. We must change this reality. What if the number 669 was the number of lives saved through education instead of the number of murders? Or the number of new homes built by socially conscious graduates to improve housing conditions in their neighborhoods? Or the number of jobs created by children who left our schools as entrepreneurs—ready to not only choose, but to create choices?

When we commit to a system that promotes educational equity—we put our values into action. We create pathways to true liberty and destroy old pipelines to prisons. We make tangible the promise of our constitution. We make the gift of democracy work for all. I do not want to watch another documentary that details the ways that systems limit opportunity and cut down life. I want to contribute to a new reality where education is the pathway to equitable possibilities, civic agency, and freedom for all. Our collective will and action can make this happen.

References

Camera, L. (2015, October 7). Stagnant City Schools Are Failing Minorities. Retrieved from www.usnews.com/news/blogs/data-mine/2015/10/07/report-stagnant-city-schools-are-failing-minorities.

Gorski, P. (2019). Avoiding Racial Equity Detours. *Educational Leadership*, April, 56–61.

Gross, T. (2017, May 3). A "Forgotten History" Of How the U.S. Retrieved from www.npr.org/2017/05/03/526655831/a-forgotten-history-of-how-the-u-s-government-segregated-america.

Heifitz, R., Grashow, A., & Linsky, M. (2009). *The Practice of Adaptive Leadership: Tools and Tactics for Changing Your Organization and the World.* Cambridge, MA: Harvard Business Press.

Horton, M., Freire, P., Bell, B., Gaventa, J., & Peters, J. (1990). *We Make the Road by Walking: Conversation on Education and Social Change.* Philadephia, PA: Temple University Press.

London, M. (2013). Ted Talks Education. TED Talks Education. Retrieved from www.pbs.org/wnet/ted-talks-education/speaker/malcolm-london.

Pippin, T., & College, A. S. (2017). What Would We Be Doing if We Weren't Doing This?: A Journey in Democratic Departmental Practices. *International Journal of Critical Pedagogy,* 8(1), 237–259.

W. Edwards Deming Institute. (2020). Quote by W. Edwards Deming. Retrieved from https://qoutes.deming.org/authors/W._Edwards_Deming/quote/10141.

Weil, M., & Escobar, G. (1991, December 25). D.C. Sets Homicide Record. Retrieved from www.washingtonpost.com/archive/politics/1991/12/25/dc-sets-homicide-record/f3b9c1d0-f9d1-4ed1-b3fb-73b56abf6f9d.

Chapter 6

Beyond Privilege

Using Student Perspectives to Create a More Equitable System

Jinni Forcucci, Kristen Nichols, and Karli Sunnergren

I (Jinni Forcucci) began teaching high school English a little over 23 years ago, naively believing that my job was to lead: to respond to student inquiry, offer resources, provide a communal environment, prepare youth for a rewarding future. What I didn't know was the most effective and impacting educators would be the students who laugh and cry, who struggle and thrive in my rural Delaware classroom. It is because of these brilliant and selfless scholars, who courageously share truths, that I am becoming the advocate all learners deserve. It is because of their argumentative essays, heartfelt narratives, transformative digital stories and courageous conversations that I realize my most important responsibilities as an educator: to listen, to self-reflect, to grow, and to provide a climate that connects humanity while disrupting the systemic racism that pervades our institutions.

Last spring, my seniors composed argumentative texts that considered how external factors influence agency, and as usual, I was educated and humbled by their candor and introspection. Writing in our room where curiosity, empathy, and evidence are required; where risk-taking is rewarded; and where the goal is to attain both cultural literacy and cultural proficiency, my young rhetoricians compose because the process prompts increased understanding, potential persuasion and valued progress. They believe in changing the world, but they also believe in exploring self. Imagine what our schools might look like if we adults followed their lead. Imagine if we all journeyed toward understanding our personal biases and their impacts on how we discipline, how we academically place students, how we build curriculum. Imagine if we collectively liberated.

Kristen Nichols and Karli Sunnergren are two recent graduates from Sussex Technical High School in Georgetown, DE, who have been integral to my journey. While their aspirations for their respective futures are impressive, and you'll inevitably be inspired by their accomplishments, it is their ability to fearlessly and authentically detail their personal experiences in an inequitable educational system that will move you the most.

In the paragraphs that follow, you'll read personal accounts of how our schools have impacted two gifted, compassionate, and hopeful young women. You'll meet Kristen, a thoughtful academic, who details a system that forces her to hide frustration and discomfort in hopes of discovering academic achievement and self-pride. And then you'll meet Karli, an impassioned overachiever, who grew up in the exact same system, a system that rewards her whiteness.

My emphatic hope, while you read, is that you honor their truths by reflecting on your own. Then consider how your experiences shape your approach to instruction and connection. Ask yourself if your own implicit bias has ever interfered with a child's ability to succeed. Continue your journey, as I try to do each day, toward identifying and working against the racist policies and procedures that ensure inequitable outcomes. Be honest with yourself.

Kristen

I started the elementary school year as an excited, motivated, hopeful child. My teacher, while she was kind and compassionate, had no idea the impact her first words would have on me.

"Are you sure this is your name?" she asked with a puzzled expression.

My motivation was immediately disrupted as I realized she'd likely never met a black child without a punctuated name. She had predicted the color of my skin based on my name, and she was dumbfounded when I wasn't her expectation.

We present our schools as safe havens that equally educate and prepare the next generation for the future. Parents send their children every day, trusting that their loved ones will be educated in a welcoming environment and encouraged to grow. Unfortunately, this is not the case for many of America's children of color. As an African American student, I have felt the hardship that occurs when students feel like an unwanted and underestimated minority.

From as early as kindergarten, curricula cater to white children. In fact, one teacher suggested that my ancestors were discovered in huts and brought to this nation, where they learned to be integrated into a thriving society. What she described did not sound so bad – in fact, it sounded good. The idea of giving people places to live in exchange for work sounded fair.

Then I realized she was talking about slavery.

My ancestors were enslaved. They were taken away from their homes in chains, crowded onto boats, and sailed to tiny shacks where they were abused. They were forced to work in fields and take care of the very people that captured them. But my teacher never said this.

When children receive inaccurate and/or false history lessons, they're taught that white people are superior. My white classmates had the chance to feel the enlightenment and pride in their race that was constantly stripped away from me as a student of color. As a result, I began to hate school.

Instead of arriving willing to learn, I came with distorted notions of education that ultimately hindered my experience.

I noticed other students of color having the same experience. Though I
was miserable, I continued to overachieve in hopes of one day being rewarded with the validation of my culture, just like my white classmates.
Unfortunately, many of my black and brown peers did not feel the same
way. As a result, their grades and hopes diminished. Watching as my white
classmates enjoyed cultural and racial celebration hurt more and more each
day. We would study white scientists, teachers, musicians, and politicians.
We learned of all the diverse accomplishments of white people. When it
came to my culture, however, the only time I heard mention of black people
was when they were in states of oppression or succeeding on athletic fields.
While my white peers were encouraged to pursue careers in anything they
desired, my black classmates and I were provided only two paths: let the
system hold us back or keep fighting for the chance to be seen.

As middle school approached and the cultural divide between races
became concrete, someone finally took notice. In an effort to reverse the
damage created by the educational neglect I'd felt for over seven years, the
diversity project was created. The project was a month-long lesson based on
discovering differences and varying aspects of other cultures. It seemed successful; it opened us up to beautiful discourse and knowledge of holidays
and traditions we would have never had otherwise. It was a great introduction to other cultures. Now, looking back I realize that this only looked at
diversity from the surface. We could have built upon this experience every
year by looking deeper into cultures, observing their history and truly
understanding how they live – the hardships they face on a day to day basis.
Yet, we never did another diversity project again. I suppose those teachers
were satisfied with their single attempt to expose us to diversity.

Without any follow up, students were not able to apply the acceptance
and empathy they had briefly learned. Bias and racism are not simple subjects. They cannot be fought with a single diversity project. Over time the
project hindered students of color as they began to feel more disconnected
from their white classmates. Many began to feel as if diversity was a topic
that they could learn for an exam and then never touch on again.

They felt forgotten. We felt forgotten. I felt forgotten.

The students of color that had worked so hard to catch up fell behind
again. I, however, could not help but feel slightly guilty as I found myself
achieving with my white counterparts.

My family's emphasis on education prompted my success. As a child, my
dad would read me to sleep every night; his favorite genre to read was history. He educated me with the truths of Harriet Tubman, Rosa Parks and
Ruby Bridges. I learned from an early age that school and home were
opposites. I saw school as a fanciful world filled with characters like Amelia
Bedelia, Junie B. Jones, and Ramona and Beezus, instead of a world of

strong black leaders like those my father preached about. I am so grateful that I had this opportunity, that I learned about my history before I was taught the whitewashed curriculum from my white teacher in a predominantly white school – all while feeling like I had to keep my blackness behind my family's door.

I was fortunate, but many students like me do not learn the value of education at all. Many come home and have to help raise their siblings. Many, outside of school, do not know the next time they will eat. Many don't even have a home to go to after school. With so much going on outside school, many of these children cannot focus in class. And, for children of color who come to school already feeling ostracized by the curriculum and the environment, the days become more and more of a challenge. Instead of trying to understand their experiences, many teachers just label children as lazy. These students, like all students, need to be uplifted, but the current system constantly undermines their identity and sets them up for a future of inferiority.

Education should not be solely focused on English, math or science. Instead, it should educate students on the world around them. Educators have developed an "ignorance is bliss" mindset toward differences or seem to think that ignoring curriculum that takes on culture and race is a better route – a favor to their students. We need to end this approach and inform children about ALL cultures from a young age. Teachers must be culturally proficient, which I know is complex, but when they are and introduce this proficiency to children at an early age, students are more likely to learn and embrace the lessons. The sooner we introduce the next generation to cultural proficiency, the sooner we destroy the opportunity gap for students of color, the sooner we invest in the future, and the sooner we work toward real equality.

Karli

I'd love to attribute my academic achievement solely to innate intelligence and my hunger to learn. I'd like to believe that I'm at the top of my class because I've worked the hardest, studied the most; because I'm the smartest, and I've made sacrifices that no one else is willing to make. And to be honest, I do lose sleep studying, forego food for the library, and drain myself emotionally from the pressures and stresses that come with overachievement. However, to celebrate my academic success without considering the privilege that's helped me to get there is unfair and misinformed.

Privilege and access are the agency that have defined my life and allowed me to find academic success. I'm the product of a system that was designed to work for people exactly like me. I'm white with educated, healthy, supportive parents. I have everything I need, and most of what I want.

In fact, I'd be remiss if I didn't note that my access has given me an undeniable advantage when it comes to academic achievement. All of the "standardized" tests and assignments that determine student success aren't standard at all – they were designed

with a person exactly like me in mind. I was taught almost exclusively by teachers that reflected my ethnic and cultural background. It's dangerous to make education a competition. It's devastating to make it an unfair one.

It's important to understand that I don't feel angry about my own access. Rather, I'm angry because not everyone has the same advantages. I'm angry that privilege is such a factor in a system that claims to offer equal opportunity. I'm incredibly grateful for the opportunities I've been given and for my parents' hard work, so I make every effort to use my privilege for good. However, if every child was given even a semblance of what I've been given; a safe, healthy environment that fosters learning, values what is relevant to the child's life and culture, and offers love and support unconditionally; what could be achieved?

When privilege stops predicting academic success, the students we recognize as brilliant and exceptional and valuable will increase exponentially because all students, from all ethnic and cultural backgrounds, will reap the benefits of access that students like me have taken for granted our whole lives. And then what, you ask? Curious, enlightened children will become changemakers and advocates. Society and culture will be uplifted by their ideas, their policies, and the stories they have waited so long to tell. New writers, thinkers, scientists and teachers will emerge, and our children will be inspired by leaders who truly represent them. Then, anything is possible.

I know that as a white person, it's often difficult and uncomfortable to talk about privilege. In fact, being able to avoid the conversion or deny it entirely is a privilege in itself. However, it is dangerous and irresponsible not to accept opportunities to spread awareness and act to preserve one's own comfort.

I know that I can join and leave the conversations surrounding privilege, racism, and justice with little to no consequence for myself; however, the discomfort in I feel in acknowledging my position is insignificant in comparison to the discomfort that children of color are constantly subjected to in American school systems, healthcare systems, culture and society.

Oftentimes, people of color don't have the luxury of fighting inequality and racism when it suits them. So, if you are a white person seeking to combat racism, here is my call to you: don't just take a stand when it suits you, when it's easy, or when it's comfortable. Don't take action when you have an audience, but then maintain the status quo when no one is watching. Don't accept racist systems because they're "too hard to change." Don't believe that you're doing your part because you've "never called anyone the N-word" or "not hired someone because they're black" (true words that have been spoken to me). Most importantly, don't walk away from the conversation, even when you misstep or when you are confronted with painful truths. Your discomfort and awareness change the conversation.

Your actions help liberate and uplift. YOU start to become part of the solution.

It's a lot to ask, but like black and brown people have done for so long, I'm asking. We're demanding. People of color have been sharing their stories of oppression, injustice, and pain from the moment that we started inflicting those upon them. Now, you have an opportunity to use your privilege and amplify their already-powerful voices. Now, you are faced with a choice of either being anti-racist or perpetuating the most devastating systems this nation has ever known. There's only one correct decision. It's up to you to make it, and then act on it.

Conclusion by Jinni Forcucci

I often hear teachers suggest that all kids feel valued or included in their classrooms. They explain that "not seeing color" results in equal treatment, and ultimately, equal access to success. I offer this to those who share these sentiments: black and brown children want you to see their color. They want you to celebrate it. To "not be seen" in totality is to not be understood. We cannot ignore a defining part of a child's identity, nor can we believe that race, as a social construct, has not shaped the experiences of youth in our schools. Kristen could not have been clearer. She was treated equally, yet that treatment failed to provide her the inclusive and culturally responsive environment she deserves.

Most teachers do not intend to hurt the children of color who count on them for rigor, representation, and support; but until they're held accountable for their biases and until they intentionally work toward dismantling institutionalized racism, our scholars will suffer. Until we ask our students, and sincerely engage in pointed discourse about the impact of race on systems, on climate, on curriculum, on community, we lull ourselves into a space where loving our learners is enough. I've lived in that space, where I believed my sincerity and heartfelt connection to each individual writer and reader in my English classroom gave me ethos. When my love for the kids, however, wasn't changing the pervading gaps I still see in discipline, AP enrollment, and communal comfort I realized I wasn't affording opportunities that equally engaged them. I needed to learn more about inequitable systems, about the socializing Eurocentric lens that white-centered my perspectives, and about how my "best" wasn't enough.

If a flipped system is to be effective in laying the foundation for a healthy, equitable democracy, we must first be willing to acknowledge that this nation's systems have, historically and by design, subordinated people of color. We must then name the ways we've intentionally and/or unintentionally supported these policies and practices in our schools and communities.

Then, with confidence and certainty, we must lead a movement that calls for increased diversity in our teacher workforce, for teacher preparation programs that center equity and culturally responsive practice, and for intensive administrative and school staff training that inspires collective liberation. Finally, we must lead this flipped system in a way that proves we've listened and learned from the most important population in the educational system: our students. When the current people of influence listen to teachers the way teachers listen to the student, maybe our system can begin to heal and rebuild in the ways that Kristen and Karli imagine.

These insightful truth tellers have made sincere calls to action, perhaps prompting you to consider a perspective that does not align with what you know—or maybe offering you a reality that parallels your own. How you respond to their calls, though, and the steps you choose to take or not take are up to you. But know this—if your journey toward becoming more racially responsive and informed ends when you put down this text, our students' journeys will be halted too.

Chapter 7

The Day After

Education and Equity after the Global Pandemic

Andy Hargreaves

The Great Disruption

Many critics of educational policy have been arguing that it's time to *flip the system* from one that has increased inequity through reduced public invest-ment, market competition, and online alternatives to teaching, to one that strengthens the hand of government, promotes professional and community-based collaboration, and supports the value of face-to-face teaching. Now, suddenly, and catastrophically, a global pandemic has happened, the world has flipped, and temporarily, at least, this has totally flipped our educational systems too. No schools, no tests, more online learning rather than less, kids at home all day with their parents, and parents in lockdown with each other and their kids. What does this mean? What can we learn from it? And once this is all over, as it may be even by the time this book is out, how will things look, the day after, when everyone goes back to school again?

1918
1929
1945
1989
9/11
2020

In the future, in modern history classes, these dates will mark moments when the world changed forever. The (misnamed) *Spanish Flu* pandemic, the *Great Depression*, the end of *World War II*, the collapse of the *Berlin Wall*, the attack on *The World Trade Center*, and now the *Coronavirus* crisis, when we really did stop the world so we could try to get off: all these things fundamentally altered how we live. How we think about fairness, openness, security, peace, community, the role of government, and the health of our nations—all these are indelibly affected by national and global crises, chan-ges that impact everybody, and how we respond to them.

Flipping from School to Home

As I write this piece, just coming out of 14 days of self-isolation into weeks and perhaps months of protracted social distancing, everyone everywhere seems affected by COVID-19 in some way or other, and that includes in education. Right at this moment, you may be a teacher scurrying around trying to put together online courses and lessons for your students. But you may also be all too aware that some of your kids don't have computers at home, or Wi-Fi, or even paper and glue. You may have been locked out of your school for health and safety reasons when you came back from spring break and so you're without a lot of resources that you need in order to plan. You may have kids of your own at home while you're trying to do all this. You or a family member might even be sick yourself. And then you'll be worried about kids for whom home is never a safe place—where there's anger, tension, or not enough food. And now there will be parents who have been thrown out of work without employment or health benefits, or parents who still have big jobs with lots of responsibility who are working from home while their kids are running around like hyperactive Muppets.

Meanwhile, your district or state department may be sending you contradictory information, insufficient information, or a surfeit of information about how to respond. When one principal emailed his teachers about what to do and got to "eleventhly," it was clear that top-down micromanagement had gone too far. As one parent's rant that went viral reminded us, perhaps sometimes we need to "turn it down, foot off the gas, leave them be" (Strauss, 2020).

But, someday soon, we will come out of this, and when we do, what will it mean for public education, and especially for equity? To understand this, we first need a quick reminder of the importance of educational equity along with some additional thoughts and reminders about the association between inequity and social class. Then, I'll address some equity issues we will need to anticipate and confront after the pandemic.

Education, Equity, and Social Class

Across the U.S., about 80% of the differences in student achievement, or in achievement gaps as we have come to know them, are explained by factors outside the school (Berliner, 2006). Educational inequalities in the U.S. are some of the greatest in the developed world and economically, as well as educationally, those inequalities are widening. The reasons for this have been attributed to the system's failure to be responsive to race, diversity, immigration, second language learning, learning disabilities, emotional and mental health problems, and so on. But cutting across them all is one key factor: social class and poverty.

North Americans, including Canadians, find it difficult to talk about the idea and importance of social class. Social class—understood in terms of working mainly with your hands, having little control over your work, employment conditions that offer no benefits or security, or being paid very low wages—is, whatever a person's color, race, or sexuality, one of the greatest determinants of educational achievement.

In both the U.S. and Canada, race and diversity have dominated the national agenda of equity and inclusion. It is diversity instead of equity, or diversity as a synonym for equity, rather than social class inequality, that dominates the educational and social policy agendas. But Joan Williams (2017), author of *White Working Class*, regards the apparent classlessness of North American society as a fiction. It is a consequence of what she calls the *class cluelessness* of U.S. society in particular. For Williams, this class cluelessness is a relatively recent phenomenon. "Over the past, 40-odd years, elites stopped connecting with the working class, whom prior generations had given a place of honor" (p. 2), she observes.

U.S. policy makers have stopped referring to social class, or, following President Barack Obama, have lumped almost everyone into the catchall category of "middle class." Yet, in his book on *The White Working Class*, Justin Gest (2018) points out that while 2019 figures show that among 437 members of Congress, 131 are women, 53 are African American, 50 are Hispanic or Latino, and 20 are Asian American, Indian American, or Pacific Islanders, only 2% of members of U.S. Congress claim working class backgrounds. This aspect of (under) representation is not even recorded on the official Congressional website. It is invisible.

Class matters. Anne Case and Angus Deaton (2017, 2020) have undertaken a landmark, large-scale study of changing levels of mortality and morbidity (chronic pain and illness) in the U.S. white working class. Under the grim heading of *Deaths of Despair*, they set out how white working class Americans have been dying of suicide, alcoholism and drug abuse at rapidly accelerating rates that exceed those of other age groups and other ethnicities, and that are actually the inverse of the declining mortality and morbidity rates that characterize other developed economies. Since the turn of the century, "after decades of improvement, all-cause mortality rates among white non-Hispanic men and women in middle age stopped falling in the United States and began to rise" (p. 398).

Importantly, as David Leonhardt and Stuart A. Thompson (2020), acknowledge in their *New York Times* review of Case and Deaton's research, "the black working class is hardly thriving—and deaths of despair have surged among them in the last few years (too). Overall life expectancy remains significantly higher for whites than blacks. So, of course, do incomes and wealth." But Case and Deaton point out, middle-age black working-class mortality and morbidity rates have actually been improving since the turn of the century, while rates for the middle-age white working class have been trending sharply in the other direction, especially among "those without a college degree" (p. 431).

Globally, these trends seem unique to the United States. Case and Deaton show that while, in 1990, "U.S. whites had much lower mortality rates from drugs, alcohol, and suicide than France, Germany, or Sweden," after 2000, "while mortality rates in the comparison countries converged to about 40 deaths per 100,000, those among U.S. white non-Hispanics doubled to 80" (p. 408).

Class matters for all ethno-cultural groups, including but also extending beyond the white working class. In *Our Kids*, Robert Putnam (2015) notes that "by the opening of the twenty-first century, the class gap among students entering kindergarten was two to three times greater than the racial gap" (p. 162). Over time, related factors like residential sorting, or *de facto* class segregation, shunt "high-income and low-income students into separate schools" (p. 162) where they end up mixing with people of their own kind. The inequalities widen even further as these kids progress towards the end of high school. It is "as if the poor kids had weights attached to their feet that grew heavier and heavier with each step up the ladder" (p. 188).

These patterns of inequality also manifest themselves in trends regarding upward social mobility—the chance young people have to move up in the world in relation to their parents. In *The Spirit Level*, Richard Wilkinson and Kate Pickett (2011) compared rates of social mobility from working class origins to middle class jobs in developed economies, and found that the U.S., with one of the highest levels of economic inequality, also had the worst rates of social mobility from one generation to the next. The U.S. also had some of the highest levels of alcoholism, drug dependency, early pregnancy, obesity and incarceration—all indicators of overall low levels of wellbeing. For people born after the mid to late 1970s, social mobility rates are not improving and are even showing signs of deterioration.

Critics of educational inequality like Diane Ravitch (2011) and David Berliner (2006) list the many reasons for this: income inequality, market choice of schools, residential segregation of communities and lack of mixing among kids, decline of public funding and of social supports for families, an "arms" race among the middle class of purchasing enriching experiences for their kids (Major & Machin, 2018); runaway levels of college tuition fees, weak health care, poor quality housing, parents with increasingly insecure jobs, and so on—in short, poverty.

Until recently, economic and educational inequality has been most manifest in large cities. However, in recent years, with intense focus, and the benefits of local economic and philanthropic investment, cities like Boston and Long Beach have been making a comeback through economic and educational regeneration (Mourshed, Chijioke, & Barber, 2010; Johnson, Marietta, Higgins, Mapp, & Grossman, 2015).

By contrast, the impact of *rural* poverty on educational achievement and opportunity is also now attracting the overdue attention of policymakers and researchers (Beckman & Gallo, 2016; Cohen, 2014, Strange, Johnson, Showalter, & Klein, 2012). Former manufacturing towns (FMTs) whose industries have forsaken them are also just starting to be recognized as one of the new faces of poverty and disadvantage, including in education (Levey, 2015). Lack of educational opportunity and achievement is stubbornly persistent in FMTs that the old economy has abandoned and that are cast adrift from the resources of financial and social capital that are more readily available in the big cities. In the U.S., as well as the UK, and Canada too, former manufacturing towns and their working-class families have become the forgotten communities of our time.

In FMTs or "third-tier cities," characterized by "high unemployment rates, a declining population rate, and high poverty rates" (Siegel & Waxman, 2001, p. 9), poverty and inequality have slipped under the official radar. Indeed, although there are official designations for urban, rural and suburban environments in U.S. national statistics, there is no category for FMTs. They have no official identity.

The point of retrieving the importance of social class in narratives of social and educational inequity is not to pit class against race or other kinds of marginalization. Indeed, in the late 1980s and early 1990s, Kimberle Crenshaw (1989) and Patricia Hill Collins (1990), who introduced the concept of *intersectionality,* pointed out that a white middle class woman who had been the victim of domestic violence, for example, was positioned very differently in terms of how she could access resources and how people represented and responded to her, compared to a poor woman of color who might also not have English as her first language and might even be an undocumented immigrant. "The violence that many women experience," Crenshaw argued, "is often shaped by other dimensions of their identities, such as race and class" (p. 1242). Both Crenshaw and Hill clearly understood that one of the key aspects of intersectionality was social class.

But subsequently, it is the other aspects of intersectionality that have come to the fore, and the working class and all its needs have been forgotten. It is time to get past this *class cluelessness,* as Joan Williams (2017) calls it, so as to engage with how class is deeply embedded in the effects that poverty has on all students' achievement and wellbeing. The relevance of all this to positive educational change, to flipping the system in a constructive way, is no more evident than in how we can think about *The Day After* the pandemic when there will be an opportunity to look at social class, and responses to inequity, with new eyes.

These Are the Days We'll Remember

Here are five predictions about what may lay ahead for student equity beyond COVID-19. They come in no particular order of priority.

I There Will Be More State Integration of Digital Technology

During COVID-19, districts, schools, teachers, parents and students themselves have been scrambling around to find technology that might support their learning. Technology and publishing companies have also been throwing out materials, websites and resources, usually free of charge, for people to access. Teachers and schools have been at very different stages with their familiarity and comfort with digital technologies and online learning. At the end of the pandemic, however, all educators should have some basic familiarity with and begin to get a direct sense of where technology adds value to, and where it subtracts from teaching and learning. But haphazard improvisation, inequitable access to devices and Wi-Fi, and the market confusion of online offerings (even though some of them are very good) should and will push state governments to set up their own large-scale digital capabilities to organize their internal and these external resources in a coherent way to support and not replace teachers.

Uruguay, for example, with a population of 3.5 million (about the size of Connecticut) has had an arm's-length government innovation agency, PLAN CEIBAL since 2007. Every child in the country, irrespective of their family circumstances, has been given a personal device and an internet connection. This has stimulated more than a third of the country's schools to develop innovative projects in which innovation and learning, not technology, are in the foreground—and CEIBAL supports these. Technology has supplemented and stimulated teaching and teachers; not replaced them. It has been made available to all students, not just some of them. During the first week of school closures in Uruguay, use of the CEIBAL platform increased by 1100 percent (Plan Ceibal, 2020).

This is what U.S. states need to do now for increased, equitable technological capacity—not traditional resistance to technology, nor a market-driven, Wild West of competing alternatives, but a coherent state-driven approach that will enhance teaching and learning for all students. From *The Day After*, there's an opportunity for technology to become an innovative and inclusive part of state systems to support existing teaching, rather than an outsourced and inequitable market alternative to it.

2 The Idolatry of Online Learning Will Weaken

During the pandemic, teachers, schools and parents have started to distinguish between online learning and on-screen learning. Online may sometimes be continuous on-screen learning—like a math game, for example. But with a lot of kids already on screens for 9 hours or more a day, they really don't need more of that. However, online or remote learning can also be used to set up an activity including making collages from pasta, doing origami, or constructing a robot, for example. The deficiencies of online learning will show up during COVID-19 among poorer and more vulnerable students who can't concentrate or self-regulate, who have family noises and distractions, who haven't learned English yet, and who are all trying to learn on different devices, or without devices, at the same time in the same house. Online will still have a place, but we'll stop overselling it.

3 Teachers Will Come Back in

Even before COVID-19, Diane Ravitch (2020), in *Slaying Goliath*, illustrated how both red and blue states had started to reinvest in their teachers, and that the days of politicians demeaning teachers as an excuse to set up private or charter-based alternatives, are no longer supported by the public, and have passed. If you don't like public education, or public school teachers, try having everyone teach their own kids at home, and see how long they can sustain that before they start climbing the walls with frustration. Teachers, and not just health workers, are some of the great unsung heroes of COVID-19: preparing resources for remote learning, reviewing their kids' work, connecting with them and their parents to make sure they are OK, all while they themselves often have kids of their own at home. But they, as well as the parents, ultimately know it's not enough. Parents will start to see that teaching isn't easy. It's hard. It's hard enough when you have two or three kids. Now, many will surely realize how hard it is when you have 25 or 30 kids to teach all day. On *The Day After,* we'll take many of our essential workers less for granted, and teachers will absolutely be among them.

4 Extra Supports Will Be Needed when School Starts up Once More

During the weeks and months of being at home and away from school during the pandemic, students will have lost the reassuring face-to-face support of their teachers. Many young people will have experienced poverty and stress. They may have seen family members become very ill, or worse. They might have had little or no chance to play outside. Where there are toxic family relationships, some children will have been particularly vulnerable. Many will have lost the habits that schools teach them. More than a few will exhibit the signs of post-traumatic stress disorder. And the learning gaps will undoubtedly widen between children from poorer and better off homes respectively. In middle class families like my own where my wife, a retired principal, has structured lessons and activities along with playing times every day for our three young grandchildren, children might benefit from the smaller group attention and get even further ahead than they might have done at school. In families without books, or without parents who can read or who know how to support their children's learning, children will return to school after long spells of boredom, having eaten the wrong kinds of food, and spending hours on end on smart-phones or playing video games. So, there will need to be a concerted effort, extra time, and additional resources and support to close the gap and support the weakest learners and the most vulnerable children again.

5 Demand for Vocational Education May Grow

This is my highest risk prediction, but here is what's behind it. One of the things the global pandemic and lockdown in many areas has exposed is the vulnerability of an economy to being one driven by the service and consumer sector domestically, while manufacturing has been increasingly outsourced abroad, to the detriment of many traditional U.S. communities and working-class towns and cities. Reliance on parts, materials and ingredients from thousands of miles overseas has created scarcities in medical and other urgent supplies. So, like Germany, some U.S. states at least, might well look at providing partial state support to bring back some manufacturing, make some of our best industry locally sourced, just like our best food, and create a more diversified and better-balanced domestic economy between manufacturing and services. This could mean a renewed demand for vocational skills and training and higher status for the schools that provide it. It might also mean we can start to talk about building a strong and dignified working class again that takes pride in its labor, has the respect of our communities, and isn't only associated with deficits and poverty. None of this will happen automatically, but it is a way forward that some states and nations might seriously consider.

Days of Our Lives

Social class inequity in education always matters. It's what many teachers fight against all the time, in every way they can. To be working class does not mean to be poor, or only that. But because of the decline of manufacturing and associated declines in social and community support, class and poverty have become increasingly interlinked. Class intersects with other aspects of marginalization like language and ethnicity. It is also becoming an increasing problem in the epidemic of "deaths of despair" among the white working class in rural communities, small cities, and former manufacturing towns.

The working class—black, white, Hispanic, Native American, and more—has always benefited less than middle and upper classes from educational opportunity and social mobility. Crises like the global pandemic do not immediately remedy these inequities. They expose and exacerbate them. The pandemic has affected everybody, but it has not affected everybody in the same way. Access to healthcare, testing and ventilators has not been distributed equally. And the same will have been true for opportunities for learning and support for mental health problems—since as Bob Putnam points out, while a crisis as simple as drug addiction can hit any family, middle class families have networks of lawyers, counsellors and other sources of help that just do not exist for their working class counterparts.

Online and remote learning will work well when the homes know what to do and have access to the financial, technological and human resources, as well as their own knowledge and know-how to enable their children to learn as well as and sometimes even better than they might at school. But in cramped apartments, or with troubled families, and cast adrift from their teachers, counsellors and other support workers, many working class young people will fall further behind their peers and suffer more mental and emotional wounds in the process.

So now is the time not only to think about the best immediate responses to COVID-19, important as these are. It's also vital to consider what we need to do *The Day After* the pandemic to rectify what will be even wider educational inequities, to relieve the post-traumatic stresses of pain and suffering that too many vulnerable young people will have encountered, and to build a better and more equitable system with strong government support in the future.

After World War II, in the U.S. and the UK (the country that raised me), the spirit of having to endure a common crisis and to pull together to get through it, left a powerful legacy. This was manifest in things like the GI Bill, greater high school opportunities, homes for returning soldiers, widened access to college, and a 30-year period when income inequalities narrowed, social mobility improved, and more Americans had a greater chance to actually live the American Dream. From the very first *Day After*, this is what the U.S. state and Federal Government needs to do once more. Bring back a proud working class, eliminate poverty, and create better, fairer, opportunities for all supported by a strong and compassionate government.

References

Beckman, P. J., & Gallo, J. (2016). Rural education in a global context. *Global Education Review*, 2(4), 1–4. Retrieved February 10, 2018, from http://ger.mercy.edu/index.php/ger/article/viewFile/238/15.

Berliner, D. (2006). Our impoverished view of educational research. *Teachers College Record*, 108(6), 949–995.

Case, A. & Deaton, A. (2020). *Deaths of despair and the future of capitalism*. Princeton, NJ: Princeton University Press.

Case, A. & Deaton, A. (2017). *Mortality & morbidity in the 21st century*. Brookings Papers on Economic Activity. Providence, RI: Brookings Institution, March 17. Retrieved from www.brookings.edu/wp-content/uploads/2017/08/casetextsp17bpea.pdf.

Cohen, R. (2014). What ails rural philanthropy, and what must be done. *Nonprofit Quarterly*. Retrieved February 10, 2018, from http://nonprofitquarterly.org/2014/12/04/what-ails-rural-communities-philanthropy-what-must-be-done/.

Collins, P. H. (1990). *Black feminist thought: Knowledge, consciousness, and the politics of empowerment.* New York: Routledge.

Crenshaw, K. (1989). Mapping the margins: Intersectionality, identity politics, and violence against women of color. *Stanford Law Review,* 43(6), 1241–1299.

Gest, J. (2018). *The white working class: What everyone needs to know.* Oxford: Oxford University Press.

Johnson, S., Marietta, G., Higgins, M. C., Mapp, K. L., & Grossman, A. (2015). *Achieving coherence in district improvement: Managing the relationship between the central office and schools.* Cambridge, MA: Harvard Education Press.

Leonhardt, D. & Thompson, S.A. (2020). How working-class life is killing Americans. *New York Times,* March 6. Retrieved from www.nytimes.com/interactive/2020/03/06/opinion/working-class-death-rate.html.

Levey, A. (2015). A world without work. *The Atlantic,* August/September. Retrieved from www.theatlantic.com/magazine/archive/2015/07/world-without-work/395294.

Major, L. E. & Machin, S. (2018). *Social mobility and its enemies.* Harmondsworth: Pelican Books.

Mourshed, M., Chijioke, C., & Barber, M. (2010). *How the world's most improved school systems keep getting better.* New York: McKinsey & Company.

Plan Ceibal (2020). COVID-19 in Uruguay: Educational disruption and response. Retrieved from http://atrico.org/wp-content/uploads/2020/03/Plan-Ceibal-contingency-plan-coronavirus-MFR-V-0.6.pdf.

Putnam, R. D. (2015). *Our kids: The American Dream in crisis.* New York: Simon & Schuster.

Ravitch, D. (2011). *The death and life of the great American school system: How testing and choice are undermining education.* New York: Basic Books.

Ravitch, D. (2020). *Slaying Goliath: The passionate resistance to privatization & the fight to save America's public schools.* New York: Knopf.

Siegel, B., & Waxman, A. (2001). *Third-tier cities: Adjusting to the new economy.* Somerville, MA: Mt. Auburn Associates.

Strange, M., Johnson, J., Showalter, D., & Klein, R. (2012). Why rural matters 2011–12: The condition of rural education in the 50 state s. Retrieved from www.ruraledu.org/articles.php?id=2820.

Strauss, V. (2020). "If we don't die of corona, we'll die of distance learning." *Washington Post Answer Sheet,* March 20. Retrieved from www.washingtonpost.com/education/2020/03/22/if-we-dont-die-corona-well-die-distance-learning-israeli-mom-with-four-kids-home-loses-it-heres-her-rant.

Wilkinson, R., & Pickett, K. (2011). *The spirit level: Why greater equality makes societies stronger.* New York: Bloomsbury Publishing.

Williams, J. C. (2017). *White working class: Overcoming class cluelessness in America,* Cambridge, MA: Harvard Business Press.

Chapter 8

Closing the Rural Opportunity Gap

Lindsey Jensen

Braden[1] is a twelfth-grade student in rural Illinois who had high aspirations to attend Yale. Despite being the president of his class, involvement in a plethora of extracurricular activities, countless hours of volunteer work, and a GPA well above 4.0, Braden was recently rejected. Braden's mother disclosed:

> We knew it was a shot in the dark. After all, kids from rural Illinois don't go to Yale. It's impossible to compete with the elite high schools in large cities, and we knew when we filled out the application that it would never happen. I just wish that Braden didn't feel like such a failure.

Half of school districts, one third of schools, and one in five students can be found in rural areas just like Braden's (White House Rural Council, 2011; National Center for Education Statistics, 2016). Much of the narrative surrounding equity and education is directed at urban school districts, where serious issues do need attention (Barrett et al., 2015; Bouck, 2004). While poverty is often associated with these urban areas, it actually exists at higher rates in rural American counties (Schaefer et al., 2016). Rural schools are often left out of research and policy discussions, exacerbating poverty, inequity, and isolation (Lavalley, 2018). This leads to fear, stagnation, and a population of students ill-equipped for life outside of their rural communities. If we truly want our school system to support a thriving democratic society, teachers must demand equitable opportunity and outcomes for all students, including those living in America's rural areas.

Rural Economies and Career Options: The Achievement Gap

In rural communities, a student's destiny is often influenced by their parents' experiences. Generational poverty and geographic isolation can lead to a lack of exposure to opportunities and perspectives from outside the local area. For some students, this can mean low expectations and bleak prospects for upward social mobility.

Consider Bailey, another 12th grade student from rural Illinois. Like Braden, she was hardworking and committed to academic success. Bailey never considered enrolling in college, though. She assumed her future was predetermined—living on public assistance like her parents in the same town. Her teacher, however, saw her potential and recommended her for a scholarship. Through this, Bailey was able to experience life beyond her community and find success through opportunities she previously didn't know existed.

Rural communities, driven by economic forces, often value education directly linked to skills needed in their local workforce (Atkin, 2000, 2003; Hektner, 1995; Morris, 2012). Consequently, higher education is often disregarded as less necessary than it is in more urban or suburban areas. Rural students have historically held lower enrollment rates in higher education than their counterparts in other geographic locales (Stone, 2017). As Biesta explained in Chapter 3 of this volume, healthy democracy depends on our education system balancing qualification for jobs after graduation, contributing and interacting with society, and self-knowledge. When education systems in rural areas amplify focus on technical skills at the expense of academic, artistic, or cultural pursuits, they eliminate opportunity for our children to develop as holistic individuals and intellectually engaged members of our democratic society.

This is not to say that workforce competencies are not vitally important aspects of education, or that the goal for every student should be to go to college. However, an overemphasis on vocational training in rural schools while schools in other areas are overemphasizing preparation for college widens the gap between the experiences of living in these areas. It leads to division, as residents of rural, urban, and suburban areas increasingly understand their "America" to be something different.

Rural students who choose to pursue higher education degrees, fearful that the local economy cannot support their career aspirations, rarely return to their home communities, exasperating the gap (Bryan & Simmons, 2009; Demi et al., 2009; Hektner, 1995; Means et al., 2016; Stone, 2017). Thus, higher education becomes a source of outmigration where students earn degrees but do not use that education to benefit the rural communities from where they came (Petrin et al., 2014). According to Mathis:

> The 20th century [saw] a continuous movement of the best and brightest of rural children away from their roots. They don't come back as often as they leave. The result is that the remaining young rural citizens do not have as high a level of education nor as high a level of income. Thus, it is also an economic out-migration. The remaining population is less likely to support education. They have less financial capacity to support education, even if they have the will. The result is a refined distillation of poverty and low-end jobs [resulting] in greater social inequities.
>
> (Mathis, 2003, p. 9)

Undoubtedly, this phenomenon fuels rural students' apprehension toward higher education, especially if students have a desire to reside in their hometowns.

The growing education gap has contributed to much of rural America's perception of academics and those with higher degrees as "others" and "liberal elites." J. D. Vance (2016) speaks to this phenomenon in his memoir, *Hillbilly Elegy*. On one of his first visits home to Ohio after studying at Yale, Vance saw a woman at a gas station wearing a Yale t-shirt. He asked her if she attended. She divulged that her nephew did and then reciprocated the question. J. D. instantly became conflicted about where he wanted to place his allegiance. Did he identify as a Yale Law school student or as "a Middletown kid with hillbilly grandparents?" Ultimately, he made the decision to lie out of embarrassment for his own success. Later, he realizes he "lied to a stranger to avoid feeling like a traitor" (Vance, 2016, p. 205).

The growing negative rural perception of higher education has given rise to much of the anti-intellectualism fueling climate change denial and anti-science sentiment in politics, as well as a political will for candidates who are "regular folk", uneducated, or who scorn those with higher degrees. It likely contributed to the delay in believing scientists who warned of the severity of the recent Coronavirus pandemic, costing countless lives. This anti-intellectual trend is damaging our national ability to have educated, nuanced conversations about complex topics, imperative to healthy democratic governance.

Isolation and Respect for Diversity

It should come as no surprise that the majority of rural students are White (Showalter et al., 2017). Because rural school districts, like their urban counterparts, face challenges of racial inequity, teachers in these areas have enormous responsibility to expose students to the realities of other areas. Respect for plurality is a prerequisite for healthy democracy, and it only occurs where it is explicitly a focus. Unfortunately, many rural teachers feel unprepared to tackle issues of race and diversity in areas where there is so little. Even when recognizing the importance of this work, teachers often lack the professional development and preparation to be fully equipped to broaden their students' horizons.

The majority of children in rural schools navigate an entire school day without ever seeing a teacher of color. We know teachers of color positively impact student achievement—especially for students of similar backgrounds. Schools with diverse staff, however, are beneficial to *all* students. In an *Education Week* essay, Gloria Ladson-Billings affirms:

> I want to suggest that there is something that may be even more important than Black students having Black teachers and that is White students having Black teachers! It is important for White students to

encounter Black people who are knowledgeable ... What opportunities do White students have to see and experience Black competence?

(Gloria Ladson-Billings cited by Ferlazzo, 2018)

Teacher Recruitment and Retention

A quality education system that promotes the health of the community is only possible if it is able to recruit and retain quality teachers. Rural children are disproportionately taught by novices. As teachers develop their craft and become more effective, they often leave for higher-paying teaching jobs in affluent, suburban schools. As a result, rural students experience a revolving door of rookie teachers—especially children with special needs. Attracting quality special education teachers in rural areas is incredibly problematic (Mathis, 2003) "because of their geographical location, culture, and lack of resources" (as cited in Brownell et al., 2018, p. 4; National Rural Education Association, 2004; Rosenkoetter et al., 2004; Ryan, 1999; Schwartzbeck & Prince 2003).

Carrie, a third-year special education teacher loved everything about working at a rural school, except for the paycheck. Faced with the responsibility of paying off her student loans, she was forced to take a job in a higher paying district in a suburb just outside of Chicago. "There was no way I could afford to teach in rural Illinois. As a result, I caved to the pressure to take a higher-paying job in an area that I didn't necessarily want to live in, but that could grant me the financial stability I need."

Mental Health and the Rural Opioid Epidemic

Economic stressors and lack of local mental health services increase the risk of opioid use in rural areas (SAMHSA, 2018). Furthermore, people living in these areas are more likely to have jobs involving physical labor, which contributes to more legal prescriptions for opioids to manage pain and opportunities for addiction and abuse. This abundance of available opioids "can lead to self-medication and drug-sharing, which—combined with a reduced understanding of how to use and discard medications, recognize side effects, and avoid drug interactions—can increase rates of addiction and overdose" (SAMHSA, 2018).

Drug-related deaths are 45% higher in rural areas than in urban areas, and rural Americans are twice as likely to die from opioids as their urban counterparts. "Rural grandparents are more likely than their urban counterparts to be raising a grandchild because their adult child is addicted to opioids ... [which] increases financial, mental health, and other challenges— particularly if the grandchildren have physical or cognitive problems resulting from their parents' opioid abuse" (SAMHSA, 2018). The impact on families and children inevitably is felt in classrooms, affecting school culture and the future wellbeing of the greater community.

Despite this issue disproportionately harming rural communities, only 10% of opioid treatment resources nationwide are located in these settings (SAMHSA, 2018). According to Monnat and Rigg (2018) of the Carsey School of Policy at the University of New Hampshire, these infrastructure challenges include "disproportionately fewer hospitals and less access to mental health treatment, drug treatment, prevention, and harm reduction programs" (p. 3).

A significant contributor to youth substance abuse in rural America is the lack of recreational opportunities, and although "strong family support can improve the odds of recovery, social and family networks in rural areas also facilitate prescription drug diversion (sharing, trading, selling). Indeed, in regions with widespread and intergenerational economic disadvantage … opioids sometimes serve as a form of currency" (Monnat & Rigg, 2018, p. 1). Because rural labor markets are less diversified than urban ones, they are more vulnerable to economic shifts due to high-wage, high-skill service, finance, and technology-based jobs which are more prevalent in urban America (Monnat & Rigg, 2018). The outmigration of highly skilled and college-bound young adults and multigenerational economic distress leave most rural communities unable to find the financial and human capital needed to combat the opioid problem.

Solutions

To address the inequities in rural schools, we must capitalize on their strengths and avoid a deficit mindset. One of the great strengths of rural schools is that they have the capacity to recruit their own graduates to come back and teach. Thus, strong public policy for recruiting and supporting educators in rural communities is paramount. This includes support for "grow-your-own" programs, recruitment efforts, mentoring programs, and meaningful professional development. An equal amount of emphasis should be placed on creating powerful partnerships between "grow-your-own" programs and neighboring universities to provide future teachers with feasible options—as well as financial support through the cultivating of scholarships and financial incentives—to make teaching a viable option in geographic locations where novice teachers suffer from a lack of affordable housing and inadequate salaries. Perhaps these incentives could include free college tuition to high school students entering teacher prep programs, and who commit themselves to teaching in their communities for the first four years of their careers.

Solutions to the problems which plague rural communities can essentially be summed up in one word: partnerships. Rural schools are the foundation of their communities, and the education they provide is the foundation of our democracy. Rural districts should engage frequently within their communities to create powerful partnerships between school, community, and home. They must create coalitions to assess the extent of opioid abuse and develop a community response that ensures prevention and treatment services. Exchange opportunities need to be built so rural students have the opportunity to engage with diverse students in urban areas and children from cities and the suburbs are given the opportunity to better understand the lived experiences of their rural counterparts.

No solution can be implemented without financial resources. Rural schools cannot thrive without equitable funding formulas, which are currently overly dependent on local property taxes. State funding formulas are generally inadequate to meet specific rural needs, and this problem is often under-recognized in state and federal calculations. "Part of the solution lies in rural economic development, increased state aid shares, less reliance on local property taxes and more progressive systems of tax collection and distribution" (Mathis, 2003, p. 9).

If we respect and leverage the strengths of our rural communities, and at the same time fully-equip them with the necessary tools to broaden students' worldviews and diversify student experiences in the process, we can empower students to seek and create opportunities both inside and outside of their rural communities. This will help to bridge the gap between rural, suburban, and urban districts. If we get this right, we can bring together people from different regions of the country, promote nuanced conversations about educational equity, and save our democracy.

Note

1 Names of students and teachers have been changed.

References

Atkin, C. (2000). Lifelong learning-attitudes to practice in the rural context: A study using Bourdieu's perspective of habitus. *International Journal of Lifelong Education*, 19(3), 253–265.

Barrett, N., Cowen, J., Toma, E., and Troske, S. (2015). Working with what they have: Professional development as a reform strategy in rural schools. *Journal of Research in Rural Education*, 30(10), 1–18.

Beeson, E., and Strange, M. (2000). Why rural matters: The need for every state to take action on rural education. *Journal of Research in Rural Education*, 16(2), 63–140.

Bouck, E. C. (2004). How size and setting impact education in rural schools. *The Rural Educator*, 25(3), 38–42.

Brownell, M. T., Bishop, A. M., & Sindelar, P. T. (2018). Republication of "NCLB and the demand for highly qualified teachers: Challenges and solutions for rural schools." *Rural Special Education Quarterly*, 37(1) 4–11.

Bryan, E. & Simmons, L. (2009). Family involvement: Impacts on post-secondary educational success for first-generation Appalachian college students. *Journal of College Student Development*, 50(4), 391–406.

Demi, M., McLaughlin, D., & Snyder, A. (2009). Rural youth residential preferences: Understanding the youth development-community development nexus. *Community Development*, 40(4), 311–330.

Ferlazzo, L. (2018). The importance of "white students having black teachers": Gloria Ladson-Billings on education. *Education Week Teacher*. Retrieved from https://blogs.edweek.org/teachers/classroom_qa_with_larry_ferlazzo/2018/02/the_importance_of_white_students_having_black_teachers_gloria_ladson-billings_on_education.html.

Gettinger, A. (2019). A big reason rural students never go to college: Colleges don't recruit them. *Hechinger Report*. Retrieved from https://hechingerreport.org/a-big-reason-rural-students-never-go-to-college-colleges-dont-recruit-them/.

Hektner, J. (1995). When moving up implies moving out: Rural adolescent conflict in the transition to adulthood. *Journal of Research in Rural Education*, 11(1), 3–14.

Lavalley, M. (2018). Out of the loop. *Center for Public Education*. Retrieved from https://education.wsu.edu/documents/2018/12/center-public-education-rural-schools-report.pdf/.

Mathis, W. J. (2003). Equity and adequacy challenges in rural schools and communities. *The Annual Meeting of the American Education Finance Association*, 1–17.

Means, D., Clayton, A., Conzelmann, J., Baynes, P., & Umbach, P. (2016). Bounded aspirations: Rural, African American high school students and college access. *The Review of Higher Education*, 39(4), 543–569.

Monnat, S., & Rigg, K. K. (2018). The opioid crisis in small town America. *Carsey Research*, 135, 1–6.

Morris, E. W. (2012). *Learning the hard way: Masculinity, place, and the gender gap in education*. New Brunswick, NJ: Rutgers University Press.

National Center for Education Statistics (2016). *Rural education in America*. Retrieved from https://nces.ed.gov/surveys/ruraled.

National Rural Education Association (2004). *Raising the alarm: Critical issues in rural education*. Retrieved from www.nrea.net/awards%20&%20otherNREA%20Position%20Paper%20I.doc.

Pappano, L. (2017). Colleges discover the rural student. *The New York Times*. Retrieved from www.nytimes.com/2017/01/31/education/edlife/colleges-discover-rural-student.html.

Petrin, R., Schafft, K. & Meece, J. (2014). Educational sorting and residential aspirations among rural high school students: What are the contributions of schools and educators to rural brain drain?. *American Educational Research Journal*, 5(2), 294–326.

Rosenkoetter, S. E., Irwin, J. D., & Saceda, R. G. (2004). Addressing personnel needs for rural areas. *Teacher Education and Special Education*, 27, 276–291.

Ryan, S. (1999). Alaska's rural early intervention preservice training program. *Rural Special Education Quarterly*, 18(3/4), 21–28.

SAMHSA (2018). *Opioid issues and trends among older adults in rural America*. Retrieved from https://dsamh.utah.gov/pdf/OA%20Conference/Key%20Facts%20OPIOID%20ISSUES%20AND%20TRENDS%20AMONG%20OLDER%20Adults%20in%20Rural%20America.pdf.

Schaefer, A., Mattingly, M. J., Johnson, K. M. (2016). Child poverty higher and more persistent in rural America. *Carsey Research*, 97, 1–8.

Schwartzbeck, T. T., & Prince, C. D. (2003). *How are rural districts meeting the teacher quality requirements of no child left behind?*Charleston, VA: Appalachia Educational Laboratory. Retrieved from www.ael.org/snaps/aasa-aelreport4.pdf.

Showalter, D., Klein, R.. Johnson, J., & Hartman, S. L. (2017). *Why rural matters 2015–2016: Understanding the changing landscape.* Washington, DC: Rural School and Community Trust.

Stone, A. N. (2017). Rural students and higher education: An overview of challenges and opportunities. *Texas Education Review*, 5(1), 1–9.

Vance, J. D. (2016). *Hillbilly elegy.* New York: HarperCollins.

White House Rural Council (2011). *Jobs and Economic Security for Rural America.* Washington, DC: White House. Retrieved from https://obamawhitehouse. archives.gov/sites/default/files/jobs_economic_security_rural_america.pdf.

Chapter 9

Market Forces and Erosion of Education as a Public Good

Widening Equity Gaps

T. Jameson Brewer and Amanda U. Potterton

Education as a Public Good

Education, and public education in particular, has long been understood as a foundational component for the maintenance of a democratic society. And while public education can be understood as a foundational component of society, it is not alone in the long list of services that are considered public goods. Police, firefighting, public sewer, libraries, roads, military, street lights, and more are all understood to be services that benefit every member of society both broadly and individually. That said, while a family may never need to call on the services of their local fire department, most families understand the importance of maintaining such public goods through tax support and public oversight.

In the case of 19th-century firefighting, this was a hard-learned lesson, as cities once understood firefighting to be an individualistic good (Landers, 2016) overseen by a myriad of private fire insurance companies, of which the first was established in 1752 (Anderson, 2019). Fire brigades were at the time organized by private insurance companies to respond to fires at homes that carried that company's insurance policy. Fires that broke out in homes that were uninsured—often as a result of not having the financial means to have such insurance—were left to the individual homeowner and any benevolent neighbors to help extinguish. In fact, drawing on the spirit of competition that is endemic in a marketplace, competing firefighting brigades would often resort to unfriendly tactics and even brawls in the streets to prevent a competing insurance company from being able to put out a fire, thus damaging the company's reputation and sales (Dupuy, 2009). This reality was captured in the 2002 Martin Scorsese film *Gangs of New York* that depicted such brawls. The film portrays a firefighter from one brigade using a crate to hide a fire hydrant so that the competing company could not put out the fire (Landers, 2016).

Cities eventually became more densely populated, and a developing colonial society reimagined firefighting to no longer be an individualistic good best left to the whims and forces of a competitive marketplace. Rather, publicly funded and operated firefighting became a mainstay in the quiver of public services best understood as benefiting the collective good. Moreover, as a public good, the service was extended to all citizens regardless of their ability to pay for such protections.

Such public goods are now funded through taxation, at varying progressive amounts based on financial ability, and provided to all equally in our democratic society. Truly, few in our society would suffer the suggestion that firefighting be turned back over to the whims of a marketplace in order to benefit from the forces of competition and choice between providers. Lest we return to the style illustrated in *Gangs of New York* (2002), most would not entertain the suggestion of turning over policing, military, and libraries to private and competing companies, because the results would not seek first to serve all in a civic society and would, by default, become inaccessible to many given the socioeconomic equity gaps in U.S. society. This would breed corruption in the same manner that privatized firefighting once fostered (Dupuy, 2009). Nevertheless, when it comes to education and schooling in the 21st century, many are quick to adopt the very same dispositions of marketization that we would never entertain with any other public good. When we discuss marketization in this chapter, we are referring to privatization efforts whereby economic gain is a driving goal.

As the U.S. changed over time, the education of every child eventually came to be understood as a necessary endeavor that was funded and overseen with public money and interests for the maintenance of society (Spring, 1996, 2011; Urban & Wagoner, 2009). It has long been implied that the benefits of education are extended well beyond the individual to her broader community, state, and nation. In short, educative experiences that benefit the individual student's ability to read, write, and engage in civic democracy benefit the student themselves but, in turn, provide societal and economic benefits to society through training and socialization of future generations. This is similar to the way a public firefighting service benefits an individual if their home is on fire, but also the broader society. In all, if fire or ignorance is left unchecked, they will spread, leaving negative consequences for the larger community.

Education as an Individualistic Good

Contrary to this perspective of public service for the common good, though, is one that conceives of education as an individualistic good, or commodity, that can be acquired through and exchanged for value across an education marketplace. That is, the experiences, choices, curriculum, and pedagogy involved in a student's education should be individual choices made by individual parents (rather than by a collective society of parents and citizens) via educational marketplaces that suit the perceived individualistic needs of their child(ren). While marketization in education purports to provide families with school choices to best suit their individualistic needs, this approach is often couched in the rhetoric of equality, wherein charter schools and school vouchers allowed for private schools are heralded by some advocates as a means by which class and racial equity gaps might be addressed (see, for example Catt, DiPerna, Lueken, McShane, & Shaw, 2019; and a critique from Brewer, 2019). In many ways, the market approach to ameliorating systemic inequity and inequalities in U.S. schools suggests that a focus on the individual is the best solution for systemic problems.

Of course, the approach to schooling as a public enterprise that benefits the common good has not always provided equitable opportunities for all students. Specifically, varied and inequitable educational opportunities have been a mainstay in the U.S. public education landscape to the point that it troubles a good-faith belief in how our understanding of education as a common good has not historically extended to students who are not of relative affluent means or White (Berliner, 2013; Bowles & Gintis, 1976; Brewer & Myers, 2015; Fischer et al., 2008; Frankenberg & Lewis, 2012; Grusky, 2008; Holme, 2002; Jencks & Phillips, 1998; Jencks et al., 1972; King, 2005; Kozol, 1991; Lareau, 2003; Massey, 2007; Massey & Denton, 1993; Newman & Chin, 2003; Orfield & Eaton, 1996; Rich, Cox, & Bloch, 2017; Sacks, 2007; Shapiro, Meschede, & Sullivan, 2010; Swartz, 1990; Wiggan, 2007). Said another way, claims made about the collective and common good benefit of education—even those we make here—require a caveat that the colonial U.S. "collective good" has long had a troubled history.

While equitable educational opportunities have yet to be realized throughout the U.S. education system (a point we take up further below), the practice of free-at-the-point-of-delivery and compulsory education that is accessible to all, regardless of financial status, represents a conception of education as both beneficial to the individual *and* the collective good given the public access, public funding, public delivery, public oversight, and the societal benefits of having an educated populace. It is through the mechanism of public schools that society is able to exercise a democratic compromise on what future generations should know (e.g., the curriculum), how they should know it (e.g., pedagogical standards), and to what end such knowledge and pedagogy are useful to society (e.g., the continuity of an educated populace). Conceptions of education as an individualistic good for the purpose of it being understood solely as an individualistic good (Friedman, 1955, 1997, 2002) as well as the belief that an individualistic approach to schooling by way of choice on an open marketplace as a means to attenuate inequality (Greene, 2001; Greene, Forster, & Winters, 2005; Greene & Winters, 2003; Mathews, 2009; McShane, 2014; McShane, Wolf, & Hitt, 2018; Moe, 2001; Thernstrom & Thernstrom, 2003; Walberg & Bast, 2003), stand in dramatic contrast to understanding the service towards civic life as a common and public good.

Market Forces in Education

Few idioms are as prolific in U.S. culture than some iteration of an expression that public schools have failed (Berliner & Biddle, 1995). Finding roots in the shock-response to the Soviet Union's placement of Sputnik into orbit, many elected officials and the media in the U.S. have exhibited a dedication to asserting, decade after decade, that public schools are a dismal failure and, further, that this has resulted in our seemingly slow victories in the space race, to economic downturns as suggested in *A Nation at Risk* (National Commission on Excellence in Education, 1983), and to contemporary evaluations that find public schools lacking in some way (deMarrais, Brewer, Atkinson, Herron, & Lewis, 2019; Goldstein, 2014). The metric on which this perceived failure is based sometimes shifts—often in search of data points that provide justification for ideologically driven education reforms. Consider, for example, how school voucher and charter school proponents have begun to move the goalposts on using testing to evaluate choice models to measurements that appear more supportive (see Lubienski & Brewer, 2018). However, across the political and policy landscape, using test scores to compare the academic outcomes of students within a school, compared to other schools, and for international comparisons, remains popular. This is despite the knowledge that testing can be a problematic metric for "proving" that schools have failed and are in need of reforming (Darling-Hammond, 1991) because of the limitations of drawing generalizable conclusions about the quality of education received (Cline & Small, 1994; Lack, 2011; Olsen, 2015; Sacks, 1999). Further, test scores have the potential to marginalize low-income students and students of color (Cunningham, 2019). Shifting the goalposts of assessing the quality of education away from testing because of the problematic nature of testing is one thing; shifting the goalposts in search of other metrics that appear—however surface level—to justify privatization of education by way of vouchers or charters is something else entirely.

Outside of wanton generalized claims of failure, test scores have long served as an artifact justifying the need to reform public schools and, in the case of marketization, reform them through the competitive forces of an educational marketplace. Despite these scores being economic and racial data in disguise, reflecting unequal opportunities (Reardon, 2011, 2013), following the passage of No Child Left Behind (NCLB), testing has become even more prolific and has brought with it more serious consequences for the perception of failure (Ahlquist, Gorski, & Montano, 2011; Anagnostopoulos, Rutledge, & Bali, 2013; Carter & Lochte, 2017; Dworkin & Tobe, 2015; Kumashiro, 2015; Mehta, 2013; Wagle & Theobald, 2011; Willis & Sandholtz, 2009). Built into NCLB was the assumption that multi-year failure by a school or school district was an artifact of a failure of education being provided by the local and state government such that the school or district could, and would be, turned over to charter school oversight (Berliner, 2013; Carr & Porfilio, 2011; Hursh, 2011).

Lagging U.S. student academic performance on international tests such as the PISA and domestic achievement gaps continue to generate questions about the effectiveness of traditional public schools and their relation to U.S. economic interests as explicated in *A Nation at Risk*. However, when it comes to international scores, lagging U.S. scores can be a misleading metric, since the disaggregation of student economic status reveals a more complex explanation and indicator for variance in student scores. As David Berliner noted, "in a country as heterogeneous and socially and ethnically segregated as ours, mean scores of achievement are not useful for understanding how we are really doing in international comparisons" (Berliner, 2006). Moreover, Berliner noted that disaggregating U.S. scores on international tests such as the PISA "reveals something very important about inequality in the United States [because] if the educational opportunities available to White students in our public schools were made available to all our students," (p. 963) our scores would be among the highest in the world. And yet, because all students, regardless of economic background, are lumped together in score reporting, the role of teachers is often at the heart of the rancorous discussion about the degree to which public schools in the U.S. are seemingly failing to prepare students—thus justifying low pay and the rise of alternative approaches to training teachers and school choice mechanisms that purport to employ better methods of recruiting, retaining, measuring, and paying teachers (Labaree, 2010; Lahann & Reagan, 2011).

There are a variety of educational delivery systems in the educational marketplace that purport to provide improved education through innovation and forced improvement for educational competitors under the threat of losing students to rival schools or school systems. Broadly, the main school choice options available in the educational marketplace are: (1) homeschooling; (2) charter schools—both nonprofit and for-profit; and (3) school vouchers.

1   Homeschooling is the oldest form of schooling and has become an increasingly popular choice for educating children for religious and/or political motivations (Brewer & Lubienski, 2017a).
2   Charter schools operate using public tax financing but are privately operated by boards or individuals. Charter schools were initially casted as an opportunity to throw off the burdensome bureaucracy of public schools to allow teachers to develop innovative pedagogical approaches and, in turn, share those insights with traditional public schools (Shanker, 1988). Developments in the charter movement (not in every case, but inmany) include corporate-style coopts and attitudes that approach teaching and learning in competitive methods that are not collaborative. Charter schools often employ pedagogical techniques that include drill-

and-kill teaching (Horn, 2016; Vasquez Heilig, Brewer, Kim, & Sanchez, in press) and highly rule-ordered behaviorist classroom management (Goodman, 2013; Lack, 2009; Stahl, 2019). Despite being publicly funded, charters often do not provide transportation for students or a full range of services for students with learning disabilities (Garcy, 2011).

3   School vouchers (often organized as a direct voucher or some iteration of a tax credit, which Welner (2008) calls a "neovoucher") provide the financial support for students to subsidize the costs of private school tuition with the full per-student allocation earmarked for the public school or some portion of that amount.

In the iterations of school choice outlined above, all three approach education from the disposition that education is best understood as an individualistic good where families can, and should, pick and choose an educational option that they feel best suits their desires (curricular, topical focus, or religious) without regard for the impacts that such a decision has on other students or the society at large. More specifically, despite the mountains of evidence that all students benefit from attending racially and economically diverse schools (Brewer & Lubienski, 2017b), charter school proponents argue that the exacerbation of racial and economic segregation that occurs as a result of school choice (Frankenberg, 2011; Frankenberg & Lewis, 2012; Frankenberg & Siegel-Hawley, 2011; Vasquez Heilig, Brewer, & Williams, 2019) is simply "in line with a properly functioning charter sector" (Hatfield & Malkus, 2017, p. 20).

Market Forces and Equity

Advocates of charters and school vouchers have largely pushed them as a mechanism through which students trapped in generational poverty (often seen as a résult of failed public schools due to failing test scores) can "escape" by attending a school that focuses on success. The marketing of educational markets—or "edvertising" as coined by DiMartino and Jessen (2018)—often targets students of color as charters and vouchers are presented as a service to be leveraged to end structural racism and generational poverty. Notable conservative intermediary organizations such as the American Legislative Exchange Council (ALEC) have likewise promoted school vouchers as a mechanism that could benefit non-White students in their goal of "escaping" failing public schools (deMarrais et al., 2019; Lubienski & Brewer, 2013). Though, it is important to point out that ALEC has, in recent years, suggested that its historical and contemporary support for vouchers was less interested in aiding poor non-White students as it was more about helping White students self-segregate into private schools in a post-*Brown* era (Persson, 2015). ALEC has invested great interest and time promoting vouchers for middle-class families who, they believe, might otherwise face a financial burden in paying for private schooling (Persson, 2015). However, an increased focus on provisions for middle-class families fails to acknowledge that many families living in poverty might not have the ability to top up vouchers to afford private tuition even with any vouchers or extra educational savings accounts. Powers and Potterton (2017) concluded, after an evaluation of tax credit and voucher programs in various U. S. locations, that:

> Taken together, the results from these studies indicate that if tax credits and voucher programs are available to all families, the more advantaged families in a given context are the ones likely to take advantage of and benefit from them. That some of the stratifying effects of private school choice programs can also be mitigated by policy design will be a challenge to policy makers intent on expanding such programs.
>
> (Powers & Potterton, 2017, p. 140)

In the quest to reimagine public education as an individualistic commodity rather than a common good, some educational reformers have long sought to create such educational marketplaces where individual customers (students and parents) are able to actualize a choice among myriad school options that provide varying services and attend to specific niche desires in educational curricula. The ideas driving these reforms include an assumption that a service provider (school), as a result of the competitive nature of a marketplace, will force another provider (school) to improve its services. This process, according to the logic, represents first-order and second-order impacts, whereby the improvements made by one school provider will attract more customers (students) given the improved nature of its service. This is the first-order effect that benefits the customers (students) who attend the improved educational services offered by the winning provider (school). The loss of students to the other provider (school), or even just the threat of losing students to another provider, will, according to the market logic, force providers (schools) to improve lest they continue to lose students on the open market.

Despite all of this logic, the realization of school choice within a marketplace often does result in students being left without the financial ability to actualize a choice option in the open educational marketplace. For example, even within the context of a fully-subsidized school voucher provision to attend a private school that covers the entire cost of the private tuition, the family often must provide their own transportation or volunteer hours, making attendance impossible for those who are less than affluent. Similarly, while charter schools are largely understood as public schools given that the funding is public tax dollars, many charter schools do not provide transportation for students and, in most cases, do not provide a full litany of services for students, as noted above, with special needs or English language learners (Potterton, 2013). These students, despite the logic of markets, are without equal choice. As a result, research has indicated that school vouchers and charter schools exacerbate racial and economic segregation and have the potential to isolate students with special needs and language learners in public schools (Orfield, Frankenberg, & Associates, 2013).

Overall, as school choice schemes bolster and subsidize the ability of the relatively affluent (and mostly White) to de-integrate and self-segregate themselves away from public schools, those same public schools can be left with less financial resources and with less buy-in from all of the families living in a community (Orfield et al., 2013; Renzulli & Evans, 2005). This can result in an environment that is less conducive to pedagogical innovations as class sizes increase in a response to having to operate with less money. Less money for the school also means a higher per-student cost ratio for operating busses, electric bills, teaching and support staff, and more.

These issues, of course, all have a direct impact on student learning and subsequent outcomes. As public schools are systematically defunded by shifting public tax monies into the hands of private operators by way of charters and vouchers, public schools suffer, which can cause morale to decline among educators and student scores to drop even further. No longer benefiting from broad public tax financing, community support, and parental social capital, public schools may become the thing that reformers claim they are: steadily declining. In contexts such as these, manufactured myths about public schools might proliferate (Berliner & Biddle, 1995; Berliner & Glass, 2014). Of course, public-favoring stories are circulating and, indeed, may be growing (Malin, Potterton, & Lubienski, in press). Still, choice-favoring discourse and justification for a perceived need to move away from public schools in favor of charter schools and vouchers can contribute to, in a self-fulfilling downward spiral, defunding that leads to decreased outcomes, and, further, that provides cover to denounce education as a public good (Malin et al., in press). Moreover, given that minority and poor students are often the ones unable to utilize the full benefits of school choice, the academic outcomes of non-White and non-affluent students in public schools can reinforce the façade that school choice is needed specifically to provide equity for minority students.

Historical Shortcomings of Schools Achieving Equity

As described above, individualistic and competitive approaches to public education that drive market-based education reforms are necessarily strong determiners of inequity in schools. The premise of choice in a market-driven system, wherein parents, if they have resources and are able to access them, enroll their children into schools of their choosing, assumes that the schools that are chosen by fewer parents will eventually close. This is not the only assumption. Another assumption within this framework is that parents will choose schools based on achievement within the school which, based on the above discussion, typically includes test scores or other standardized measures of achievement. This, however, is a problematic assumption because parents often choose schools for a variety of reasons that are not always related to achievement measures, and these choices include a complex array of factors (Garcia, 2008; Potterton, 2020). Choice systems can, and have, deepened inequity as described by Orfield:

> The idea of school choice has a tangled history. It is an idea that has taken many shapes, under the banner of the same hopeful word, one that seems to have a simple positive meaning but embodies many contradictory possibilities. Choice has a thousand different faces, some treacherous, some benign. It includes the creation of charter and magnet schools, voluntary transfer programs under state and federal regulation, choice-based desegregation plans, transfer rights under No Child Left Behind (NCLB), and voucher programs. The distinctions and this history are important to understand because forgetting what has been learned about choice systems that failed means repeating mistakes and paying the costs. There is no reason to keep making that error.
>
> (Orfield, 2013, p. 3)

While we know that the first use of vouchers was to avoid integration—in other words, for the purpose of segregation—there are also examples of educators who, in the 1970s, attempted to create diverse schools via magnet schools (Orfield, 2013). Still, as overt desegregation plans were abandoned as race issues became less prominent in discussions around these schools, diversity issues were also minimized (Orfield, 2013). These changes in priorities matter in an important way because they determine the larger discourse, strategies, and allowances of policymakers who have power and, ultimately, affect practitioners and the students whom they serve as well as the discourse surrounding the need to reform schools by way of marketization.

In all, we assume the perspective in this chapter that there are educational policies and practices over time that have been affected (and reproduced) by market- and neoliberal-based shortcomings, including those related to race, class, and gender inequities in larger society. As Dixson, James-Gallaway, Cardenas, and Perkins-Williams (2019) point out, it is via a broader set of powers, policy, and decision-makers that school choice continues to reproduce race, class, and gender inequities. That said, we also acknowledge that there is a tendency for proponents of school choice policies and practices to romanticize public education as an entity that has never itself been riddled with inequity and barriers for students from various socioeconomic status, and we know that this is not true because there is restricted access to neighborhood public schools based on religion, race, ethnicity, and residency (Shircliffe, Dorn, & Cobb-Roberts, 2006).

What Markets and Individualization Mean for the Public and Common Good

At the core of questions surrounding the marketization of education and the elevation of privatization over public schooling options is a fundamental question about the purpose and benefits of education. Understood as a common good, public education, with its requisite public oversight, operations, and efforts to equalize (albeit, not fully realized), assumes the benefits of education to be broader than the individual. Also, and perhaps more importantly, public education accentuates the notion that there is a collective obligation towards providing quality, equal, and equitable resources for all students. When education is conceived as an individualistic commodity best bought and traded in the open educational marketplace, the locus of responsibility and obligation (both morally and financially) shifts away from the collective community and becomes centered on the individual. As such, if we shift our conception of public education away from being understood as the cornerstone of U.S. democracy into a reimagining of it as an individualistic good, we will likely reinforce the very inequalities and inequities that educational reformers suggest might be ended through market solutions.

Retaining an understanding of education as a public good is a fundamental prerequisite for those legitimate calls for equity reforms. If schooling is in the best interest of the society at large, the onus to improve rests with the society and, thus, has the best chance at collective improvement. Reimagining education as an individualistic good ultimately releases society and communities of their shared obligation to our children by putting the onus for improvement squarely into individual hands—which can only further exacerbate inequality as such practices would reify and reinforce the socioeconomic and racial disparities that are already a problem in U.S. society, its schools, and within its democracy writ large.

References

Ahlquist, R., Gorski, P. C., & Montano, T. (Eds.). (2011). *Assault on kids: How hyper-accountability, corporatization, deficit ideologies, and Ruby Payne are destroying our schools*. New York: Peter Lang Publishing.

Anagnostopoulos, D., Rutledge, S., & Bali, V. (2013). State education agencies, information systems, and the expansion of state power in the era of test-based accountability. *Educational Policy*, 27(2), 217–247.

Anderson, A. G. (2019). The development of municipal fire departments in the United States. *The Journal of Libertarian Studies*, 3(3), 331–359.

Berliner, D. C. (2006). Our impoverished view of educational reform. *Teachers College Record*, 108, 949–995.

Berliner, D. C. (2013). Effects of inequality and poverty vs. Teachers and schooling on America's youth. *Teachers College Record*, 115, 1–26.

Berliner, D. C., & Biddle, B. J. (1995). *The manufactured crisis: Myths, fraud, and the attack on America's public schools*. Reading, MA: Addison-Wesley.

Berliner, D. C., & Glass, G. V. (2014). *50 myths and lies that threaten America's public schools: The real crisis in education*. New York: Teachers College Press.

Bowles, S., & Gintis, H. (1976). *Schooling in capitalist America*. New York: HarperCollins.

Brewer, T. J. (2019). NEPC review: The 123s of school choice: What the research says about private school choice: 2019 edition. Retrieved from https://nepc.color ado.edu/thinktank/school-choice.

Brewer, T. J., & Lubienski, C. (2017a). Homeschooling in the United States: Examining the rationales for individualizing education. *Pro-Posições*, 28(2), 21–38.

Brewer, T. J., & Lubienski, C. (2017b). NEPC review: Differences by design? Student composition in charter schools with different academic models. Retrieved from http://nepc.colorado.edu/thinktank/review-charters.

Brewer, T. J., & Myers, P. S. (2015). How neoliberalism subverts equality and perpetuates poverty in our nation's schools. In S. N. Haymes, M. V. d. Haymes, & R. Miller (Eds.), *The Routledge handbook of poverty in the United States* (pp. 190–198). New York: Routledge.

Carr, P. R., & Porfilio, B. J. (2011). Audaciously espousing hope within a torrent of hegemonic neoliberalism. In P. R. Carr & B. J. Porfilio (Eds.), *The phenomenon of Obama and the agenda for education: Can hope audaciously trump neoliberalism?* (pp. xvii–li). Charlotte, NC: Information Age.

Carter, J. H., & Lochte, H. A. (Eds.). (2017). *Teacher performance assessment and accountability reforms: The impacts of EdTPA on teaching and schools*. New York: Palgrave Macmillian.

Catt, A. D., DiPerna, P., Lueken, M. F., McShane, M. Q., & Shaw, M. (2019). The 123s of school choice: What the research says about private school choice. Retrieved from www.edchoice.org/research/the-123s-of-school-choice.

Cline, R., & Small, R. C. (1994). The problem with U.S. education: Too much criticism, too little commitment. *The English Journal*, 83(7), 21–24.

Cunningham, J. (2019). Missing the mark: Standardized testing as epistemological erasure in U.S. schooling. *Power and Education*, 11(1), 111–120.

Darling-Hammond, L. (1991). The implications of testing policy for quality and equality. *The Phi Delta Kappan*, 73(3), 220–225.

deMarrais, K., Brewer, T. J., Atkinson, J. C., Herron, B., & Lewis, J. (2019). *Philanthropy, hidden strategy, and collective resistance: A primer for concerned educators*. Borham, ME: Myers Education Press.

DiMartino, C., & Jessen, S. B. (2018). *Selling school: The marketing of public education*. New York: Teachers College Press.

Dixson, A., James-Gallaway, C., Cardenas, N. D., & Perkins-Williams, R. (2019). Critical perspectives on school choice: An examination of race, class, and gender in school choice policies. In M. Berends, A. Primus, & M. G. Springer (Eds.), *Handbook of research on school choice* (pp. 73–86). New York: Routledge.

Dupuy, T. (2009). Firefighting in the 1800s: A corrupt, bloated, private for-profit industry. Retrieved March 12, 2020 from www.huffpost.com/entry/firefighting-in-the-1800s_b_247936.

Dworkin, A. G., & Tobe, P. E. (2015). Does school accountability alter teacher trust and promote burnout? In J. H. Ballantine & J. Z. Spade (Eds.), *School and society: A sociological approach* (5 ed., pp. 183–192). Los Angeles, CA: Sage.

Fischer, C. S., Hout, M., Jankowski, M. S., Lucas, S. R., Swidler, A., & Voss, K. (2008). Inequality by design. In D. B. Grusky (Ed.), *Social social stratification: Class, race, and gender in sociological perspective* (pp. 49–53). Boulder, CO: Westview Press.

Frankenberg, E. (2011). Charter schools: A civil rights mirage? *Kappa Delti Pi Record*, 47, 100–105.

Frankenberg, E., & Lewis, T. (2012). School segregation then and now. In R. Ognibene (Ed.), *A persistent reformer: Jonathan kozol's work to promote equality in America* (pp. 1–19). New York: Peter Lang.

Frankenberg, E., & Siegel-Hawley, G. (2011). Choice without equity: Charter school segregation and the need for civil rights standards. *Education Digest*, 76(5), 44–47.

Friedman, M. (1955). The role of government in education. Retrieved www.schoolchoices.org/roo/fried1.htm.

Friedman, M. (1997). Public schools: Make them private. Retrieved www.cato.org/pubs/briefs/bp-023.html.

Friedman, M. (2002). *Capitalism and freedom.* Chicago, IL: University of Chicago Press.

Garcia, D. R. (2008). The impact of school choice on racial segregation in charter schools. *Educational Policy*, 22(6), 805–829.

Garcy, A. M. (2011). High expense: Disability severity and charter school attendance in arizona. *Education Policy Analysis Archives*, 19(6).

Goldstein, D. (2014). *The teacher wars: A history of America's most embattled profession.* New York: Doubleday.

Goodman, J. (2013). Charter management organizations and the regulated environment: Is it worth the price? *Educational Researcher*, 42(2), 89–96.

Greene, J. P. (2001). Vouchers in Charlotte. *Education Next, Summer 2001.*

Greene, J. P., Forster, G., & Winters, M. A. (2005). *Education myths: What special interest groups want you to believe about our schools—and why it isn't so.* Lanham, MD: Rowman & Littlefield Publishers.

Greene, J. P., & Winters, M. A. (2003). When schools compete: The effects of vouchers on florida public school achievement. Retrieved from www.manhattan-institute.org/html/ewp_02.htm.

Grusky, D. B. (Ed.) (2008). *Social stratification: Class, race, and gender in sociological perspective.* Boulder, CO: Westview Press.

Hatfield, J., & Malkus, N. (2017). *Differences by design? Student composition in charter schools with different academic models.* Washington, DC: American Enterprise Institute.

Holme, J. J. (2002). Buying homes, buying schools: School choice and the social construction of school quality. *Harvard Educational Review*, 72(2), 177–205.

Horn, J. (2016). *Work hard, be hard: Journeys through "no excuses" teaching.* Lanham, MD: Rowman & Littlefield.

Hursh, D. (2011). More of the same: How free market-capitalism dominates the economy and education. In P. R. Carr & B. J. Porfilio (Eds.), *The phenomenon of Obama and the agenda for education: Can hope audaciously trump neoliberalism?* (pp. 3–22). Charlotte, NC: Information Age.

Jencks, C., & Phillips, M. (Eds.). (1998). *The Black-White test score gap.* Washington, DC: Brookings Institution Press.

Jencks, C., Smith, M., Acland, H., Bane, M. J., Cohen, D., Gintis, H., … Michelson, S. (1972). *Inequality: A reassessment of the effect of family and schooling in America.* New York: Basic Books.

King, J. E. (2005). A transformative vision of Black education for human freedom. In J. E. King (Ed.), *Black education: A transformative research and action agenda for the new century* (pp. 3–17). Mahwah, NJ: Lawrence Erlbaum Associates.

Kozol, J. (1991). *Savage inequalities: Children in America's schools.* New York: Crown Publishing Group.

Kumashiro, K. (2015). Review of proposed 2015 federal teacher preparation regulations. Retrieved from http://nepc.colorado.edu/thinktank/review-proposed-teacher-preparation.

Labaree, D. (2010). Teach For America and teacher ed: Heads they win, tails we lose. *Journal of Teacher Education,* 61(1–2),48–55.

Lack, B. (2009). No excuses: A critique of the knowledge is power program (KIPP) within charter schools in the USA. *Journal for Critical Education Policy Studies,* 7 (2), 126–153.

Lack, B. (2011). Anti-democratic militaristic education: An overview and critical analysis of KIPP schools. In R. Ahlquist, P. C. Gorski, & T. Montano (Eds.), *Assault on kids: How hyper-accountability, corporatization, deficit ideologies, and Ruby Payne are destroying our schools* (pp. 65–90). New York: Peter Lang Publishing.

Lahann, R., & Reagan, E. M. (2011). Teach For America and the politics of progressive neoliberalism. *Teacher Education Quarterly,* 38(1), 7–27.

Landers, J. (2016). In the early 19th century, firefighters fought fires … and each other. Retrieved March 6, 2020 from www.smithsonianmag.com/smithsonian-institution/early-19-century-firefighters-fought-fires-each-other-180960391.

Lareau, A. (2003). *Unequal childhoods: Class, race, and family life.* Berkeley, CA: University of California Press.

Lubienski, C., & Brewer, T. J. (2013). Review of report card on American education. Retrieved from http://nepc.colorado.edu/thinktank/review-report-card-ALEC-2013.

Lubienski, C., & Brewer, T. J. (2018). Review of "Do impacts on test scores even matter? Lessons from long-run outcomes in school choice research: Attainment versus achievement impacts and rethinking how to evaluate school choice programs." Available at http://nepc.colorado.edu/thinktank/review-goalposts.

Malin, J. R., Potterton, A. U., & Lubienski, C. (in press). Language matters: K-12 choice-favoring and public-favoring stories. *Kappa Delta Pi Record.*

Massey, D. S. (2007). *Categorically unequal: The American stratification system.* New York: Russell Sage Foundation.

Massey, D. S., & Denton, N. A. (1993). *American apartheid: Segregation and the making of the underclass.* Cambridge, MA: Harvard University Press.

Mathews, J. (2009). *Work hard, be nice. How two inspired teachers created the most promising schools in America.* Chapel Hill, NC: Algonquin Books.

McShane, M. Q. (2014). *Education and opportunity*. Washington, DC: AEI Press.

McShane, M. Q., Wolf, P., & Hitt, C. (2018). Do impacts on test scores even matter? Lessons from long-run outcomes in school choice research: Attainment versus achievement impacts and rethinking how to evaluate school choice programs. Retrieved from www.aei.org/publication/do-impacts-on-test-scores-even-matter-lessons-from-long-run-outcomes-in-school-choice-research.

Mehta, J. (2013). How paradigms create politics. *American Educational Research Journal, 50*(2), 285–324.

Moe, T. M. (2001). *Schools, vouchers, and the American public*. Washington, DC: The Brookings Institution Press.

National Commission on Excellence in Education. (1983). A nation at risk: The imperative for educational reform. In C. Kridel (Ed.), *Classic edition sources, education* (4th ed., pp. 169–174). New York: McGraw Hill.

Newman, K. S., & Chin, M. M. (2003). High stakes: Time poverty, testing, and the children of the working poor. *Qualitative Sociology, 26*(1), 3–34.

Olsen, R. (2015). *The toxic myth of good and bad teachers*. Retrieved January 16, 2017 from www.richardolsen.me/b/2015/05/the-toxic-myth-of-good-and-bad-teachers.

Orfield, G. (2013). Choice and civil rights: Forgetting history, facing consequences. In G. Orfield, E. Frankenberg, & Associates (Eds.), *Educational delusions? Why choice can deepen inequality and how to make schools fair*. Berkeley, CA: University of California Press.

Orfield, G., & Eaton, S. (1996). *Dismantling desegregation: The quiet reversal of brown v. Board of education*. New York: The New Press.

Orfield, G., Frankenberg, E., & Associates (Eds.). (2013). *Educational delusions? Why choice can deepen inequality and how to make schools fair*. Berkeley, CA: University of California Press.

Persson, J. (2015). ALEC admits school vouchers are for kids in suburbia. Retrieved August 17, 2015 from www.prwatch.org/news/2015/07/12869/alec-school-vouchers-are-kids-suburbia.

Potterton, A. U. (2013). A citizen's response to the president's charter school education proclamation: With a profile of two "highly performing" charter school organizations in Arizona. *Teachers College Record*. 17309.

Potterton, A. U. (2020). Parental accountability, school choice, and the invisible hand of the market. *Educational Policy, 34*(1), 166–192.

Powers, J. M., & Potterton, A. U. (2017). The case against private schooling. In R. Fox & N. Buchanan (Eds.), *The wiley handbook of school choice* (pp. 131–148). Hoboken, NJ: Wiley.

Reardon, S. (2011). The widening academic achievement gap between the rich and the poor: New evidence and possible explanations. In G. J. Duncan & R. J. Murnane (Eds.), *Whither opportunity?: Rising inequality, schools, and children's life chances* (pp. 91–116). New York: Russell Sage Foundation.

Reardon, S. (2013). The widening income achievement gap. *Educational Leadership, 70*(8), 10–16.

Renzulli, L. A., & Evans, L. (2005). School choice, charter schools, and white flight. *Social Problems, 52*(3), 398–418.

Rich, M., Cox, A., & Bloch, M. (2017). Money, race and success: How your school district compares. Retrieved April 4, 2017 from www.nytimes.com/interactive/2016/04/29/upshot/money-race-and-success-how-your-school-district-compares.html.

Sacks, P. (1999). *Standardized minds: The high price of America's testing culture and what we can do to change it.* New York: Da Capo Press.

Sacks, P. (2007). *Tearing down the Gates: Confronting the class divide in American education.* Los Angeles, CA: University of California Press.

Shanker, A. (1988). Untitled speech to the national press club. Retrieved March 12, 2020 from https://reuther.wayne.edu/files/64.43.pdf.

Shapiro, T. M., Meschede, T., & Sullivan, L. (2010). The racial wealth gap increases fourfold. Retrieved from http://iasp.brandeis.edu/pdfs/Racial-Wealth-Gap-Brief.pdf.

Shircliffe, B. J., Dorn, S., & Cobb-Roberts, D. (2006). Schools as imagined communities. In D. Cobb-Roberts, S. Dorn, & B. J. Shircliffe (Eds.), *School as imagined communities: The creation of identity, meaning, and conflict in U.S. history* (pp. 1–32). New York: Palgrave Macmillan.

Spring, J. (1996). *American education* (7th ed.). New York: McGraw Hill.

Spring, J. (2011). *The politics of American education.* New York: Routledge.

Stahl, G. (2019). Critiquing the corporeal curriculum: Body pedagogies in "no excuses" charter schools. *Journal of Youth Studies, Advanced Online Publication.*

Swartz, D. (1990). Pierre Bourdieu: Culture, education, and social inequality. In K. J. Dougherty & F. M. Hammack (Eds.), *Education and society: A reader* (pp. 70–80). San Diego, CA: Harcourt Brace Jovanovich.

Thernstrom, A., & Thernstrom, S. (2003). *No excuses: Closing the racial gap in learning.* New York: Simon & Schuster.

Urban, W. J., & Wagoner, J. L. (2009). *American education: A history* (4th ed.). New York: Routledge.

Vasquez Heilig, J., Brewer, T. J., Kim, A., & Sanchez, M. (in press). A digital ethnography of Teach For America: Ethnographic analysis of the truth for America podcast. *Urban Education.*

Vasquez Heilig, J., Brewer, T. J., & Williams, Y. (2019). Choice without inclusion? Comparing the intensity of racial segregation in charters and public schools at the local, state, and national levels. *Education Sciences*, 9(3), 1–16.

Wagle, T., & Theobald, P. (2011). Connecting communities and schools: Accountability in the post-nclb era. In P. R. Carr & B. J. Porfilio (Eds.), *The phenomenon of Obama and the agenda for education: Can hope audaciously trump neoliberalism?* (pp. 249–263). Charlotte, NC: Information Age.

Walberg, H. J., & Bast, J. L. (2003). *Education and capitalism: How overcoming our fear of markets and economics can improve America's schools.* Stanford, CA: Hoover Institution Press.

Welner, K. G. (2008). *Neovouchers: The emergence of tuition tax credits for private schooling.* Lanham, MD: Rowman & Littlefield.

Wiggan, G. (2007). Race, school achievement, and educational inequality: Toward a student-based inquiry perspective. *Review of Educational Research*, 77(3), 310–333.

Willis, J., & Sandholtz, J. (2009). Constrained professionalism: Dilemmas of teaching in the face of test-based accountability. *Teachers College Record*, 111(4), 1065–1114.

Part III

Healthy Students, Healthy Schools, and Healthy Communities

There is perhaps no other American institution that mirrors our communities as well as public schools. Issues in the community manifest themselves in classrooms, and shortcomings in education are likewise reflected in the societal fabric outside schools. Because of this symbiotic relationship, education must be used as a tool to meet each child's holistic needs rather than only being used to develop them academically. A failure to focus on the whole child leads to more than an incomplete education for that student— the ripple effects spread outward until they impact everyone.

At the same time as helping students discover themselves and their unique talents, our public schools must help them look outward at how they can have a positive impact on the community. True education includes application, problem-solving, and service. It incorporates the arts and humanities, subjects that allow us to appreciate the beauty around us, relate to others, and use our talents to share the best of ourselves with others. When we get education right it is personalized, but not isolating. When education and public schools are used as a vehicle for improving both individual students and the community, the bond between them is solidified. The positive repercussions also radiate outward.

Most importantly, as you will see in Part III, public education is at its best it serves as a vehicle to heal societal wounds that present themselves in our communities.

Sean Slade (Chapter 10) begins by giving an in-depth look at whole child education, and why a focus on social-emotional learning and wellbeing in schools is necessary for students to fully grow as participants in a democracy.

Next, **Mairi Cooper** (Chapter 11) explains how her students were able to find their purpose, create a culture of democratic activism, and use the design process to expand their impact into the community.

In Chapter 12, **Mandy Manning** shares her experiences teaching refugee and immigrant students and gives us insight into the ways education of those who come to our country makes our communities stronger.

Lastly, in Chapter 13, **Kelly Holstine** and **Beth Davey** examine the impact of trauma on our students, and share how schools and teachers can help those who have suffered trauma become healthier and more successful

Chapter 10

Educating the Whole Child

Sean Slade

There are four core reasons, explored in this chapter, why a focus on health and wellbeing is a necessity for schools in order for our education system to fulfill its role as the foundation of our democracy. Any one of these reasons should be adequate enough for school leaders, teachers, and educational policy makers to ensure that our schools are safe, healthy learning environments. When presented collectively they form an overwhelming case that a focus on the holistic wellbeing of our schools, staff, and students is necessary for the health of our society.

Health and Wellbeing are Fundamental

There is the fundamental understanding that health and wellbeing is a prerequisite for our own personal growth, development, and learning. Abraham Maslow in his landmark publication *A Theory of Human Motivation* (Maslow, 1943) highlighted the role of a hierarchy of needs where one is required in order to allow the next to grow or develop or mature. In short, the physiological needs of health, safety must be ensured before the individual can focus on the more psychological or cognitive needs. In education terms, the child or learner must be healthy and safe before they can focus on what they are learning and understand why they are learning it. *Self-Actualization*, where learners meet their full potential, can only be achieved if we support learners, ensure their needs are met, and build upon each layer of the hierarchy.

This understanding has helped form the basis for the original Coordinated School Health Model (Allensworth & Kolbe, 1987); the growing understanding of the link between health and academic achievement (Marx, Wooley, & Northrop, 1998); and the development of launch of the Whole School, Whole Community, Whole Child Model (ASCD & CDC, 2014).

> Human needs arrange themselves in hierarchies of pre-potency. That is to say, the appearance of one need usually rests on the prior satisfaction of another, more pre-potent need.
>
> (Maslow, 1943)

The health and wellbeing of the learner, including the physical, social, and emotional safety, is a requirement for learning. If the child is not well, they may not even be at school. If they are in pain, have vision issues, or feel unsafe, we cannot expect them to learn, collaborate, or grow into new ideas and experiences. The health and wellbeing of the learner are paramount, and if health needs are not met it undoubtedly will impact learning.

This was highlighted in the 2010 publication by Charles Basch, *Healthier Students Are Better Learners: A Missing Link in School Reforms to Close the Achievement Gap*—a meta-analysis of the key health and learning research findings over the past decade.

> No matter how well teachers are prepared to teach, no matter what accountability measures are put in place, no matter what governing structures are established for schools, educational progress will be profoundly limited if students are not motivated and able to learn. Health-related problems play a major role in limiting the motivation and ability to learn of urban minority youth, and interventions to address those problems can improve educational as well as health outcomes. Healthier students are better learners.
>
> (Basch, 2010, p. 4)

Basch highlighted seven health disparities, that if addressed would improve educational attainment across the U.S., according to his research and analysis even without making changes to the teaching and learning process. These seven disparities are (1) *vision*, (2) *asthma*, (3) *teen pregnancy*, (4) *aggression and violence*, (5) *physical activity*, (6) *breakfast*, and (7) *inattention and hyperactivity*. While individual communities and schools have localized issues these seven were highlighted to showcase the influence health and wellbeing have on learning and the education system more broadly.

> Recent research in fields ranging from neurosciences and child development to epidemiology and public health provide compelling evidence for the causal role that educationally relevant health disparities play in the educational achievement gap that plagues urban minority youth. This is why reducing these health disparities must be a fundamental part of school reform.
>
> (Basch, 2010, p. 4)

Health and Education are Symbiotic

Due to the symbiotic relationship between health and education, improving one very likely improves the other. As is too often the case in our system, this also means restricting one likely restricts or harms the other. We are a composite of everything that makes us whole—more than the sum of our content knowledge, more than our Body Mass Index (BMI), more than our ability to socialize, collaborate, or interact. We are all of these things and more, and the education community is coming to realize that each of these facets will aid, boost, and influence our growth and development, as well as our ability and motivation to learn.

Although reforms have compartmentalized the learner by subjects, grade levels, and sectors, we have started to understand how interconnected we truly are. Social and emotional well-being, whether related to empathy or self-worth, can affect the student's ability to collaborate, communicate, co-construct learning, understand differing perspectives, and create new value. It can also affect the individual's use and development of their cognitive skills (Chernyshenko, Kankaraš, & Drasgow, 2018). Health, similarly, affects ability, which affects self-worth, which affects socialization, which affects knowledge acquisition, which affects educational outcomes, the likelihood for economic prosperity, and long-term health.

We must appreciate this interconnectedness, seek to blend what has been siloed, and weave what makes us whole.

> When students receive both the education and health interventions that they need, academic performance and educational achievement levels improve. Graduation from high school is associated with better health and an increase of six to nine years in average lifespan. As income levels increase, positive health behaviors and health outcomes are enhanced. Post-secondary education leads to even healthier lives by improving earning power, social status, and cognitive ability, which in turn influences positive lifestyle choices, an enhanced understanding of health issues, and better negotiations within the medical care system. Better adult health status improves the health status of future children.
>
> (SOPHE-ASCD, 2010)

A Focus on Health and Wellbeing Supports Effective Teaching and Learning

A focus on health and wellbeing in the school creates the optimal environment for effective teaching and learning. This is aligned with, but distinct from the two reasons already discussed.

Schools that focus on the health and safety of their students, staff, classrooms, and schools are creating the optimal climate and culture for effective teaching and learning. We may use different terms, phases, and accountability measures across sectors, but we are frequently discussing the same thing—a positive, connected, safe and supportive learning environment, where students are physically healthy, feel socially and emotionally safe, and have a sense of belonging.

Schools and classrooms that are focused on developing a positive climate where the teachers holistically know their students have been shown to increase learning. Additionally, classrooms where students have a sense of belonging have been shown to increase academic test scores (Basch, 2010; CDC, 2009; Comer, 1984), improve self-esteem (DeWit et al, 2011); and reduce student absenteeism (Basch, 2010; CDC, 2009). Environments where students feel supported in taking risks and learning from failure foster experimentation, promote creativity, and increased understanding of what is being taught (Benard, 2004).

> A Review of Educational Research analysis of 46 studies found that strong teacher-student relationships were associated in both the short- and long-term with improvements on practically every measure schools care about: higher student academic engagement, attendance, grades, fewer disruptive behaviors and suspensions, and lower school dropout rates. Those effects were strong even after controlling for differences in students' individual, family, and school backgrounds.
>
> (Sparks, 2019)

Education Should be Holistic, with Whole-Child Focus

A primary role of education is to nurture, develop and grow the individual so that they are able to be effective, resourceful and active members of their community and society. This requires developing children holistically, and not just academically. The skills, competencies, and knowledge required by business and by society requires an education system that develops children socially, emotionally, physically, and cognitively. It can be argued that civic and spiritual development should be added to this list. Education is more than a content delivery system and must fulfill the role of developing individuals for success in their lives and in their futures.

> What is the purpose of education? This question agitates scholars, teachers, statesmen, every group, in fact, of thoughtful men and women. The conventional answer is the acquisition of knowledge, the reading of books, and the learning of facts. Perhaps because there are so many books and the branches of knowledge in which we can learn facts are so multitudinous today, we begin to hear more frequently that the function of education is to give children a desire to learn and to teach them how to use their minds and where to go to acquire facts when their curiosity is aroused. Even more all-embracing than this is the statement made not long ago, before a group of English head-masters, by the Archbishop of York, that "the true purpose of education is to produce citizens."
>
> (Roosevelt, 1930)

The purpose of education has always been to every one, in essence, the same—to give the young, the things they need in order to develop if an orderly, sequential way into members of society.

(Dewey, 1934, 1)

How Do We Do This?

Understanding rationale for a whole-child approach in education leads us to an obvious question: How can this approach be implemented? Many available logic models suggest a similar process—raise awareness, garner support, set outcome goals, and showcase current successes.

One Approach and Two Models

In 2007 ASCD (formerly the Association for Supervision and Curriculum Development) launched its Whole Child approach, based on five tenets of Healthy, Safe, Engaged, Supported, and Challenged, which in turn were based on Maslow's hierarchy of needs. The Whole Child launch set to recast "the definition of a successful learner from one whose achievement is

Table 10.1 Steps for Implementation of Whole-Child Approach in Education

Raising Awareness	• *Reaffirm education's focus on developing the whole child* • *Engage leadership and staff discussions about the purpose of education* • *Discuss and own your "why" of education*
Garner Support	• Understand the role that school leadership plays in forming a positive school-wide climate • Reaffirm the role that teachers have in developing and growing positive relationships with their students and across their school-community • Showcase the role that the arts, music, drama, physical education play in both engaging learners and developing skills, attributes and attitudes beyond the academic
Set Outcome Goals	• Highlight the role that a positive school climate and culture play in effective teaching and learning. • Outline the relationship between education gains and engagement in learning (and vice versa) • Set outcome goals across multiple measures and areas
Showcase Successes	• Highlight actions that educators are already doing to ensure a positive school climate and a safe, supportive learning environment. • Showcase how and where stakeholders—across key sectors such as health and education—are supporting the child. • Engage cross sector stakeholders in conversations around practices, processes, and policy.

measured solely by academic tests, to one who is knowledgeable, emotionally and physically healthy, civically inspired, engaged in the arts, prepared for work and economic self-sufficiency, and ready for the world beyond formal schooling" (ASCD, 2007, p. 4).

In conjunction with this ASCD called for an acknowledgement of the interdependent nature of health and learning.

> We call on communities—educators, parents, businesses, health and social service providers, arts professionals, recreation leaders, and policymakers at all levels—to forge a new compact with our young people to ensure their whole and healthy development. We ask communities to redefine learning to focus on the whole person. We ask schools and communities to lay aside perennial battles for resources and instead align those resources in support of the whole child. Policy, practice, and resources must be aligned to support not only academic learning for each child, but also the experiences that encourage development of a whole child—one who is knowledgeable, healthy, motivated, and engaged.
>
> (ASCD, 2007, p. 8)

Since its launch in 2007 this approach has expanded to incorporate 10 Indicators per Tenet (total of 50 Indicators) delineating the meaning and makeup of each Tenet. It has expanded into national and state resolutions in the U.S.; has been incorporated into state level Every Student Succeeds Acts; adopted by schools, districts, and networks globally; and most recently a free network that provides tools and resources for all schools globally focused on a Whole Child approach to education (ASCD, 2020).

In addition, in 2014 ASCD in collaboration with the U.S. Centers for Disease Control and Prevention (CDC) launched what has been termed the next evolution of coordinated school health. The Whole School, Whole Community, Whole Child (WSCC) model combines and builds on elements of the traditional coordinated school health approach and the whole child framework. This model was developed —in collaboration with key leaders from the fields of health, public health, education, and school health—to strengthen a unified and collaborative approach to learning and health.

The new model responds to the call for greater alignment, integration, and collaboration between education and health to improve each child's cognitive, physical, social, and emotional development. It incorporates the components of a coordinated school health program around the tenets of a whole child approach to education and provides a framework to address the symbiotic relationship between learning and health.

The focus of the WSCC model, with the Whole Child approach at its core, is an ecological approach that is directed at the whole school, with the school in turn drawing its resources and influences from the whole community and serving to address the needs of the whole child.

Whether or not schools and communities use a Whole Child framework or the Whole School, Whole Community, Whole Child Model, they both encompass the same approach framework and similar paths and processes to help ensure that schools and their communities are healthy, safe, engaged, supported, and challenged.

Summary

Why do teachers choose to teach? For most it is not the love of an algebraic formula, or a semicolon, but rather a belief in the potential of children and youth. New teachers believe that education holds one of the best opportunities for people to fulfill their potential, improve their status, and in turn improve their and our communities and societies. They appreciate the unearthed potency that working with children and youth holds and become wary if this potential is ignored.

Unfortunately, too many in-service teachers are not asked to reflect on their purpose for teaching or their power to affect positive change. Too often, their internal motivations remain an untapped resource and an underutilized vehicle for empowering themselves, and in turn each of the students they teach. This can change if we flip our current system.

Meeting the holistic needs of all students requires a new debate on the purpose of education across all stakeholders. It requires us putting the needs of each child, each learner, at the center of this discussion. It requires teachers to be empowered with ownership and agency over the important decisions that impact their students. It requires students to be active owners of their own education. It requires a more democratically infused system. It requires a flattening of established hierarchies, restrictive accountability systems, and decision-making processes. It requires change, and change is difficult.

The wellbeing of our students, our schools, our communities, and our democracy demands that we meet the challenge.

> If the whole child were truly at the center of each educational decision, we would create learning conditions that enable all children to develop all of their gifts and realize their fullest potential. We would enable children to reconnect to their communities and their own diverse learning resources, and we would deeply engage each child in learning. Finally, if the child were at the center, we would integrate all the ways children come to know the natural world, themselves, and one another, so that they can authentically take their place in creating a better future for all.
>
> (ASCD, 2007)

References

Allensworth, D. & Kolbe, L. (1987) The Comprehensive School Health Program: Exploring an Expanded Concept. *Journal of School Health*, 57(10).

ASCD. (2007) *The Learning Compact Redefined: A Call to Action*. Alexandria, VA: ASCD. Retrieved from www.ascd.org/ASCD/pdf/Whole%20Child/WCC%20Learning%20Compact.pdf.

ASCD. (2020). ASCD Whole Child Network. Retrieved from www.ascd.org/programs/The-Whole-Child/Whole-Child-Network.aspx.

ASCD & CDC (2014) *Whole School, Whole Child, Whole Community collaborative approach to learning and health*. Alexandria, VA: ASCD.

Basch C. E. (2010) Healthier Students Are Better Learners: A Missing Link in School Reforms to Close the Achievement Gap. Retrieved from www.equitycampaign.org/i/a/document/12557_EquityMattersVol6_Web03082010.pdf.

Benard, B. (2004) *Resiliency: What We Have Learned*. Oakland, CA: WestEd.

CDC (2009) *School Connectedness: Strategies for Increasing Protective Factors Among Youth*. Atlanta, GA: U.S. Department of Health and Human Services. Retrieved from www.cdc.gov/healthyyouth/protective/pdf/connectedness.pdf.

Chernyshenko, O. S., Kankaraš, M., & Drasgow, F. (2018). Social and Emotional Skills for Student Success and Well-being: Conceptual Framework for the OECD Study on Social and Emotional Skills. Retrieved from www.oecd-ilibrary.org/education/social-and-emotional-skills-for-student-success-and-well-being_db1d8e59-en.

Comer, J. P. (1984) Home-School Relationships as They Affect the Academic Success of Children. *Education and Urban Society*, 16(3), 323–337.

Dewey, J. (1934) Individual Psychology and Education. *The Philosopher*, XII, 1–6.

DeWit, D.J., Karioja, K., Rye, B. J., & Shain, M. (2011) Perceptions of Declining Classmate and Teacher Support Following the Transition to High School: Potential Correlates of Increasing Student Mental Health Difficulties. Psychology in the Schools, 48(612), 556–572.

Marx, E., Wooley, S., & Northrop, D. (1998) *Health Is Academic: A Guide to Coordinated School Health Programs, National Association of Secondary School Principals*. Reston, VA: ASCD. Retrieved from www.ascd.org/ASCD/pdf/siteASCD/publications/wholechild/wscc-a-collaborative-approach.pdf.

Maslow, A. H. (1943) A Theory of Human Motivation, Originally Published in Psychological Review. Retrieved from http://psychclassics.yorku.ca/Maslow/motivation.htm.

Roosevelt, E. (1930) Good Citizenship: The Purpose of Education. *Pictorial Review*, April.

SOPHE-ASCD. (2010) Reducing Youth Health Disparities Requires Cross-Agency Collaboration Between the Health and Education Sectors. Retrieved from www.sophe.org/SchoolHealth/Disparities.cfm.

Sparks, S. (2019) Why Teacher-Student Relationships Matter: New Findings Shed Light on Best Approaches. *EdWeek*, March 12. Retrieved from www.edweek.org/ew/articles/2019/03/13/why-teacher-student-relationships-matter.html.

Chapter 11

Flipping the System for Students
A Primer for the Classroom Teacher

Mairi Cooper

We exited the school bus, walked across the cracked concrete bridge, opened the bullet-proofed doors, and began to sort out how to get the instruments through the metal detectors. My students were entering the County Jail for the first time.

"2,300 inmates but only 300 have been convicted. The rest can't afford bail and are awaiting trial. If they plead, it will be 6 to 8 months. If they don't, it will be at least a year." Our host was sharing these facts as we prepared to go to the performance space.

We played for 30 minutes before the guards allowed audience members to ask questions. My students, mostly white and middle class, listened as the predominantly black and Hispanic lower-class audience eagerly asked about how the instruments and orchestra worked.

"When I get out of here, how do I find pretty violin music to listen to?"

"Would I be able to learn one of these instruments?"

"Why do you wave that stick in the air?"

The evening ended with the inmates being escorted out by pod, or group. When the guards called for the veterans' pod, my students all spontaneously started calling out "thank you for your service."

One man started to cry as he said to the guard, "They saw me as a vet— not an inmate."

Three years ago, my students staged a revolution.

I had spent the previous two years in and out of my classroom as the Pennsylvania Teacher of the Year. I visited schools across the Commonwealth, delivered dozens of speeches, met President Obama, attended Space Camp and slept an average of about four hours per night. Everywhere I went, I took a picture of my orchestra, "flat orchestra," with me. Ironically, the experience flattened my actual orchestra. As I was exposed to the best teachers in the nation and learned of the amazing work being done in their classrooms, I was doing some of the worst teaching of my career. I was exhausted and felt inadequate. Of course, this is when a group of my students decided to challenge me.

Before every concert my full orchestra gets only one vital opportunity to practice together. Usually I only get to teach students in smaller groups, so this practice is sacred. When a group of sophomores requested that I allow them to miss this full-orchestra session to study for an AP test, I denied their request. An assistant principal overrode my decision and I had no recourse but to allow them to miss the rehearsal. We would give a successful concert the next day, but I knew that my orchestra team was broken. I was reeling.

Why after 16 years of teaching would students question the importance of this rehearsal? Why did they not care about the quality of the concert? Why would they take an elective class that they clearly did not value? What did they hope to learn from their time in orchestra?

Little did I know that by diving into self-reflection of my own practice, and asking these questions of my students, I would flip my classroom system, putting my students in charge of their own learning.

Step One: Defining Purpose—The WHY

It took me three weeks to garner the courage to ask my students the most difficult question. If they didn't care about the concert that they were producing, then why were they taking orchestra?

Fine arts teachers are frequently asked to defend the purpose of their content area within the broader curriculum and so are generally well-versed in describing and defending the value of the arts. I was struggling to identify the purpose of teaching music rooted in the white European aristocracy through standard rehearsal techniques. In asking my students to identify their purpose for taking orchestra, I was also seeking to rediscover my own purpose. To my surprise, as my students began to answer my initial questions, other deeper and more fundamental questions began to emerge about the broader purpose of public education. In a fitting twist, I had inadvertently ceded democratic autonomy over the most fundamental part of my classroom to my students: my educational philosophy.

America's founding fathers were clear about the importance of education within a democratic republic. Jefferson (1816) famously wrote, "If a nation expects to be ignorant and free in a state of civilization, it expects what never was and never will be." For Jefferson, as for many of the Founding Fathers, education is critical in creating an informed citizenry.

John Adams (1785) shaped a philosophical and economic argument for public education when he wrote, "The whole people must take upon themselves the education of the whole people and must be willing to bear the expenses of it. There should not be a district of one mile square, without a school in it, not founded by a charitable individual, but maintained at the expense of the people themselves." He viewed education as a vehicle for social mobility. In a letter to his wife, he stated:

> I must study Politicks and War that my sons may have liberty to study Mathematicks and Philosophy. My sons ought to study Mathematicks

and Philosophy, Geography, natural History, Naval Architecture, navigation, Commerce and Agriculture, in order to give their Children a right to study Painting, Poetry, Musick, Architecture, Statuary, Tapestry and Porcelaine.

(Adams, 1780)

They acknowledged the *power* of public education, while simultaneously arguing about the *purpose* of that education. Along with my students, I was trying to find that power and purpose for our orchestra.

Three weeks after that fateful concert, I nervously met my students at the door, asking them to respect the chamber of silence. Authenticity was required for the exercise and at this stage I wanted to hear from each individual. They were surprised to find seats spread out with Post-It notes and Sharpie Markers on each chair. An enormous "WHY" was written on the board. This was totally new, and they were curious. I sat down in the center of the room and recounted the stages of their revolution from my perspective. I acknowledged that I had failed them and that our "union" needed reformation. My language was purposeful. I wanted them to understand that we were embarking on a new journey together.

Our next step would be to establish a collective purpose for the ensemble. I did not read them statistics about the importance of arts education in developing the mind. I did not share Daniel Pink's assertion that "The future belongs to ... creators and empathizers, pattern recognizers and meaning-makers. These people ... will now reap society's richest rewards and share its greatest joys" (Pink, 2012). Rather, I honored their voices, their ideas, and their solutions. We had a brief conversation to establish exactly what we needed to identify.

I shared, "Since 3rd grade, our curriculum has been structured around performing for our parents. We love our parents and want to perform for them. But there must be more."

So, what should be the purpose of our performances? Each student wrote their "WHY" on a post-it note and plastered it on our wall. Many wrote several notes. By the end of the day, the wall was covered. Our journey had begun.

The Post-It notes fell easily into three categories; concerts for educational purposes, concerts providing live music for community members who normally would not have access, and concerts designed to develop an audience for orchestra performances. We sorted the Post-it notes and considered if anything was missing. Only then did somebody shout out "what about the sheer joy of playing?"

The wall quickly became flooded with new notes, and we had our fourth, and final, category.

These four categories became our "pillars." If any concert did not satisfy one of these categories for the collective majority, then we would not perform. For anyone involved in a revolution, ideology is critical. Flipping a system, whether it is in your classroom, your school, or the public education system in America, requires a strong collective philosophical belief. In my classroom it eventually developed into a mission statement.

> *The Fox Chapel Area High School Orchestra's mission is to spread joy, promote artistry and create unity within and beyond our community.*

Step Two: Developing a Process—The HOW

On Sunday mornings, I find myself listening to talking heads discussing the myriad of issues in public education from teacher retention, pension plans, and standardized testing to school choice. As questions of equity arise, John Dewey's words ring in my ears:

> Most of us live in a world in which everyone has a calling and occupation, something to do. Some are managers and others are subordinates. But the great thing for one as for the other is that each shall have had the education which enables him to see within his daily work all there is in it of large and human significance.
>
> (Dewey, 1899)

Over the din of arguments about college and career preparation, I think of Thomas Friedman's writings (2009):

> The jobs of the new middle will require you to be a good collaborator, leverager, adapter, explainer, synthesizer, model builder, localizer, or personalizer and these approaches require you, among other things, to be able to learn how to learn, to bring curiosity and passion to your work, to play well with others, and to nurture your right-brain skills.
>
> (Friedman, 2009)

As educators, our job is to create both an informed citizenry and to prepare our students for the ever-changing face of the future. The world is evolving rapidly, and our education system must adapt at the same pace. The difficulty arises in the *how*. *How* do we prepare our children for careers that have not yet been created? *How* do we change our current educational structure to meet the needs of a future that has yet to emerge?

The success of creating a philosophy had renewed my spirit and restored my relationship with my students. Then the panic set in. Exactly *how* would my students' vision become a reality? *How* would this impact my curriculum? What steps would I need to connect my students' new philosophy with a process and product? I quickly realized that we would be "building the plane as we were flying it," and I had no blueprints to follow.

My sleepless nights were spent researching project-based learning and Stanford University d-School's 5-stage model for design thinking, which mirrors the processes of creating and practicing music (see https://dschool.stanford.edu). Unwittingly, I had already engaged my students in the first two steps of the process: empathizing and defining the problem. Next was the third step, ideation—the act of creating.

Using our newly recognized "pillars" as a foundation, I asked my students to imagine concerts in regional venues. From turnpike plazas to Comicon and the zoo, they opened their imaginations to new possibilities. Any concert they created needed to look substantially different than a typical concert. They needed to design them for their identified audience, be that toll collectors or lions. I showed them the website for purchasing music, taught them how to use our own music library, and asked them to consider how we would teach and learn the music. Did we need the same program for a number of concerts? Would a program on space at the Science Center translate to a program at a Dinner for the Blind? We talked about inviting pop-up audiences to our more traditional concerts. Could we help them get to our high school? The problems were as manifold as the possibilities. It was incredibly exciting and extremely messy. When my students left for the summer I was left with the mess—half-built concerts for over a dozen venues with multiple musical programs.

If there is one thing that educators universally understand it is the power of a strong curriculum. A good curriculum mitigates the mess. My school district has trained us extensively in the principles of McTighe and Wiggins's (2008) backward design. In my earlier years of teaching, I had identified discrete skills that I wanted my students to understand, know, and apply when they left my classroom. I wanted them to have good bow grips, play in tune, and interpret pieces of classical music. With these as my goals, I designed learning plans that built bridges from where my students were to where I wanted them to be at the end of twelfth grade. Now, my goals had shifted.

The words of Dewey and Friedman drove me forward. I was determined to teach the *whole* child on a daily basis by focusing on goals that kept their futures paramount:

- In the future students will work in environments that require complex solutions to difficult issues. They will need to identify problems, analyze them, and create solutions. We must teach them critical thinking and problem solving.
- In the future students will change careers, not simply jobs, multiple times before retirement. As they move between these careers, they not only need to be able to process new information but also entirely new systems. We must teach them to think in terms of processes, not simply basic constructs.

- In the future students will need to be good team members and clear communicators. We must teach them to express themselves and also to *listen to others*. We need for our students to develop empathy and collaboration skills.

I began to understand that discrete skills already embedded in my curriculum were simply in the wrong place. My students were choosing the final product, but I needed to guide the intermediary steps. The skills were not the final goal, but they were critical for building the bridges to the future. Realigning my curriculum was guided by the passions driving my students. The "how" began to materialize.

Step Three: Creating a Product—The WHAT

As we began the first season of newly designed "pop-up concerts," I was keenly aware that failure was not only possible, but inevitable. I was not concerned about failing myself, nor was I really concerned about my students failing. We would all survive. My concern was that our relationships with the community would become strained and this would impact the support for the arts. In much the same way that core curriculum teachers are evaluated by test results, music programs are judged by performances. If my students reached out to the local library but failed to follow through, performed poorly, or were thoughtless, the impact could be devastating for our entire arts program. I worked to create a system where my students could take risks but we maintained our goodwill with the community.

Each event during that year was a prototype. I had to step back and let students accept responsibility so that they could be nurtured in taking risks. If they were passionate about a particular event, they could create a committee, design the content, select the music and create a relationship with the community partner. A senior was selected to oversee all of the projects. Her role was to coordinate repertoire and scheduling between the groups. I served as an advisor.

In this role, I taught how to program music, how to integrate books into programs, and how to work on a committee. Most of the time, I simply said "What do you think?" or "That sounds interesting." During that first year, I communicated with community partners after the students had contacted them. This created a safety net for me and the program.

Were all of our events successful? Absolutely not. After a concert at a retirement home, one of the residents walked up to a student and said, "you really should have learned your part before coming here." I never had to ask that student to practice again. At the same time, my students have created beautiful moments for children, elderly and people who are struggling.

Step Four: Rinse and repeat

Every May we begin the process again. We start by analyzing the data. We scour through the evaluations of each pop-up concert, review programs, and discuss viewpoints. We go back to the basics. The Post-It notes resurface and the wall gets covered once again with our purpose. We re-evaluate the pillars and our mission statement. The mission statement is always revised; the pillars generally are not. We brainstorm venues. We democratically vote on areas of focus for the next year. We establish committees to create programs. We create contacts. We create concerts.

Mostly, we create light for others to step into.

The 300 elementary students had been spellbound as my high schoolers, dressed in Disney costumes, performed for them. We had one piece left, Moana, when my student who had organized this particular event improvised. While introducing the piece, she taught the entire room how to conduct. En route back to the violin section, she informed me that we should play the piece twice, once for the kids to practice conducting and a second time so that we could give individuals an opportunity to conduct the orchestra. I watched over my shoulder and noticed one little 7-year-old girl sitting upright in her seat and conducting with both hands throughout the entire piece. I asked this little girl to be our first conductor. She approached the stage and I was surprised as almost every teacher began to video her on their phones. She was spectacular, but this seemed odd to me. Only later did I learn that the previous year this incredible child had witnessed her mother being murdered and had pulled her younger sister out of the house, saving her life. It had been a difficult year for her to connect at school but in this moment, in this concert, she had connected. My students made that possible. They created light and she stepped into it.

Chapter Addendum

Shortly after I wrote this chapter the COVID-19 Pandemic significantly changed how we live and teach. A week ago, our school district abruptly closed after a student was suspected of having coronavirus. The teachers had two days to prepare online classes before we began to teach. On the first day of our new reality, I awoke to an email from a student inquiring about the possibility of creating "virtual" pop up concerts for isolated elderly. That evening 45 students met by videoconference to brainstorm a series of concerts. They identified their targeted audiences and divided into groups to plan. They have sourced music, conferenced with a children's librarian about obtaining a copyright release, and written music recording app engineers to ask for additional access. My role? To set up video conferences and be quiet. I wonder if they know that in this time of great uncertainty, they are creating light for their teacher.

References

Adams, J. (1780). Letter from John Adams to Abigail Adams, May 12. 2 pages. Original manuscript from the Adams Family Papers, Massachusetts Historical Society.

Adams, J. (1785). From John Adams to John Jebb, 10 September 1785. Retrieved from https://founders.archives.gov/documents/Adams/06-17-02-0232.

Dewey, J. (1899). *The School and Society: Being Three Lectures*. Chicago, IL: University of Chicago.

Friedman, T. L. (2009). *The World is Flat: A Brief History of the Twenty-first Century*. Bridgewater, NJ: Paw Prints.

Jefferson, T. (1816). Thomas Jefferson to Charles Yancey, 6 January 1816. Retrieved from https://founders.archives.gov/documents/Jefferson/03-09-02-0209.

Pink, D. H. (2012). *A Whole New Mind: Why Right-Brainers Will Rule the Future*. New York: Riverhead Books.

Wiggins, G. P., & McTighe, J. (2008). *Understanding by Design*. Alexandria, VA: Association for Supervision and Curriculum Development.

Chapter 12

Immigrant and Refugee Education

Strengthening Our Communities

Mandy Manning

Our democracy is strongest when our communities are healthy, and our communities are strongest when everyone is educated, included, and valued. Immigrants and refugees are our neighbors, our colleagues, and fellow members of our cities and towns. They bring invaluable perspectives, skills, and talents that make us better. If we appreciate each person for the value they add to our communities, rather than focusing on our fears and anxieties about differences, we all grow stronger. This work starts in our schools. Including and educating our refugee and immigrant community members is fundamental to our democracy and prosperity.

Twenty-four students from nine different countries entered my Newcomer Center classroom at the start of last school year. They spoke seven languages and had limited English proficiency. During our time together I witnessed students' bravery, resilience, focus, and grace, learned through the challenging journey that brought them to my class. Kids with little in common bridged differences to become friends and allies—united by their transition to living and studying in the U.S.

War, persecution, and violence displaced seventy-one million people in 2018, many of them like my students (Westerman, 2019). This is two million more than the year before, and a 65% increase over the last decade. 140 million more face the same fate due to climate change by 2050. Displacement is a global crisis.

About one-fifth of the world's migrants live in the United States, unsurprising because most refugees and immigrants relocate to the wealthiest nations. In 2018 we remained the largest recipient of new asylum-seeker applications, accepting more than 254,000 (Radford, 2019). More than 40 million people living in the U.S. were not born here. Just as my students have enriched my life as a teacher, these immigrants add value to our communities and American society.

Immigration trends are shifting, and I see this in my classroom. Prior to 2017, the majority of my students were refugees. Now, only a handful are. The U.S. is developing and enacting policies to reject refugees and asylum seekers. Our government is preventing more people from finding safe haven as they are forced to flee their homes. In 2016–2017, we received the most refugees we ever had in a single year (84,995), while in 2018–2019 we welcomed the fewest (22,491).

Limiting the rights of immigrants to seek asylum as a refugee, through accessing temporary protective status, or by requesting asylum negatively impacts those fleeing dangerous environments and harms our economy and democracy. Fleeing dysfunctional political situations makes asylum seekers/refugees more likely to embrace American ingenuity and ideals of liberty.

This is exemplified by the families of my students. One of my Sudanese students is the only daughter of 10 children. Her father labors on the production floor of a local farm equipment factory, a major industry and economic catalyst in Eastern Washington. The majority of workers in the factory are immigrants, like 17% of the U.S. civilian labor force. Immigrants have provided half the growth in our workforce in the past decade and have started 40% of Fortune 500 companies (Collins, 2019). As the number of refugees declines positions like those in the farm equipment factory cannot be filled, impacting production and weakening our economy.

The Sudanese family's older children are academically successful, and the three oldest now attend university. The eldest is in graduate school, studying international relations and communications, and my student is about to graduate university and begin a promising career. Most of the family members have now become naturalized citizens.

Every year I witness first-hand the optimism, the struggle, the determination, the trauma, the civic participation, the prejudice, and the community involvement described above. The issues are complex, but the lived experiences of my students and their families are real. Their ability to use education as a means to better themselves and their new home is just as real.

This family, like so many others, recognizes the opportunities afforded them by being welcomed into our community, and are working hard to ensure they are giving back. They are representative of the majority of families with which I've worked—believing in the freedom and potential promised by sanctuary in the U.S. While there has been a decrease in voting rates for U.S. born Americans in the past few decades, rates of immigrant voter registration increased by 6% between 1996 and 2012 (Collins, 2019).

Considering how much immigrants contribute to the economy and their dedication to civic participation, providing migrant children with a quality education should be a priority. Immigration has contributed to higher incomes, lower poverty, and lower unemployment in our communities. A study of counties with high levels of immigrants between 1850 and 1920 shows they "enjoy 13 percent higher per-capita income today than [counties] that did not host any new immigrants," which "led to early industrial development and long-run prosperity, which persists today" (Jacobs, 2019). Arguably more important than their labor or skills, immigrants bring diversity, which contributes to better decision-making, problem solving, innovation, and the new perspectives that make progress possible (Phillips, 2014).

Yet, the United States has a shameful history with immigrant education. It wasn't until the 1974 Supreme Court decision, *Lau v. Nichols*, that schools began providing support for non-native English speakers. This decision found that failing to provide language support for students with limited or no English language proficiency violated the Civil Rights Act of 1964. Despite the Supreme Court's ruling, English learner programs are still largely inconsistent among geographical regions and in areas with varying concentrations of immigrant students.

This inconsistency harms our students, our communities, and our nation. Roughly one in ten students in the United States are English learners. Though refugee resettlement has decreased in recent years, immigrant populations as a whole have increased—resulting in new challenges as greater numbers of both documented and undocumented students enter rural, suburban, and urban schools.

Trends show that quality education is key to helping America's immigrants improve themselves and society. In 2017, immigrants were three times less likely than those who were born in the United States to have completed high school. Yet, they were just as likely to have at least a bachelor's degree (Radford, 2019). These statistics, which seem at odds with each other point to a reality that I've seen in my own students. Given proper support, immigrants often achieve academically. The barrier for them is not knowing English.

Once immigrant students are able to overcome the language barrier, they are usually very successful in part because migrant parents, often highly educated in their country of origin, tend to have high academic expectations of their children (DeRuy, 2017). More than one in five highly skilled people emigrate.

Welcoming immigrant students into our school communities also provides exposure for U.S. born students. UNESCO (2018) tells us, "Education can mediate negative portrayals [of immigrants and refugees] by providing political knowledge and critical thinking skills to decipher fact from fiction." In addition, exposure to diverse viewpoints and experiences challenges our perceptions and makes us more empathetic.

In recent years my students have experienced wide-spread anti-immigrant and anti-refugee rhetoric. Even within my own school students are harassed, particularly if they wear outward representations of their cultures or beliefs, such as wearing a hijab. They've been told to go back to their countries and generally made to feel unwelcome, especially if they are not white. This has increased a sense of insecurity for all students, immigrants and U.S. born. No one feels safe, which impacts growth, confidence, and community. When we are isolated, none of us thrive.

To combat this fear I work daily to create connections between all my students, regardless of birthplace. I organize lessons in which students share their cultures and experiences with one another, provide opportunities to appreciate differences, and connect through their commonalities. This increases a sense of belonging for all students. These small steps, while helpful, are not enough to combat the messaging and anti-immigrant stance of the current United States government.

Anti-immigrant sentiment and the political action that feeds off it are driving policies that devastate children and their ability to get the quality education they need to be successful. Current U.S. immigration policy utilizes child separation from parents as a means of deterring immigration into the country (Currier, 2018), often detaining minors in subpar facilities for as long as 93 days without access to legal representation (UNESCO, 2018). In 2019 alone, 69,550 immigrant children were in the custody of the Department of Health and Human Services and afforded limited or no schooling. Missed classes, though, are only one of the many negative consequences.

An indirect, but potentially more harmful impact is the trauma that is inflicted on these children in the process. Educators across the nation have reported an increased number of students in their classrooms with trauma (Acosta & Ellis, 2019). In many cases, this has been inflicted through experiences upon arrival to the U.S. and being detained at the border (Cardoza, 2019). Physical manifestations include digestion issues, headaches, exhaustion, severe mood swings, and difficulty managing emotions. These children exhibit high anxiety, depression, and difficulty forming positive relationships with peers and teachers.

Contrary to public perception, children locked in detention centers are not usually deported. Instead, they are often thrown into a overwhelmed foster care system as unaccompanied minors and attend schools in our communities. Policies that harm these children also wound our communities.

Terrorism is often cited as justification for anti-immigration policies but focusing on education is arguably much more effective. While displaced people are particularly vulnerable to radicalization, education has been shown to be an effective way to combat violent extremism (De Silva, 2017; UNESCO, 2017). According to UNESCO (2018):

- Preventing the emergence of extremism is a key line of defense against terrorism.
- By promoting respect for diversity, peace, and economic advancement education can be a buffer against radicalization.
- Exclusion from education can increase vulnerability.

Our national security depends on supporting immigrant students' language acquisition and development of knowledge and skills needed to move beyond high school. Students in the English learner Newcomer program consistently graduate four years after arriving in the United States. Most of my students continue to post-secondary education. They've become sociologists, dental hygienists, teachers, nurses, mechanics, construction workers, and civic-minded citizens who give back to our community.

It is imperative to welcome newcomers and to provide them with a positive and supportive intercultural educational experience. Our educational aim must not be assimilation. Rather, we must help students learn about themselves and their cultural identity, about America's democratic values, about the skills and competencies they need to be successful here, and how these things intersect. Educating and supporting immigrants as they become members of our communities strengthens our nation. Our economic, political, and cultural influence is grounded in our respect for plurality. America is her best when we all have the opportunity to prosper.

References

Acosta, O., & Ellis, W. (2019, February 20). Student Trauma Is Widespread: Schools Don't Have to Go It Alone. Retrieved from www.edweek.org/ew/articles/2018/02/26/student-trauma-is-widespread-schools-dont-have-to-go-alone.html.

Cardoza, K. (2019, November 18). How Schools Are Responding to Migrant Children. Retrieved from www.edweek.org/ew/articles/2019/04/10/how-schools-are-responding-to-migrant-children.html.

Collins, L. (2019, March 29). America Should Naturalize More Immigrants to Benefit Economy. Retrieved from https://thehill.com/opinion/immigration/435308-america-should-naturalize-more-immigrants-to-benefit-economy.

Currier, C. (2018, September 25). Prosecuting Parents—and Separating Families—Was Meant to Deter Migration, Signed Memo Confirms. Retrieved from https://theintercept.com/2018/09/25/family-separation-border-crossings-zero-tolerance.

DeRuy, E. (2017, February 8). The Myth of Immigrants' Educational Attainment. Retrieved from www.theatlantic.com/education/archive/2017/02/the-myth-of-the-immigrant-paradox/515835.

De Silva, Samantha. (2017). *Role of Education in the Prevention of Violent Extremism*. Washington, DC: World Bank Group.

Jacobs, T. (2019, March 12). Areas Where More Immigrants Settled a Century Ago Have Stronger Economies Today. Retrieved from https://psmag.com/economics/new-evidence-that-immigration-is-good-for-america.

Phillips, K. W. (2014, October 1). How Diversity Makes Us Smarter. Retrieved from https://www.scientificamerican.com/article/how-diversity-makes-us-smarter.

Westerman, A. (2019, June 19). Nearly 71 Million People Forcibly Displaced Worldwide As Of 2018, U.N. Report Says. Retrieved from www.npr.org/2019/06/19/733945696/nearly-71-million-people-forcibly-displaced-worldwide-in-2018-says-u-n-report.

UNESCO. (2017). *Preventing Violent Extremism through Education: A Guide for Policy-makers*. Paris: UNESCO.

UNESCO. (2018). *Migration, Displacement and Education: Building Bridges, Not Walls*. Paris: UNESCO.

Radford, J. (2019, June 17). Key Findings about U.S. Immigrants. Retrieved from www.pewresearch.org/fact-tank/2019/06/17/key-findings-about-u-s-immigrants.

Chapter 13

Impact of Trauma on Our Youth

Kelly D. Holstine and Beth Davey

Trauma, Education, & the Brain

I helped to design and open Tokata Learning Center in Shakopee, MN, in 2012.[1] Mary,[2] one of my students, was creative, kind, caring, and intelligent. She loved animals, journaling, talking about TV shows, and giving hugs.

When Mary was emotionally triggered, she felt like the world was against her. Anything we said felt like a personal attack. She would yell, throw things, and punch walls. Her rage would cause cracks in her relationships. Mary's reactive behaviors would push others away and decrease her chances of receiving the feelings of love and belonging that she so desperately craved. With the exception of a few connecting moments (when she wasn't triggered), Mary mostly felt lonely, scared, and disconnected.

Her mother disappeared when she was younger, and her father never recovered. His pain came out sideways onto Mary as verbal abuse and neglect. She self-medicated with drugs and alcohol, but neither of those helped her to feel any better.

*As a result of her childhood trauma, Mary had an **Attachment Disorder**, which made having healthy relationships with other people extremely difficult. She desperately wanted to be seen and to feel like she mattered, but when her Attachment Disorder kicked in her reality was skewed and she couldn't remember that we cared about her.*

Although Mary was supposed to be a senior, her earned credits placed her at a sophomore grade level. She enrolled, dropped out of school, and re-enrolled several times before it became too difficult to adapt to the school's social expectations and she finally quit. She was intelligent and competent, but her frequent emotional outbursts made it almost impossible for her to function in an academic setting.

When students feel like the world is against them, it is difficult for them to get into their "learning brains" and to be productive at school.

*Everyone has an **Attachment System**. It is created based on how parents and caregivers respond to their children's distress. This internal working* *model directly impacts a person's ability to cope and survive. It is how children learn to keep themselves safe when faced with danger and is one of the most powerful predictors of social and emotional behavior (Therapist Uncensored, 2018). Your Attachment System impacts how you relate to and interact with yourself and others, your emotional regulation and distress tolerance, your self-confidence & self-worth, and your mental, emotional, and physical health.*

Infants and children who experience a disruption in attachment to their primary caregivers are likely to develop an Attachment Disorder. This disruption can be caused by abuse, neglect, separation, or maltreatment (including receiving inadequate care in an institutional setting). Attachment Disorders inhibit one's ability to build healthy attachments to other humans and can create a myriad of psychological and behavioral effects (Therapist Uncensored, 2018).

I have met hundreds of students who struggle in similar ways to Mary because of their childhood trauma. As a teacher, I attempt to find the causes of students' behaviors while still holding them responsible for those behaviors. Compassionate accountability strengthens relationships, improves school culture, and increases self-awareness and self-worth.

* * *

Trauma can be broadly defined as a distressing event or pattern in a person's life, and the impact of various traumas are felt in our schools and communities. Students across the United States are afflicted with negative experiences that shape their understanding of the world and personal identity within it. Community-wide trauma and American income disparity are increasing as systemic injustices marginalize entire communities. Yet, trauma is not isolated to one socioeconomic bracket, neighborhood, or life situation; individuals experience trauma across all spectrums of our society.

Educators have the opportunity to serve each student who walks through their classroom door. It is imperative, therefore, that teachers are knowledgeable of the effects of trauma on brain development. When a young person experiences a traumatic event or pattern, the brain releases hormones as an act of protection (National Scientific Council on the Developing Child, 2014). Some hormones, like adrenaline, can help individuals find safety in dangerous situations. Others, like cortisol, are released in the brain to help the body react with urgency.

In particular, cortisol has a unique impact on the development of the young brain. As young people grow, they acquire new experiences and rational processing which develop areas of the frontal lobe, particularly the prefrontal cortex. A healthy brain is able to process information through rationalization rather than reaction. When a young person's brain is continuously bombarded by protective cortisol releases, however, the development shifts away from the frontal lobe and instead grows the limbic system. This system includes the hippocampus, often associated as a center of memory, and the amygdala, which prompts survival instincts. The result is young people who have experienced a high quantity of trauma are molded to react through emotion and fear rather than conscious processing.

We must educate ourselves on basic neurological operations and their relation to a student's success in school if we want to effectively serve each student. One way that child psychologists have begun to categorize traumatic events is through identifying Adverse Childhood Experiences, or ACEs. Originating in 1985 with research from Dr. Vincent Felitti, the ACEs system assigns a score to individuals based on categories including forms of abuse, substance abuse in the household, systemic racism, and family incarceration. Individuals with higher scores are more likely to develop chronic health conditions, fall into substance abuse, and have a shortened life span (CDC, 2019).

Childhood trauma manifests in a number of ways. Students may appear physically agitated when presented with various stimuli, while others may "shut down" and withdraw from participation. Others still may react to redirection with immediate survival instincts, physically escalating or leaving the classroom altogether.

Trauma as an Equity Issue

I was a tomboy as a kid. What that meant to me was that I didn't want to look girly. But, parts of my personality were feminine, and I was OK with that. This REALLY confused people- and it still does. I wanted to dress like a boy and play with adventure people and trucks. But I also wanted to talk about my feelings and know what everyone around me was thinking and feeling, too. I still do.

As a kid, I got hit, kicked, spit on, harassed, and called names all throughout my elementary and middle school years. As a highly sensitive and gender nonconforming human, I was easy prey. And even though I have since learned that bullies are often the ones with unresolved trauma, it still felt awful to be treated like crap.

I was not allowed to be a tomboy anymore once I entered 9th grade. I had to wear feminine clothes and makeup; paint my nails; have long blonde, curly hair; and not leave the house without lipstick on. I felt like I was in feminine drag.

The positive side effect of my new look was that I didn't get bullied anymore. The negative effect was that pretending to be someone who I wasn't caused such deep depression that I made a plan to end my life. Fortunately, I had some friends and supportive adults who helped me to survive.

My teachers were the ones who made me feel the safest. They inspired me to want to help other people feel like they mattered, too.

My experiences have helped me to support, understand, and advocate for students and staff who do not feel accepted, valued, or seen. I know what it feels like to have someone who is supposed to care about you cause you harm.

Educational equity means finding out what every student needs to be successful and getting it for them. This includes academic needs, socio-emotional needs, and everything in-between.

It is an ongoing and dynamic process that benefits everyone. When we don't prioritize equity, our students fail. Diving into the murk of our own stories to excavate all the ways we were not cared for as kids helps us to have more empathy for the needs of others.

There is a lot I have had to improve as an educator.
I needed to learn how to challenge my own biases and make sure that my thoughts and behaviors were in sync; to increase my understanding of all the ways my privilege impacts the people around me; to replace my defensiveness, perspective gaps, and judgment with curiosity; to understand the difference between intention and impact; to let go of needing to always be the expert; to celebrate vulnerability; and to encourage authenticity in myself and those around me.

All of this work has strengthened my ability to more effectively create equity for others.

* * *

A foundation of our public education system is providing each student with access and opportunity to build a future of social contribution and personal growth. We work to ensure that our school systems provide differentiation and support services for many students. Yet, it is clear that there are gaps in our efforts. As a result of post-industrial shifts in urban settings, changing economies of our rural towns, and systemic funding inequities in communities of color, many schools and students do not have access to the services and education which they deserve (Ed Build, 2016).

Trauma knows no bounds when it comes to socio-economic status or geographical area. There are several markers, however, which can escalate into community health crises: mass incarceration of communities of color, continued marginalization of indigenous peoples, growing epidemics in opioid abuse, and the increasing wealth gap influence traumatic events in particular pockets of our society (FACT, 2019). Worse, these trends are often in communities and schools that are underfunded and under-resourced. If we hope to address this equity issue, we must consider our dedication to provide resources to all of our students. This includes additional counselors, social workers, therapists, and training for all staff members.

The core of this conversation prompts us to ask ourselves: when it comes to social and emotional health, are we giving each student what they need for success? Are we as a society willing to step with nuance while addressing these needs in community health? Are our policies and systems serving each child?

Trauma-Responsive Teaching

We got a new student at our school, Olivia, a few years ago. She hid behind her bangs and had difficulty looking at anyone. She did not know how to talk to other people without making them feel judged. Her mother had recently died by suicide. After being rejected by her extended family she became the responsibility of her 20-year-old sister. Olivia was lonely and heartbroken. She desperately wanted to connect with others but did not know how. She had been given a variety of mental health diagnoses, but she didn't understand their meanings or what to do with them.

Olivia started to slowly trust others and become more confident: she joined our leadership group, built connections with staff and students, ran the school store, became my teaching assistant, and ran our online literary magazine.

We discovered that she loved Gray's Anatomy, *guinea pigs, helping other students, and writing poetry. We learned that she was brilliant, highly organized, and creative. Olivia graduated two years ago, without bangs over her eyes and with a gigantic smile on her face. She held a golden rose that contained some of her mom's ashes.*

Olivia is now thriving at her job and has consistently been given extra responsibilities. Her supervisor told me how much they rely on her. She beautifully represents the students who used to be unaware of their gifts and have not always been given the safe support to challenge their flaws. They all have learned what feeling like they matter can do for their self-esteem.

When I designed and created an Area Learning Center (an alternative high school), I quickly learned what students who had experienced educational and personal trauma needed to thrive. They desired inclusive spaces with soft lighting, seating options, snacks, basic school supplies, and posters that represented diversity. They wanted to see themselves in what they were learning. They benefited from personalized, self-paced, voice and choice curriculum. Student engagement increased significantly when they could select texts that piqued their interest.

All humans deserve to be called by their affirmed pronouns and names and to use whatever bathroom makes them feel safe. Too many of our transgender students are not eating or drinking during the day and waiting to use the bathroom until they get home. This causes significant medical issues and acute emotional pain. A national survey revealed that 73% of LGBTQ youth have experienced verbal threats because of their actual or perceived LGBTQ identity (Human Rights Campaign, 2018). It's not enough to tell our kids that, "it gets better." We need to show them that we are making it better now.

Research and experience teach us that kids who have been victims of trauma build resiliency only when they are believed and supported by an adult. I can tell you firsthand that trauma-sensitive environments make learning much easier for everyone. And, as mandated reporters, it is our duty to protect every single one of our students. Every. Single. One.

* * *

Teachers have the opportunity to nurture and support every student who enters their door. It is our responsibility to help each student see that they are safe, that they are loved, and that they matter. Because of this, educators should address all needs in their classroom, including needs of students who have experienced trauma. A trauma-responsive educator partners with community health resources, instructs students on the functions of their own brains (i.e. frontal lobe versus limbic reactions), and explicitly teaches strategies for students experiencing dysregulation (Cole et al., 2005).

Trauma-responsive teaching benefits not only students who have experienced trauma, but the entire student population. Through intentional work in educating students on their own brain development and needs of their community, teachers can forge environments of respect, build foundations for empathy and inclusion, and impact their wider community through teaching regulation skills.

Can Education Cause Trauma?

Alternative educators work with students who are unable to find success in mainstream schools. These are students who can feel unseen and like they don't matter, causing them to "act out" in class because their needs are not being met.

Area Learning Centers have been given the unflattering nickname of "Assholes' Last Chance." Our population can consist of students with varying abilities and temperaments, but these same students are also some of the most creative and brilliant humans with whom I have ever worked. The students who arrive angry, sad, hurt, or scared reveal their authentic, vulnerable, brilliant, and beautiful selves when they feel safe and valued.

Here is the truth: these students are extraordinary human beings who are consistently underestimated and need a safe place to become the best version of themselves.

We must understand the impact of prejudice, discrimination, educational trauma, and bias (explicit and implicit). Our beliefs and actions must be consistently aligned in order to provide equity. Educators need to be trained in restorative practices and how to create culturally responsive classrooms. And, we need to heal educational and personal trauma, and never, ever, be the cause of it.

It is impossible to determine our student's needs, and thus achieve equity, if they are disconnected and distrustful. They count on us to be their advocates and their champions, and I strongly believe that ALL our kids are all OUR kids. We are all responsible for the well-being of all our students—not just the humans in our classrooms, but also the ones in our schools, our communities, our cities, our states, and in our country.

* * *

As a universal system, public education has the opportunity and responsibility to provide justice and close equity gaps for all students. Education can also cause harm through its perpetration of systemic trauma. Our national obsession with testing and performance-based tasks puts enormous stress on our young people (Heissel et al., 2018). Additionally, many available curricula affirm colonialist mindsets and do not tell complete stories of historically marginalized communities, thus rewriting history and silencing identities (Masta, 2016). Educators should also address explicit and implicit biases that impact student success and perception of safety in school.

Poorly designed or implemented discipline practices also can traumatize students. As we observe disproportionate rates of school discipline for students of color, we must consider how our intended system of educational justice contributes to the school-to-prison pipeline. Instead of no-tolerance policies of school discipline, we can choose to act in hopes of restoration rather than punishment.

Educators should engage to ensure that each student experiences justice, belonging, and opportunity in school. To do this, educators must drive conversations surrounding policies that impact student success.

Shifting Our Structures

There is reason for optimism, and it is built on teachers' love for their students.

By focusing resources, intentions, and actions on addressing epidemics of trauma we can more equitably serve each child. To do this, we must collectively prioritize the social and emotional well-being of our young people. Every school needs mental health professionals, and underserved communities require additional resources.

Educators possess a holistic perspective on social issues due to their influence and impact within a community. As professionals who interact with children impacted by inequities in health and housing, we have the perspective and knowledge to find the synthesis between education policies and wider issues. It is essential, therefore, that teachers are consulted in housing and health policies at local, state, and national levels.

There is hope for our students who have experienced trauma. It does not need to define our students. Empowering them to process their trauma in healthy ways can help them use increased empathy and compassion as assets.

We are at a crossroads. If we ignore the impact of educational and personal trauma on students, we waste precious resources and talents, contributing to further societal injustices. And yet—if we engage, problem-solve, and seek to equitably serve our students, then we can build a healthier society.

Notes

1 In this chapter, *italic text* is by Kelly D. Holstine, and roman text is by Beth Davey.
2 All student names have been changed.

References

CDC. (2019, April 2). Adverse Childhood Experiences (ACEs). Retrieved from www. cdc.gov/violenceprevention/childabuseandneglect/acestudy/index.html?CDC_AA_refVal=https://www.cdc.gov/violenceprevention/acestudy/index.html.

Cole, S. F., O'Brien, J. G., Gadd, M. G., Ristuccia, J., Wallace, D. L., & Gregory, M. (2005). *The impact of trauma on learning.* In *Helping Traumatized Children Learn: Supportive School Environments for Children Traumatized by Family Violence* (pp. 14–41). Boston, MA: Massachusetts Advocates for Children. Retrieved from https://traumasensitiveschools.org.

Ed Build. (2016). Nonwhite School Districts Get $23 Billion Less that White Districts Despite Serving the Same Number of Students. Retrieved from https://edbuild.org/content/23-billion.

FACT. (2019). Systems of Trauma. Retrieved from www.fact.virginia.gov/systems-of-trauma/.

Heissel, J., Adam, E., Doleac, J., Figlio, D., & Meer, J. (2018). Testing, Stress, and Performance: How Students Respond Physiologically to High-Stakes Testing. Retrieved from www.nber.org/papers/w25305.

Human Rights Campaign. (2018). 2018 LGBTQ Youth Report. Retrieved from www.hrc.org/resources/2018-lgbtq-youth-report.

Masta, S. (2016). Disrupting Colonial Narratives in the Curriculum. *Multicultural Perspectives*, 18(4), 185–191.

National Scientific Council on the Developing Child. (2014). Excessive Stress Disrupts the Architecture of the Developing Brain. Working paper no. 3. Retrieved from www.developingchild.harvard.edu.

Therapist Uncensored. (2018). TU78: The Stress Response System (Attachment) Across the Lifespan. Retrieved from www.therapistuncensored.com/episodes/tu78.

Part IV

Elevating Teacher Expertise into Education Decisions

A flipped education system, a flattening of the educational hierarchy, and a decentralization of decision-making power in policy decisions will not happen simply because it is a good idea, or because it is good for our students. History tells us that many great ideas and policies that were good for students lie in policy graveyards. Momentum is a powerful force, and those with power tend to consolidate it and fight to retain it. Only outside pressure brought about by activism, mobilization, public engagement, and determination can force the systemic transformation outlined in this book.

Structural changes are needed, and these must be driven from within the teaching profession. Nobody is going to do this work for us. Nobody is going to give us a pass because we are exhausted from our classroom duties. If we believe that our students deserve better, that our colleagues and our profession deserve better, and that our communities deserve better, then we must create the change we know is needed.

Teachers need to be respected and valued as the professionals that they are. At the same time, teachers must assume greater professional responsibility. To achieve a flipped system, both of these have to happen simultaneously. The chapters in Part IV give us guidance in how this is possible.

In Chapter 14, **Melissa Tomlinson** establishes that teaching is fundamentally a political profession and gives guidance on how teachers can use their political influence to bring about positive change for their students and colleagues.

Pasi Sahlberg (Chapter 15) follows by revealing that many of the innovations and reforms that are driving educational success internationally have roots in the United States, and imploring decision makers to use these successful practices in American systems.

In Chapter 16, **Tracey Fritch** shares a case study of the Sanger Unified School District, where a distributed leadership model has given teachers greater autonomy and produced outstanding outcomes for students and the community.

Noah Karvelis, one of the founders of the #RedforEd movement in Arizona, details in Chapter 17 how that grassroots movement started, and lessons that teachers can learn in working together toward positive change.

In Chapter 18, **Howard Stevenson** communicates the important role that education unions have in a flipped system, and how union renewal can make them more responsive to members and more effective.

Chapter 14

Teaching is a Political Profession

Stepping into the Arena

Melissa Tomlinson

"Just let me teach."

This has become the clarion call of educators for the past few decades as they have been burdened by overregulation, micromanagement, and top-down mandates from those far removed from classrooms. Armed with degrees in pedagogy and years of experience, teachers are well prepared to meet the needs of students in their classrooms if they are given the professional autonomy to do so. Yet, since the passage of No Child Left Behind (NCLB), there has been a trend to take away that professional autonomy. This law accelerated an intensive push to take professional decision-making out of the hands of teachers who are intimately knowledgeable about the unique needs of their students and to place it under the control of lawmakers, lobbyists, and corporations that profit off public school funding.

Perhaps just as concerning, as teachers have become overwhelmed by burdens of unintended negative consequences created by uninformed policy, they have less capacity to step into political spaces necessary to advocate for the wellbeing of our students and our public schools. Anyone who has talked with a teacher knows that the most valuable resource in our schools is time. By forcing teachers to spend time and energy on mandates that do not help their students, we are limiting their ability to do the things that would benefit our students and our schools most—in and outside the classroom.

As professionals, every teacher has two realms of responsibility. The most obvious is the practice of teaching that happens every day in the classroom. We need our teachers to be excellent practitioners. We also, however, need them to be excellent advocates for our students and our education system. This is their responsibility to our society. Teachers understand the collective and individual needs of students in a way that nobody else in our system can. Without teacher input in the political arena, our schools, communities, and students cannot meet their full potential.

Teaching is a political profession, and teachers must step into the political arena if we are to flip the system.

Teacher Autonomy

There is a difference between a profession and an occupation. Being a professional requires specialized training, expertise, and skill. It demands collaboration with other professionals, continuing education, and a responsibility to follow and help develop professional standards. It is of paramount importance that those in the teaching profession have the autonomy and independence to act on their training, expertise, skill, collaboration, and education for the benefit of those in their charge. This professional autonomy falls into two categories—individual and collective.

Individual autonomy refers to a teacher's ability to make direct decisions in her/his classroom for the benefit of students. Cribb and Gerwitz (2007) found that this type of autonomy, compared to state control of education, allowed teachers to leverage professional expertise, served as a source of job satisfaction and well-being, expanded creativity and variety within the classroom, and increased the effectiveness of individual teachers and the profession as a whole.

Evaluating the importance of individual autonomy can be done by examining a classroom that lacks it, such as one that is part of a school-wide scripted-curriculum program. These programs are designed to have teachers read from a prepared script while delivering a lesson. The scripts assume everyone in a grade level is moving at the same pace and rely heavily on rote learning that leaves little room for creativity. In these situations, the teacher is stripped of the opportunity to make normative decisions based on analysis and knowledge of their students and is unable to make important choices about meeting the varied needs of the children in their classroom. This eliminates opportunities for teachable moments that reach the students on a personal level. It destroys relationships between children and learning, students and teachers, and between classmates.

Like many issues in education, there are complexities in determining how to best provide individual autonomy. Absolute individual autonomy can have harmful consequences, especially when operating within the context of social and race demographics. In a profession that has a majority of white female educators and a high percentage of non-white students, decisions that are made in isolation within a classroom can sometimes be influenced by internal biases of the teacher. As a result, harmful practices such as unfair disciplinary procedures and higher suspension rates for students of color can occur. Teachers who don't recognize their unconscious bias may incorporate lessons that are inappropriate to the racial, or social make-up of the children in front of them. As we focus on educating teachers to be culturally responsive and mitigate harmful individual decisions, we must also look within the teaching profession collectively to develop professional standards for teacher accountability.

Collective autonomy is the ability for a profession to regulate itself and develop these standards. Just as we all want doctors developing rules for when heart surgery is required rather than insurance companies, and architects determining regulations for the safety of buildings rather than contractors, we want teachers creating the professional standards that govern classrooms and protect our children rather than corporate executives, textbook companies, or standardized test profiteers. A flipped education system balances the individual autonomy of professional teachers with the standards and accountability developed by the collective expertise found in the teaching profession.

This balance allows teachers to hone current practices that work for their students and innovate new strategies without being forced to incorporate mandated initiatives that may not have benefit. Included are educational technology trends, at times with problematic corporate ties and conflicts of interest, that have often been pushed on teachers despite a lack of research showing effectiveness. While innovation and technological relevance are important, overreliance on technology in the classroom at the expense of students' holistic needs erodes personal connections that bolster student learning. Economic factors, such as the financial benefit of placing a computer in a classroom rather than decreasing class size, can be alluring to districts that have had their budgets slashed. To maintain one's own relevance as a classroom teacher as well as protecting the standing of the greater profession, educators need to walk this line carefully, being aware of how technology can be used as a learning tool while fighting against being replaced by machines or forced into a role of merely facilitating computer programs.

Increased individual and collective autonomy for teachers allows for conversations to build consensus around what is in the best interest of our students. As Howard Stevenson will show in a following chapter on union renewal, teacher unions serve as an important space for these conversations, as well as a vehicle for the political activism needed to turn them into sound educational policy. Within teacher unions, consensus on issues drives legislative platforms, which then directs advocacy for teacher-informed policies. This is most effective in grassroots, democratic unionism models that inspire engagement and elevate the voices of those who have traditionally been marginalized. When used as a connection tool, technology can be powerful in building transformational grassroots movements within and outside unions.

Networking and Social Media

Social media has become a powerful tool in building and activating teacher networks across the country to focus on advocacy and policy change. While teachers in the United States under NCLB were feeling increasingly powerless to make the decisions they knew were best for students, anger and frustration increased. After the implementation of Race to the Top, a new

top-down federal mandate heavily focused on testing and removing autonomy from classroom teachers, many educators were looking for a way to
connect and amplify their voice in political spaces. Social media provided
the perfect way to do that.

In 2013 Badass Teachers Association (BAT) started as a closed Facebook
group. It grew exponentially as educators and public education supporters
engaged in conversations about the teaching profession and taking action for
the collective good of public education. From this Facebook group rose a
nonprofit advocacy organization that works to shape narratives around
public education by listening to those most affected by education policies.
More than just elevating the voices of educators through social media, the
organization has modeled how educators must engage in the political arena.
Members of BAT have testified about education policy and legislation at
state capitals and the U.S. Department of Education, engaged in public
education research, co-written an Amicus Brief for the *Friedrichs vs California Teachers Association* Supreme Court Case, taken roles as union leaders, and have even been elected to positions at the local and state level.

Why Teachers Need to be in the Political Arena

If you aren't at the table, you are on the menu.

Schools are bound by their budgets and public education is funded
through a political process. As much as educators may want to keep politics
out of schools, the political arena is where decisions are made that greatly
impact every aspect of public education. Without the involvement of educators that have both theoretical and experiential knowledge of the educational process and child development, decisions can, and often do, have
harmful consequences. Teachers are often reluctant to become politically
engaged because they are afraid of being perceived as too outspoken, parti-
san, or divisive. But, using our expertise and unique insight to inform education decisions is our professional and moral obligation. Involvement in
political discussions becomes easier to navigate when our central focus
remains on students and what is best for them.

Every educator must be politically engaged to meet their responsibility of
being an advocate for their students and the families in their school community. Abdication of this responsibility perpetuates an educational system
that fails to equitably provide opportunity to our children. It is only through
the inclusion and elevation of teacher expertise that we can be sure our
schools fulfill their intended role as safe spaces that prepare all students for
future success. Ceding political spaces that impact public education to non-
educators exposes our children to decisions made devoid of practical information. Worse, a lack of teachers in those spaces creates opportunity for
those seeking to dismantle public education for their own financial gain to
fill the void.

Unfortunately, due to decades of public attacks on teachers, we must convince our colleagues that they have the credibility to drive political decisions that impact their work and their students. This can be done through training, networking, and support. When educators come to the point of self-realization of their own expertise it is both empowering and inspiring. In actuality, educators develop the skills necessary to traverse multifaceted conversational terrains in their everyday classroom practice and professional workspaces. To flip the system we need to develop natural pathways for them to testify and explain to lawmakers narratives from their schools and communities.

If teacher insights and perspectives, formed through direct knowledge of our students, schools, and communities are absent from education decisions, then whose agenda will be served? If we refuse to speak up for our students and colleagues, who will?

Flipping the System

Aside from the direct benefits to students and schools, teachers must have agency in decision making for their own job satisfaction. Current teacher shortages are fueled by lack of professional autonomy (García & Weiss, 2019), and research shows our most effective and intelligent teachers are those most likely to leave the profession (Hare & Heap, 2001). To stop these alarming trends, educator voices must be heard. Otherwise, stress factors will continue to increase for educators, turnover will increase, and student learning will suffer. Exploratory research about teacher stress levels by the American Federation of Teachers and Badass Teachers Association (2015) showed that most teachers were stressed, not feeling respected, and were less enthusiastic about their career than they were when they started teaching.

Working to get educators into decision-making positions means little if these educators must leave the classroom to have influence. Such a system would perpetuate current shortcomings that stem from a lack of relevant and recent experience. Instead spaces must be created where expert teachers are given the greatest weight in educational decision making—at local, state, and national levels. The Every Student Succeeds Act (ESSA) that became federal law in 2015 provides a mechanism that mandates stakeholder engagement in the different steps of analyzing data, conducting a needs assessment, identifying root causes, and developing annual school plans. What this process actually looks like in reality reveals a lack of intention towards creating inclusive spaces where those most impacted by decisions are heard and elevated. The Center on Education Policy found only 1% of teachers felt like their opinions were factored in national education decisions while ESSA was being implemented, and only 5% felt like they had a voice in state-level policy (Rentner et al., 2016).

Imagine for a moment what it would look like if we were to flip the system. What if we let educators design the parameters under which a federal education act like this is written? To begin with, the name of the Every Student Succeeds Act would likely change. Success is subjective, defined differently for each person. At the moment, educational success is measured within corporate business terms, emphasizing the creation of future workers, corporate business managers, and cogs in the economy—an over focus on "qualification" as described by Biesta earlier in this book. But there are broader ways to look at success. Educators, who tend to look beyond economic outcomes are well positioned to recognize individual talents, the beauty of the arts, the importance of compassion, and the role these difficult-to-quantify aspects play in the health of our society. With teacher input, the parameters for measuring growth would become individualized, as the fact that children develop at different rates and in different areas would be given serious consideration.

Just as important as defining educational goals and metrics for success, we must imagine the structures to be created to elevate educator voices. What would they look like? How would they be managed? Right now, we operate in a system that does not easily accommodate the inclusion of teacher expertise. Hearings and meetings that allow for input into policies are often held during the week and during school hours. To start with, flipping the system requires schedule changes that allow teacher access to these spaces. Formal virtual meetings to provide practical context to policy decisions, held in evenings among groups of educators from states around the country, would be a significant step towards building an inclusive table. Technology and video conferencing platforms would eliminate the need for travel or for educators to take copious amounts of time away from their classroom to participate. A process like this would allow teachers access and influence without leaving their classroom positions. A flipped system would begin to alleviate current trends where those who find avenues to both have influence and stay in their teaching positions often burn out.

Truly establishing a quality, equitable school system demands flattening the hierarchy beyond teachers. School cultures and environments must change. Students must have autonomy over their learning in many of the ways that teachers need autonomy over teaching. Inspiration must replace coercion at all levels of the system. This control over their educational experiences will help students develop a personal investment in their education. By building partnerships and establishing schools as innovative spaces focused on meeting the needs of their local area, they can again become cornerstones of their communities. This would allow every dollar of public investment spent on public education to provide value far beyond the school walls.

Even these reforms, however, require teacher agency and engagement in the political arena. While parents can (and should) speak for the needs of their own children, they have a limited perspective. While community business owners can advocate for the economic requirements of their establishments, and public servants understand many community issues, they are not well positioned to understand how those intersect with child development or learning. Teachers have both a unique perspective and a vital role to play in bridging the holistic development of the many different, individual students that they interact with on a daily basis with the diverse needs in the community. Growth and progress only happen when we move beyond our comfort zones. This is true for individuals and systems. If we are to flip the system, structures and capacity must be built to allow teacher expertise to drive education decisions. These changes are unlikely to happen without public pressure and mobilization. Those in power are often reluctant to give some of it up.

This is why teachers must focus beyond classroom practice and assume greater professional responsibility in political spaces, even if it is uncomfortable. Every teacher who chooses to remain quiet during the implementation of policies that negatively impact their students and colleagues is complicit in allowing it to happen. Within schools, districts, unions, and online networks, teachers must find new ways to support and mentor each other, not only in the classroom, but also in the political arena.

We can do this. Movements like #RedforEd, explained by Noah Karvelis in Chapter 17, and BAT exemplify how the power of solidarity and grassroots collective action can move us toward these goals. We all want what is best for our students. We all want what is best for our profession. We all want what is best for our schools and communities. If we each do our part to step into the political arena and support each other, it is not difficult to imagine a flipped system with equitable and outstanding outcomes for all children. It is not difficult to imagine a future where teachers do not have to say, "Just let me teach." Perhaps in this new reality, they will say, "Just let me lead."

References

American Federation of Teachers & Badass Teachers Association. (2015). Quality of worklife survey. Retrieved from https://static1.squarespace.com/static/5d30f5468f2df10001eae004/t/5ddf15772104bb5045690381/1574901113738/worklifesurveyresults2015.pdf.

Cribb, A., & Gewirtz, S. (2007). Unpacking autonomy and control in education: Some conceptual and normative groundwork for a comparative analysis. Retrieved from https://journals.sagepub.com/doi/abs/10.2304/eerj.2007.6.3.203.

Hare, D., & Heap, J. L. (2001). *Effective teacher recruitment and retention strategies in the Midwest: Who is making use of them?* Naperville, IL: North Central Regional Educational Laboratory.

García, E., & Weiss, E. (2019). The teacher shortage is real, large and growing, and worse than we thought. Retrieved from www.epi.org/publication/the-teacher-shortage-is-real-large-and-growing-and-worse-than-we-thought-the-first-report-in-the-perfect-storm-in-the-teacher-labor-market-series.

Rentner, D. S., Kober, N., Frizzell, M., & Ferguson, M. (2016). *Listen to us: Teacher views and voices*. Washington, DC: Center on Education Policy.

Chapter 15

Lessons for the United States from International Education Systems

Pasi Sahlberg

My grandfather was American citizen. Together with thousands of other Finns, he left for New York City in the spring of 1914 to look for something that his homeland that time couldn't offer. He settled down in New York, went to war as a member of the U.S. armed forces, and obtained an engineering degree in Brooklyn's Polytech. I grew up listening to my grandfather's stories about life in the New World, his voyages across the Atlantic, and great American education.

During my initial teacher education in Helsinki, and later when doing doctoral studies in Jyvaskyla, most of the literature I read was written by American scholars and practitioners. My readings ranged from John Dewey to Elizabeth Cohen and from Howard Gardner to Linda Darling-Hammond. They, and many others, helped me to build a strong foundation for my career later on as an educator in Finland and beyond. I often thought of how right my grandfather was in his views about America.

The United States has been an educational inspiration, not only for people like me in Finland, but for many teachers and researchers around the world. American ideas about pedagogy, assessment, curriculum, leadership, and school improvement have been important for Canadians, Dutch, Australians, Singaporeans and Chinese educators as they have built world-class education systems in their countries. As a consequence, the United States has been a role-model for other countries when they reformed their education systems to better meet the needs of modern times. Many individual scholars, activists, experts, and institutions in the United States continue to lead the way in generating forward-looking thinking and solutions in education. But as a system—or systems—the United States is no longer among the most interesting places in the world.

Innovation and Improvement

An intriguing question of whether innovation in education system level can be measured was answered by the Organisation for Economic Co-operation and Development (OECD) a few years ago in its report *Measuring*

Innovation in Education (OECD, 2014). It measured the level of educational innovation in 22 countries and 6 jurisdictions, among them Indiana, Massachusetts and Minnesota.

One conclusion of the OECD's measurement of innovation between 2003 and 2011 was that "there have been large increases in innovative pedagogic practices across all countries ... in areas such as relating lessons to real life, higher order skills, data and text interpretation and personalization of teaching" (OECD, 2014). In this comparison of the education systems' internal abilities to renew itself the U.S. did not do very well compared to other participating countries. Those who know that the period covered in this measurement included the most intensive push of No Child Left Behind and Race to the Top legislations would say: "Not surprising." Market-like school-to-school competition, tougher accountability measures, and an obsession with standardized testing were the core ideas through which many American politicians tried to unlock improvement within American school system.

It was surprising, however, to see the OECD's list of the top five U.S. "innovations in pedagogic practice." They were:

1   observation and description in secondary school science lessons;
2   individualized reading instruction in primary school classrooms;
3   use of answer explanation in primary mathematics;
4   relating of primary school lessons to everyday life; and
5   text interpretation in primary lessons (OECD, 2014).

Innovation in organizational policy and practice included mostly different aspects of student assessment and standardized testing. In reality, these numerous innovations rapidly led to overloading teachers' and principals' daily work, lack of proper preparation of good laws and implantation of new practices and burn-out of many in the country's public schools. What has been missing in most school reform efforts in the United States, Australia, England and several other countries is that good innovation often means reducing teachers' workload so that they have time for new ideas. Time is a critical condition to have if we want to flip the system.

The last two decades have witnessed a notable shift from reforming education by domestic innovation to transforming it by importing international ideas for improvement. A closer look at what current high-performing school systems have in common reveals that they all (some more than the others) have taken critical lessons from other countries to transform their national policies and school-level practices. Singapore sends hundreds of students to study education in U.S. universities and encourage university scholars to collaborate in teaching and research with their American colleagues. Japan, Hong Kong and South Korea have done the same. More recently, China has also benefited from education innovation in the U.S. and other western education systems. Canadians also admit that U.S. research and innovation have been instrumental in gradually moving education in Canada forward to be world-class today.

Finland is no exception. If you want to discover the origins of the most successful practices in pedagogy, student assessment, school leadership, or school improvement in Finland, you only need to visit schools and ask teachers and principals. Most of them, including me, have studied psychology, teaching methods, curriculum theories, assessment models, and classroom management researched and designed in the U.S. in their initial teacher education programs. Primary school teacher education curricula in Finnish universities include piles of books and research articles written by American scholars and thought leaders (Hammerness et al., 2017). Professional development programs and school improvement initiatives often include invited experts from the U.S. universities to teach and work with Finnish teachers and system leaders. So common is this reliance on American educational ideas in Finland that some have come to call Finnish school system a large-scale laboratory of American education innovation (Sahlberg, 2015). The evidence shows that these innovations can work in practice.

The relatively low overall international rating of "innovation in education" in the U.S. raises an important question: Why have state or federal education authorities systematically ignored most great American educational ideas and innovation that many other countries have utilized to improve the performance of their school systems during the last decades? Of course, there are schools and districts that have understood the power and value of American expert knowledge and research. But overall, it is hard to find a school system—either a state or a district—that has systematically relied on American research knowledge in providing better public education to their children. It is interesting that, according to the OECD (2014), the U.S. exhibits only modest innovation in its education system but, at the same time, it is the world leader in generating world-class research, inventing practical solutions for school, and innovation to policy-makers, leaders and practitioners in other countries.

Shadow American School System in Finland

I have hosted hundreds of politicians, administrators and teachers in Finland during their pilgrimage to find out the drivers behind Finnish education. Often, I heard these visitors surprised how similar school cultures and classroom life are to what they were in the U.S. before the 1990s. In fact, what visitors to Finnish schools and teacher education sites witness is a wide range of American educational theories and models put into large-scale practice.

Five significant American educational ideas have been instrumental in accelerating Finland's success in teaching and learning.

1 Education for Democracy and Active Citizenship

The roots of Finland's pedagogical ideas date back to the 1860s when Uno Cygnaeus, who is sometimes referred as the father of basic education in Finland, said that in an ideal classroom, pupils speak more than the teacher. He was also a fan of practical aspects of education and insisted that both boys and girls must learn all the practical skills that people need in everyday lives. It is understandable that the pragmatic, child-centered educational thinking of John Dewey has been widely accepted among Finnish educators. Dewey's philosophy of education forms a foundation for academic, research-based teacher education in Finland and influenced also the work of the most influential Finnish scholar professor Matti Koskenniemi in the 1940s. All primary school teachers read and explore Dewey's and Kosken-niemi's ideas as part of their courses leading to the master's degree today. Many Finnish schools have adopted Dewey's view of education for democracy by enhancing students' access to decision-making regarding their own lives and studying in school (Dewey, 1916). Some visitors to Finland, among them the late Seymour Sarason, have observed that the entire Finnish school system looks like John Dewey's laboratory schools in the U.S. when they were actively alive.

2 Learning Cooperatively in Small Groups

Unlike in most other countries, cooperative learning has become a pedagogical approach that is widely practiced throughout Finnish education system. Finland's new 9-year comprehensive school launched in early 1970s was built on an idea of equal education opportunity and regular small-group learning of students coming from different family backgrounds. But it was the national curriculum reform in 1994 that brought cooperative learning as it is known now to all Finnish schools. Before that, most significant researchers and trainers of cooperative learning in the United States, including David Johnson, Roger Johnson and Elizabeth Cohen, had visited Finland to train trainers and teachers on their methods of cooperative learning. Their books and articles were translated into Finnish and shared widely to schools (Johnson & Johnson, 1984). The 1994 National Curriculum included a requirement that all schools design their own curricula in a way that would enhance teaching and learning according to constructivist educational ideas (National Board of Education, 2016). Although cooperative learning is not mentioned as an obligatory pedagogical practice in schools, there are several recommendations for teachers that make cooperative learning a common approach in all schools and classrooms in the country. Cooperative learning is also an integral element of initial teacher education in Finland and one of the most popular topics in professional learning of teachers and school leaders in Finland.

3 Children Have Multiple Intelligences

The spirit of 1970s school reform in Finland included another idea that derives from U.S. universities and scholars: development of the whole child. The overall goal of schooling in Finland was to support a child's holistic development and growth by focusing on different aspects of talent and intelligence (see Chapter 10 of this volume, by Sean Slade). After abolishing all streaming and tracking of students in the mid-1980s, both education policies and school practices adopted the principle that all children have different kinds of intelligence and that schools must find ways to cultivate these different individual aspects in balanced ways. Howard Gardner's (1983) Theory of Multiple Intelligences became a leading idea in transferring these policy principles to school practice. Again, the 1994 National Curriculum emphasizes that school education must provide all students with opportunities to develop all aspects of their minds. As a consequence, that curriculum framework required that all schools have a balanced program, blending academic subjects with art, music, crafts, and physical education. This framework moreover mandated that all schools provide students with sufficient time for their self-directed activities. Gardner's influence has also been notable in the Finnish system by conferring a broader definition of "talent." Today, Finnish teachers believe that over 90 percent of students can learn successfully in their own classrooms if given the opportunity to evolve in a holistic manner.

4 Classroom Assessment Must Have Various Forms

Without frequent standardized and census-based testing, the Finnish education system relies on local monitoring and teacher-made student assessments. A child-centered, interaction-rich whole-child approach in the national curriculum requires that different student assessment models are used in schools. Furthermore, primary school pupils don't get any grades in their assessments before they are in fourth grade. It was natural that Finnish teachers found alternative student assessment methods attractive. And, it is ironic that many of these methods developed at U.S. universities are yet far more popular in Finland than in the United States. These include portfolio assessment, performance assessment, self-assessment and self-reflection, and assessment for learning methods. Academic teacher education programs in Finland include elements of study of educational assessment and evaluation theories and also provide all students with practical knowledge and skill of how to use alternative student assessment methods in the classroom.

5 Teachers Leading and Learning from One Another

Another surprising aspect of Finnish education is that it lacks much of systematically created change knowledge that is normally expected to guide policymakers and education authorities in planning and implementing desired reforms in education. Research and development of system-wide educational reform and change hasn't belonged to the academic repertoire of Finnish educational research community. The number of research papers related to that field has therefore remained small compared to most other countries. Instead, Finnish education experts have relied on foreign sources of expertise and knowledge. A good example of an American innovation commonly in use in Finland is peer coaching that evolved in the 1980s and 1990s as a result of research and development work of Bruce Joyce and his colleagues (Showers & Joyce, 1996). Bruce Joyce came to Finland in the late 1980s to train trainers and education leaders on how the impact of professional development of teachers can be enhanced. Peer coaching—that is, a confidential process through which teachers work together to reflect on current practices, expand, improve, and learn new skills, exchange ideas, conduct classroom research and solve problems together in school—has been normal practice in school improvement programs and professional development in Finland since the mid-1990s.

Can We Flip the System?

Visitors to the U.S. often wonder why research and innovation that have improved practically every successful education system today are not used more systematically in the U.S. school systems. Yet, many international educational indicators, like the recent OECD's PISA survey 2018 (OECD, 2019) or review of innovation in education a few years earlier suggest that there is a big need to change the policies and methods currently used in the U.S. But it doesn't have to be this way. As the introduction section of this book says, the need to flip the system "is inherently a call to restore the United States education system to its roots as the foundation of American democracy."

One reason approaches used by other countries are not being implemented in the U.S. may be that schools in the U.S. are so affected by bureaucracies, politics and commercialization that schools are simply doing what they must, not what they think would be necessary to do to give all children real opportunities to learn well. One great opportunity in flipping the system in the United States is to take a closer look at how more successful education systems let the teaching profession lead the design, implementation, and evaluation of teaching and learning in schools in collaboration with system administrators and policymakers. In Canada the teaching profession, which includes both teachers and principals, has a central role through democratic procedures in deciding the directions that school systems need to go. In Finland any successful change in education requires that teachers' perspectives are carefully included in policies and strategies. Involving the teaching profession in system level leadership leads to closer engagement of teachers and school leaders in making change happen. That, in turn, strengthens the collective ownership of both teaching and learning in schools.

A message from abroad to American colleagues is this: The United States is one of the few education systems in the world that is self-sufficient enough in terms of important ideas, knowledge, research and innovation—and financial resources—to build a high quality, equitable 21st century school system for all American children. All other countries, more or less, depend on research knowledge and practical ideas that are created and tested, but not used, in the U.S. It is hard to accept the OECD's conclusion on the state of education innovation, that the greatest American innovation in organizational policy and practice in this century is student assessment, including standardized testing. Many American teachers probably shake their heads at this. High-stakes standardized testing, combined with punitive accountability is, as Diane Ravitch (2020) explains, one of the main reasons for persistent mediocrity in outcomes and prevalent inequality in American education.

The question should not be: "How can we have more innovation in education to shake up the status quo?" The real question is: "How can we flip the system in such a way that would lead to better understanding of the potential that exists within American professional and academic communities in education?"

Perhaps the most important lesson that the United States should learn from international education systems is that the solution is here already. This would immediately mean that it is more important to see which American ideas have worked elsewhere and why, then improve them based on experiences in other systems, and finally learn how to implement these ideas with the teachers in all schools.

One thing we know by now for sure: The answer is not to have more charter schools or private ownership of public schools to improve education. The message from the most successful education systems is loud and clear: Education policies should not be determined by mythology and ideology, but rather should be guided by research and evidence from home and abroad. When this is done in close collaboration with the teaching profession, it also serves the purpose of restoring American education as a foundation of democracy.

References

Dewey, J. (1916). *Democracy and education: An introduction to the philosophy of education.* New York: Macmillan.

Gardner, H. (1983). *Frames of mind: The theory of multiple intelligences.* New York: Basic Books.

Hammerness, K., Ahtiainen, R., & Sahlberg, P. (2017). *Empowered educations in Finland: How high-performing systems shape teaching quality.* San Francisco, CA: Jossey-Bass.

Johnson, D. & Johnson, R. (1984). *Circles of learning: Cooperation in the classroom*. Alexandria, VA: ASCD.

National Board of Education. (2016). *National core curriculum for basic education 2014*. Helsinki: National Board of Education.

OECD (2014). *Measuring innovation in education: A new perspective*. Paris: OECD.

OECD (2019). *PISA 2018 result: What students know and can do, vol I*. Paris: OECD.

Ravitch, D. (2020). *Slaying Goliath: The passionate resistance to privatization and the fight to save America's schools*. New York: Alfred Knopf.

Sahlberg, P. (2015). *Finnish lessons 2.0: What can the world learn from educational change in Finland*. New York: Teachers College Press.

Sahlberg, P. (2018). *FinnishEd leadership: Four big, inexpensive ideas to transform education*. Thousand Oaks, CA: Corwin.

Showers, B., & Joyce, B. (1996). The evolution of peer coaching. *Educational Leadership*, 53(6), 12–16.

Chapter 16

A Case Study in Distributed Leadership

Sanger Unified School District

Tracey Fritch

District Profile (2018–19 School Year)

Location: Fresno County, California.
Schools: 20.
Students: Approximately 12,300.
Economically disadvantaged students: 66%.
English language learners: 15%.
Ethnicity of students: 70% Hispanic/Latino, 13% White, 11% Asian, 6% Other/Not Reported.

The Challenge

In the early 2000s, Sanger Unified faced a state takeover and superintendent removal due to student achievement that ranked in the bottom 10% of the state. Seven schools and the district were declared in need of improvement under federal law (David & Talbert, 2012). Facilitating that improvement and boosting student outcomes was complicated by high rates of extreme poverty, low teacher morale, and a large percentage of English Language Learners.

Rather than focusing on test-preparation and narrowing the curriculum, district leaders focused on school culture and a *distributed leadership* model that relied heavily on teacher expertise. They moved decision-making closer to those in direct contact with students. Led by Marcus Johnson, who would be later named the National Superintendent of the Year in 2011, the district experienced a rapid turnaround and became a national model.

Today, under Superintendent Adela Jones, Sanger students continue to outperform state and national peers. The district has a graduation rate (95%) more than 10% higher than the state average and 13% higher than the rest of Fresno County, and property values have skyrocketed over 276% in the past 15 years. The district's reputation for excellence has significantly improved, leading more families to seek residency in the area. Many of the initial reforms enacted in the 2000s have been adapted to current district and community needs, but a strong focus on teacher leadership, positive school culture, and collaboration perpetuate the district's excellent outcomes.

Sanger's Distributed Leadership Model

Sanger began by partnering with the teacher's union to design and implement solutions. The district chose to focus upon three essential goals which currently remain: raising all students' achievement, closing the achievement gap toward meeting standards (particularly with English Language Learners), and ensuring a safe school environment. Initially a pilot program incorporated Professional Learning Communities (PLCs) with a small number of administrators and teachers. After seeing the success, the initiative was expanded to all schools. Superintendent Jones notes, "That really was the impetus of us starting this whole cultural transformation here, regarding our values and what's important to us" (A. Jones, personal communication, Feb. 20, 2020).

The district has emphasized the importance of PLCs by building time for them. By adjusting the school schedule, teachers are given 90 minutes per week to collaborate through an early release or late start for students. In addition, elementary and middle school teachers have common planning periods. These schedule changes were possible after assuring the community that no instructional minutes would be lost. In addition, between three and five PLC days are scheduled each school year that allow teachers to collaborate within subject areas. Within the PLCs, teachers focus on sharing effective instruction strategies, reviewing student artifacts, developing assessments, and refining the district's Multi-Tiered System of Support (MTSS), which plays a critical role in building schoolwide community and a positive culture. Teachers are surveyed after each PLC meeting to both provide feedback and decide upon the focus of future sessions.

The shift toward distributed leadership means that each principal no longer solely supervises the professional growth of each individual teacher. Instead, teachers have increased power over their own professional learning. Each PLC is headed by "lead teachers," typically identified by school administration for pedagogical excellence. Teachers are also provided the opportunity to share best practices each August through an in-house *Teachers Leading Teachers Conference*, where colleagues and administrators offer PD for each other. Jones asserts that the focus on distributed leadership, along with consistent messaging, work, and training, have created a "cultural shift" at Sanger, in which teachers were both held accountable for and empowered by a heavily supported process of evolving their practice. She believes this accounts for the dramatic increases in student achievement (A. Jones, personal communication, Feb. 20, 2020).

Multi-Tiered System of Support Model

The district's Multi-Tiered System of Support (MTSS)model places an equal value on providing academic and social-emotional support. Through embedded school psychologists in each building, a Restorative Justice approach to behavior issues that includes dedicated staff in middle and high schools, and a Community of Caring program that builds partnerships with parents and community leaders, the district focuses on the holistic needs of its students. In elementary schools, staff emphasize Social-Emotional Learning through a dedicated curriculum that is taught every Friday.

Conclusion

Between 2004 and 2010, Sanger was able to drastically turn around negative student outcomes, low teacher morale, and community perception of the district through implementation of a distributed leadership model that increased teacher agency and autonomy. Continuation and adaptation of those policies and others that flip the system in the district shift responsibility toward those in classrooms. This has allowed for sustained excellence. In 2019, 53% of Sanger students met or exceeded ELA standards on the Smarter Balanced Assessment Consortium (SBAC) exam, higher than the California state average of 51%. Sanger students also met or exceeded standards on the math exam at a rate 4% higher than state average. When compared with other districts that had similar demographic profiles, Sanger's student performance is even more exceptional. In a study of U.S. school districts with at least 10,000 students and majority Latino population, Sanger was among the top ten districts in the nation and distinguished for their exceptional Latino graduation rates (Talbert & David, 2019).

The Sanger Unified School District provides a model on how a flattened hierarchy and flipped system in a school district can produce outstanding results for students, schools, and the community.

References

David, J. L., & Talbert, J. E. (2012). *Turning around a high-poverty school district: Learning from Sanger Unified's success*. Palo Alto, CA: Bay Area Research Group and Stanford, CA: Center for Research on the Context of Teaching.

Talbert, J. E., & David, J. L. (2019). *Sanger Unified School District: Positive outliers case study*. Palo Alto, CA: Learning Policy Institute.

Chapter 17

#RedForEd and the Struggle for Our Schools

Noah Karvelis

The West Virginia Teacher Strike of 2018 resonated with teachers around the country. 20,000 teachers and public-school employees closed down schools in all 55 counties, resulting in wage increases and reduced health care costs for teachers. The same issues over which teachers had unified there were causing an exodus from the profession and low morale in my state of Arizona as well. Many of us admired the solidarity, relentlessness, and grassroots organization with which the teachers in West Virginia fought for their students and their profession. While we dreamed of replicating their success, none of us knew how to start a movement like that.

It was in the midst of that strike that I came across a Tweet from Arizona Education Association president, Joe Thomas. It read, "What do your colleagues at school want to do? Ask them tomorrow. Ask them if they saw what WV teachers and staff just did" (Thomas, 2018).

Inspired by that tweet and the movement in West Virginia, I responded explaining that the teachers in my building wanted to strike. Similar to many other faculty rooms across the U.S., my colleagues and I regularly spoke of striking in order to finally get the respect and funding that we and our students needed to be successful.

Yet, I was surprised when Joe asked me to prove that we were ready to take action. I questioned if I could actually organize the teachers in my building to show that they were capable of solidarity.

We did not have full union participation, and we were anything but a group of activists. Despite my feeling that we might be unable to accomplish much, Joe and I exchanged a few ideas about what a potential first step could be. Ultimately, we decided that I would organize the teachers in my building to all wear red on the same day. We would call it a #RedForEd day and "do it until it catches on."

Excited, but unsure, I messaged a co-worker and asked if he would help organize our campus. I also began promoting the first #RedForEd day, which was set one week later. If half of the teachers participated, I would have considered the day a success. As we circulated the hashtag and the Facebook event we created, more and more teachers agreed to participate.

I watched in shock as teachers from not only my school, but hundreds, then thousands of teachers from all across Arizona confirmed their participation.

That Wednesday, my campus was filled with red with 100% of teachers participating. When the media showed up a few hours later, I learned that our school was not an exception. Thousands of teachers across the state were in red shirts, declaring their willingness to demand the funding and conditions our students and colleagues deserved. Media outlets called it the largest teacher action in the state's history.

Broken was the isolation and fear we felt to speak up. Each of us now knew that we were not alone.

The Beginning of a Movement

In the days leading up to our first #RedForEd day, teachers and supporters began discussing ideas and finding support across the state through social media groups. A common theme kept coming up: "Don't let this one day in red be all that we do."

I knew they were right. While showing solidarity and collective action through one day's wardrobe choice was powerful, it would not be enough to bring about the changes that teachers knew were necessary. I wasn't sure where to turn for help.

Realizing that the Facebook group was bringing people together in a powerful way, I reached out to a few people who were driving conversations with bold, exciting ideas. Rebecca Garelli, Dylan Wegela, Derek Harris, and I established a new group where we hoped to bring teachers together and continue taking action. We called it "Arizona Educators United."

What Made Arizona Educators United Work?

Arizona Educators United (AEU) sought to preserve what made the first #RedForEd day successful. We hoped that we could unite teachers, give them space to engage both authentically and democratically, and ultimately create a powerful movement. We embraced two pivotal ideas.

The first was to always be democratic and ensure that the educators in the group were able to use their voices to lead the trajectory of the movement. Through a series of polls, we allowed participants to decide our demands, encouraged teachers to discuss strategy, and considered other initial steps of defining what AEU was to be.

The second vital piece of AEU infrastructure was the establishment of "site liaisons." Essentially, they were teacher-organizers for their schools. We brought them together in a group of their own, armed them with an "organizing toolkit" and developed a communications network where they would receive information from statewide leaders. Then, we turned the liaisons back to their buildings with one goal in mind: build a movement.

Through this, along with a powerful collaboration with our union, Arizona Education Association, a network of over 2,000 teachers from all parts of the state used site-specific, localized actions to help construct a community-based movement. Liaisons would communicate information about official events from our communication network to their campus, while also hosting their own events such as "standouts" (informational pickets), "walk-ins" (walking into a school alongside parents to show solidarity), and "bridge takeovers" (occupying the overpass on highways). As a result of our democratic structure, collaboration with the union, and ability to authentically engage with educators and communities, the movement grew in powerful ways in just a few short weeks.

The Escalation toward the Inevitable

To capitalize on the infrastructure we had built, we needed to grow along with the movement. Connecting teacher narrative to action in order to move public opinion was the next step. We knew this would allow us to build a larger base of support and increase political pressure before the end of the school year. The public needed to know that we were fighting to reverse the $1.1 billion deficit in the system and all of the negative impacts this financial stress placed on our students. In response, we embraced a slow escalation of tactics.

We started asking people to share the reasons why they were wearing red along with photos on social media. To protect against our message getting muddled, we requested that supporters explicitly talk about what was happening in our schools. When the governor refused to meet with leaders of our movement, our mobilization and protests were amplified through social media. Eventually, this escalation led to a 110,000-person walk-in orchestrated by AEU, the Arizona Education Association, and site liaisons across the state.

In response, the Governor released a plan that partially met one of our five demands. As organizers, we were unsure of what would happen next. Did educators still want to continue building pressure? Were they ready to strike? We held a statewide vote on a walk-out.

The response was clear. Arizona educators wanted to walk-out and continue the fight for our schools and students. We set our walk-out date for April 26, 2018.

A Walk-Out and a Challenge to Business as Usual

The walk-out date quickly approached, and the Governor still refused to meet with movement leaders. The result was a 75,000-person march on the Arizona State Capitol and a six-day walk-out which closed schools across the state.

In the end, we successfully won over $400 millionfor public education in Arizona. This amount, determined by the legislature, was set to increase teacher pay by 20% over three years. Many districts were also able to grant raises to support staff. Pressure from our coalition also led to a funding initiative on the state ballot. It also significantly impacted Arizona's 2018 elections, in which former educator Kathy Hoffman was chosen as Arizona Superintendent of Public Instruction. Our fight continues, but #RedForEd has delivered a resounding victory for students, teachers, public education, and communities in Arizona.

The #RedForEd story has expanded to include many chapters in states across the US and internationally. Each of those chapters is a story of power, solidarity, and hope. It is an example of what happens when the theories and ideas in this book are combined with grassroots organization and teachers finding their collective voice. It is my hope that we can continue to learn from our successes and our failures as we continue to fight alongside one another in a united struggle for the future of our children, our schools, and our society. As I continually told teachers in Arizona, no one is coming to save us. We must fight for the future that we deserve!

Reference

Thomas, Joe. (2018, February 28). Twitter. Retrieved from https://twitter.com/AZ1Thomas/status/968682335687159808.

Chapter 18

Education Union Renewal

The Key to Flipping the System

Howard Stevenson

Introduction

I am writing this chapter in November 2019 on the eve of an eight-day strike by my union (UCU, the University and College Union in the United Kingdom) in which we seek to challenge attacks on our pay and pensions while also confronting chronic workload problems, epidemic levels of casualization, and wholly unacceptable pay gaps that discriminate against women, colleagues of color, and disabled workers. As we strike in universities in England education, workers in Chile will be at the heart of general strike that stands against the desperate policies of the Chilean government and education reforms that seek to reintroduce the failed policies of the Pinochet era.

Although these disputes may be taking place on opposite sides of the world, they are not disconnected. On the contrary, they are intimately woven together while also building on a wave of teacher protests globally that has been made particularly visible in the U.S.A. through the extraordinary and inspirational #RedForEd movement (Blanc, 2019). All these movements, in their different ways, represent efforts by education workers to push back against the systemic reforms that have seen real terms pay decline, ever escalating workloads and increasing control over what and how teachers teach. These are the ways teachers across the world experience the new global education system. This is the system that needs to be "flipped."

In this chapter I seek to argue that there can be no "flipping the system" without recognizing the pivotal role that education unions must play in any effort to tackle the chronic problems that education workers face in very similar forms but in many different countries. To some readers of this volume the suggestion that education unions are key to flipping the system may seem improbable. Indeed, some may see unions as part of the "system" they seek to flip. I understand these concerns and I am not claiming that education unions are the only ways educators can organize together to secure changes within the current system. However I do want to return to an argument I made in the original "flip the system publication" and assert that "the system" that we work in is extraordinarily powerful and that there is no way to disrupt it fundamentally without serious coordinated and organized collective action (Stevenson & Gilliland, 2016). Such action requires mass organizations that are both independent and democratic. Education unions provide the only vehicle to mobilize the collective action required to up-end a system that desperately needs challenging.

No Flipping the System without Unions at the Centre

In recent years teachers, and others who work in education, have been subject to unprecedented degrees of control and intervention. There is increasing involvement by governments and others to determine what teachers teach, how they teach it, how they assess student learning and how teachers' work is evaluated.

This increase in monitoring, surveillance and control can look very different in different parts of the world, but despite this variation in experience the general trend can be considered a common one. Almost everywhere teachers experience diminishing control over matters that historically were considered core issues of professional concern and over which teachers have traditionally been able to exercise their professional judgement. Moreover, the monitoring and surveillance that seeks to control teachers' work also underpins the high stakes accountability model that drives teachers' workload inexorably upwards. In the globalized world of education reform being good can never be good enough. There is always more to do, there is always a higher target that must be reached.

That such developments are experienced by teachers as a shared phenomenon across the world, albeit in contextually specific forms, must serve to remind us that there is nothing accidental or serendipitous about what is happening to teachers and their work. The toxic mix of rising workloads and diminished professional control are not a quirk of history that will somehow auto correct at some point in the future, but rather they are the direct consequence of imperatives in the global political economy that focus the attention of powerful groups on education services in general, and the work of teachers specifically.

The drive to assert ever greater control over what teachers teach in part arises from education's role in (re-)producing the labor that is required by businesses and capital. This has always been an important function of education but in a world where globalized competition is intensifying the tendency is for powerful interests (which extend far beyond any narrow definition of "government") to intervene ever more directly in shaping educational outcomes. The result is that the purposes of public education become increasingly subordinated to the needs of the economy. Furthermore, the same pressures that seek to subordinate the purposes of education to the needs of the economy also seek to influence how education shapes us all as future citizens. As the world we inhabit becomes more complex and diverse those with power and resources seek ever greater control over the content of schooling.

Teachers therefore experience the twin pressures of "producing more" (more students being driven to achieve ever higher test scores) while simultaneously having less control over what it is they teach. Often the curriculum is narrowed to prioritize what is tested while teachers find themselves directed to adopt specific pedagogical methods determined by others. However, the same global pressures that drive teacher workload up also place a downward pressure on public spending which means that teachers experience ever rising targets and a drive to deliver "more" at the same time that resources for public education are being reduced. Educators are caught in a classic squeeze between rising expectations and diminishing resources.

What I have described above, very briefly, is best described as a restructuring of our public education systems along neoliberal lines. It seeks to subordinate public education to the wider demands of the economy while simultaneously cutting costs. Those parts of the system that remain public are often compelled to function more and more as if they were businesses operating in a market while other elements of the system are broken off and opened up to private companies who can "cherry pick" those parts of the service capable of turning a profit.

Education unions have often been in the vanguard of resistance to these developments, seeking to protect educator's working conditions while also campaigning to defend public education as a public good, publicly provided and driven by public service values. This is why the powerful vested interests that seek to exploit public education for private profit have worked so hard to try to undermine the ability of teacher unions to act as the collective voice of their members. From attacks on collective bargaining rights to the development of non-union charter schools, the drive to marginalize and weaken teachers' unions is clear. Such has been the power of this mobilization of powerful vested interests against education unions that for many years education unions have found themselves on the defensive (as indeed has the wider trade union movement, which is subject to many of the same pressures). This poses difficult strategic questions for education unions and in the next section I explore what these are.

Education Unions: What Is to Be Done?

In 2010 I was co-author of a book with Bob Carter and Rowena Passy in which we explored teacher trade union responses to the neoliberal restructuring of public education that I have described above (Carter, Stevenson, & Passy, 2010). In the book we identified three broad approaches that might be adopted by unions—*rapprochement*, resistance and renewal, and although any such effort to present typologies involves simplifications and compromises I believe these three different approaches provide a useful heuristic to help us understand what options exist for unions currently, and what future strategies might be adopted.

Rapprochement was the term we used to describe a situation in which unions sought to "come to terms" with the restructuring of public education and attempted to secure the best deal for their members within the parameters determined for them by that reshaped system. Within this approach unions reject an explicitly ideological analysis of the developments that frame the new educational landscape but rather adopt a more "pragmatic" approach. The task of the union is not presented as one that challenges developments in policy in any fundamental sense but rather the role of the union is to work "with the grain" of the reform agenda and to try to maximize the benefits to members within it.

A feature of *rapprochement* is that it does not involve any structural or cultural change in the union, but rather the union seeks to incrementally adapt to the changed environment, including one where its own influence may be being actively undermined. Unions that work within this tradition do not rule out taking industrial action, but are most likely to respond to attacks on their influence by seeking "partnership" type arrangements with employers or by adopting a more explicitly "service model" approach towards members (seeking to be "relevant" to members, and to offer "added value" by providing a range of services such as discount schemes, legal services and access to professional development programs).

The profound problem with this approach is that it does not deal fundamentally with structural attacks on public education and union organization. Rather the union seeks to adapt to the new landscape with its role restricted to "damage limitation." Given this more limited goal the danger is that members' confidence in the union's ability to address their grievances declines. The union itself becomes weaker, characterized by a diminishing and ageing activist base that clings to the wreckage of a system that no longer exists.

In contrast to the above, the strategy we identified as "resistance" refuses to accept the restructuring of public education with all the attacks on teacher professionalism and working conditions that accompany it. Unions that adopt this approach are more likely to have developed an analytical critique of trends in public education and are therefore more likely to position themselves "politically" (which does not necessarily mean a party-political affiliation). Such an analysis is rooted in a critique of the neoliberal restructuring of public education which sees it as inimical to the values of high quality, democratic public education for all. It also recognizes that the attacks on education workers' unions are both deliberate and determined. It is the case that unions that adopt this approach are therefore more likely to seek to robustly challenge the neoliberal restructuring of public education— oftentimes by seeking to mobilize members in forms of industrial action.

Strategies of "resistance" have considerable potential to disrupt the trajectory of neoliberal education restructuring, and certainly to defend aspects of teachers' working conditions that may be under attack. However, as a strategy on their own such approaches have been shown to have severe limitations. This is because although the union seeks to mount a challenge to the trajectory of reform it often does so as an organization that remains rooted in past structures, often with a strong emphasis on hierarchical forms of "top-down" leadership. Members are encouraged to "step up" or "step back" as and when the union organization decides. In this sense union members are seen as active participants in union campaigns, but not necessarily as genuine agents in shaping union strategy. Hence, the union's tactics may adapt to new circumstances—but this is not accompanied by a fundamental reculturing of the organization, which remains a creature of a system that often no longer exists. As with *rapprochement*, the danger is that union members do not genuinely engage with the union but rather there exists a dependency culture in which members continue to rely on a small number of activist leaders. Although campaigns of resistance can be energizing for teachers in the immediate term there is no strategy to fundamentally reinvigorate and rebuild the union.

In contrast to the above, a strategy of union renewal involves processes of both resistance and reculturing whereby unions seek to disrupt the trajectory of neoliberal reform, but this is intimately interwoven with a re-forming of the union itself as an organization focused on member participation and engagement. This approach to union development acknowledges the political nature of the attacks on public education and teachers' work, but also the attacks on education union organization. It recognizes that the only way to resist these attacks is to reconnect with grassroots members and to find new ways to draw on the capacities, skills and commitment of the organization's membership.

The defining feature of the type of union renewal being discussed here is a process of re-forming the union as one that is transformed from a mass membership organization (many members but with a few active participants) to a mass participation organization in which the active involvement of grassroots members is pivotal. However, this is not a process that can be simply "activated" from above by seeking to increase member engagement in some technical way. Rather renewal is an alchemic fusion of resistance (taking up the grievances that matter to members) and reculturing (re-forming the organization in a way that encourages and values participation). In this instance reculturing involves hard thinking about union practices that act to include, or often exclude, union members—from rethinking the culture at union meetings to creating spaces that allow under-represented groups to self-organize. Union renewal places a premium on the ordinary, everyday person to person communication of members as members learn to work together, explore common understandings and begin to understand the power of their own collective organization.

A distinctive feature of this approach to teacher trade unionism is a much-expanded conception of what are seen as "union concerns." Teacher trade unions are often presented as only being concerned with "narrow" so-called "bread and butter" issues such as pay and contracts. In truth this has often been a misrepresentation but the more dynamic form of union renewal being discussed here rejects the concept of a crude bifurcation between "industrial" and "professional" issues (the former being legitimate trade union concerns, but the latter being seen as the opposite). Rather this approach to teacher unionism sees professional and industrial issues as inseparable elements of teachers' work. The union's role is to help the teacher reclaim control of their work in whatever form it takes. An example is provided by resistance to high stakes testing in schools. This is directly responsible for driving up workload, reducing the scope for teachers' professional judgement and contributing to increased inequalities in the education system. For *all* these reasons, union campaigns against high stakes testing are legitimate union action. A practical illustration of this type of trade unionism is provided by Mort (2019) who describes how union members in her school organized for a strike to challenge the use of appraisal targets (linked to pay) being based on the scores achieved by students in standardized tests. Such a campaign shows how "industrial" and "professional" issues are inseparable as the issue is framed as a wider question of who controls teachers' work.

Another feature of this expanded conception of teacher trade unionism is a commitment to build alliances with groups outside of the union and to campaign on issues that connect with community concerns. This may be the case with very direct educational issues such as campaigns against testing, funding cuts or school privatization, all of which have attracted considerable parent, student and community support, but in other cases the issues may be those that affect students in their communities, but without being directly education related. Examples include teacher union involvement in campaigns against racist attacks in the community or cuts to community facilities. What unites these examples is a commitment to build coalitions with those beyond the union and to create the alliances that are necessary to push back against the powerful vested interests seeking to reshape education. It is fundamental to union renewal as it rejects any narrow conception of unionism, but rather sees the union as intimately involved in the democratic struggles of the local community.

Conclusion

Teachers in the U.S.A., alongside their counterparts in Chile and England, have found themselves being used as lab rats for the radical experiment that is the neoliberal restructuring of public education. Dismantling the system through establishing Charter Schools, imposing high stakes testing to rank, compare and reward or penalize and then seeking to marginalize the professional voice of teachers by undermining collective bargaining have created the conditions in which workload rises inexorably while teachers' space to exercise professional judgement is diminished. The outcomes are inevitable—teachers hope they can "hang on" but often feel they must quit or face burnout in a system that does not care about them.

There has to be an alternative to quitting or burnout (or just keeping one's head down in the hope that the problems will go away). I want to conclude by arguing that we are already seeing that alternative—that the broken system that is the global education reform movement is already being flipped. It is being flipped in countless ways, when teachers find the confidence to push back against a system they see as unjust and dehumanizing. However, it is being challenged most effectively when teachers realize that the only way to genuinely flip the system is to organize collectively, find the courage that comes from collective action and take the bold and necessary action to say that "enough is enough."

Teachers in the U.S.A., often in the most unlikely states, have begun that process. The "red state revolt" has many lessons to teach us all, but perhaps the most powerful message is that we must never allow ourselves to believe that change is not possible. That somehow "there is no alternative." It may be the case that many currently do not believe there is an alternative, or they do not believe that change is possible. The task facing all of us who seek to "flip the system" is to do the long and patient work with our colleagues to persuade them that there *is* a better way, and that if we work together, we can make change happen. Teachers' unions provide the organizational framework, and the collective, independent and democratic space, that can act as an engine of change. However, for that to happen we must all play our part in making our unions the inclusive, participatory organizations that they must be to fulfil their potential.

References

Blanc, E. (2019) *Red state revolt: The teachers' strikes and working-class politics*, London: Verso.

Carter, B., Stevenson, H., & Passy, R. (2010) *Industrial relations in education: Transforming the school workforce*. Abingdon: Routledge.

Mort, E. (2019) Winning on professional control in the workplace. Retrieved from https://educationfortomorrow.org.uk/winning-on-professional-control-in-the-workplace.

Stevenson, H., & Gilliland, A. (2016) The teachers' voice: Teacher unions at the heart of a new democratic professionalism. In J. Evers & R. Kneyber (Eds.), *Flip the system: Changing education from the ground up*. Abingdon: Routledge.

Part V

Supporting Teachers in a Flipped System

Asking our teachers to take greater collective ownership and responsibility for decision making in a flipped education system cannot happen unless we provide them with much greater support, both as people and professionals. Teachers already are stretched beyond their mental health limit. A 2017 survey revealed that 58% of teachers reported a decline in mental health because of their job. Another study found that 93% of teachers are suffering from some combination of high stress and burnout. Some of the mental health issues caused by this stress are the result of mandates created by-non educators that don't serve our students. Others are created by a lack of professional autonomy in other areas. Many teachers, especially teachers of color, teachers with physical limitations, LGBTQ+ educators, and religious minorities, feel like they are not fully accepted within our schools. Our teachers cannot do their job effectively, let alone take on a larger professional role in our education system, if they are not well. Democracy is not healthy unless schools are healthy and supported, schools are not healthy unless students are healthy and supported, and students will not be healthy until our teachers are healthy and supported.

The lack of support we currently give teachers has manifested itself as a recruitment and retention crisis. Fewer of our talented young people are choosing to become teachers. Those that do are leaving the profession well before retirement age at high rates. Many states are facing a teacher shortage created by poor policy decisions. There is not a lack of quality teacher candidates in our high schools or our communities. There is a shortage of talented young people who are willing to teach under the conditions that we have created, and a lack of professionals willing to continue in a system that does not support them. Addressing the shortage should be achieved by solving these issues, not by subjecting our children to untrained or poorly qualified replacements as has been suggested by some.

Part V includes ideas on how we can forge a path forward that addresses the recruitment and retainment issues and provides greater support for teachers.

First, **Kimberly Eckert** (Chapter 19) explains how Generation Z, the students in our high schools right now, are craving jobs that will allow them to impact their world and help others—exactly the opportunity teaching provides. She shares how Grow Your Own programs can be a tool for recruiting a diverse new generation of excellent teachers.

In Chapter 20, **Michael Peña, Winter Marshall-Allen, Carlos Avila, Melissa Collins, Alhassan Susso**, and **Jill Davidson** share experiences as educators from historically marginalized communities and give recommendations on how the system can be better designed to support all teachers.

Dan Callahan (Chapter 21) then gives insight into democratized professional development and the Edcamp model, highlighting how teachers can take control of their own growth and learning.

Lastly, in Chapter 22 **Trista Hollweck** and **Dyane Smokorowski** look at successful professional learning and development implementation in two different settings that can be used as models for schools to support their teachers and increase retainment rates.

Chapter 19

Addressing the Teacher Shortage

Recruiting our Next Generation of Teachers

Kimberly Eckert

In the Fall of 2017, I was given a new Mercedes Benz to drive as the newly named Louisiana Teacher of the Year. Leaving my 2004 Kia Spectra behind, I drove to a student-run car wash. After hugs, cheers, and congratulations my students began to realize the sweet ride was mine.

One student couldn't hide his shock: "Wait. They gave you a BENZ?! Just for TEACHING?!"

At that moment I realized exactly why we have a teacher recruitment problem. This student, who I believe loved and respected me, couldn't conceive that a teacher could possess such a symbol of prestige. To him, teachers—even really good ones—aren't Mercedes material. The Benz is for CEOs, doctors, Instagram influencers, or rappers.

If teachers are not valued by students or the public, how can they fulfill the role of helping our next generation build a healthy democracy and society? Lack of respect for teachers runs deep and has been eroding for years. For a flipped system, driven by teacher expertise, to be successful we must reverse this trend and recruit talented young people into teaching.

Teacher Shortage or Teacher Crisis?

Our country now faces critical teacher shortages. No matter how many times teachers are given platitudes affirming their value and importance, public support to demand widespread policies that protect teacher wellbeing and elevate their expertise has not materialized. Teachers are leaving the profession and fewer young people are choosing to teach. The lack of talented, professional teachers threatens both our education system and our democracy.

Over half of teachers polled in 2019 say they do not want their own children becoming teachers, citing poor pay, stress, and lack of respect (PDK Poll, 2019). American teachers, who spend more than 40 hours per week and more time working than peers in most other industrialized countries (NCES, 2018), report factors like lack of professional autonomy, inadequate support, poor school leadership, and safety concerns are causing high rates of attrition (Taie & Goldring, 2019). In fact, 46% of teachers report high daily stress during the school year, among the highest rates of any profession (Gallup, 2014). Greatest attrition comes from poorly prepared teachers, those in high-poverty and high-minority schools, teachers of color (disproportionately placed in these schools), teachers in urban areas, and teachers in Southern States (Sutcher, Darling-Hammond, & Carver-Thomas, 2016).

At the highest reported levels of all time, 54% of parents don't want their children to become teachers, most often citing poor pay and benefits (PDK Poll, 2018). Although teacher pay appears to be a common factor between parents and teachers telling youngsters to avoid teaching, further examination suggests the lack of respect and low value placed on teachers by society are more of a deterrent, even if implicit. There are many careers that require the same level of degree and have similar or lower salaries than teachers: Social workers, news reporters, public interest attorneys, nurses, theologians, and degree-required positions in the police force. Yet, these fields are not met with the same level of outright detraction when young people announce intention to join their ranks.

This reality is reflected in the declining numbers of teacher preparation programs. Although an increase of 3 million students is expected in the next decade, teacher preparation programs have seen a 35% reduction in new enrollments since 2009 (Sutcher, Darling-Hammond, & Carver-Thomas, 2016). This disconnect is most severe in math and science content areas, special education, and schools with higher percentages of minority students and poverty. Because districts handle shortages by cancelling classes, increasing class size, and relying on unskilled teachers, accurate data on the effects of the teacher shortage is difficult to obtain.

To address this crisis, creating a strong teacher workforce must start before college. Grow your own (GYO) programs like Educators Rising, a high school Career and Technical Education (CTE) program, offer opportunities for schools to encourage bright, creative young people to try out teaching (see www.educatorsrising.org/the-mission). In addition to helping schools and communities mitigate the teacher shortage through direct recruiting, GYO programs allow for development of leadership skills transferable to other contexts.

Appealing to Generation Z

Despite the offer of free pizza and an energetic announcement for our first Educators Rising meeting, only ONE kid showed up. He was the only student in the school willing to admit wanting to be a teacher, and even he was unsure. I reflected on my original messaging and revised the announcement:

> Are you interested in changing the world? Do you see yourself in a career making a lasting impact on people, changing lives, saving lives

and helping create stronger societies? If so, join us to discuss your place in an exciting new class/club we are offering.

Changing the language to reflect what teachers DO was enough to pack the next recruitment meeting. As new Educator Rising classes began forming across Louisiana in 2018, I had to help teacher leaders craft similar messages to avoid the same issues I had in my initial attempt to fill a class.

Generation Z, those born between 1994 and 2010, tend to seek opportunities to make a positive difference in their world (Broadbent et al., 2017). The majority want to have an impact through their jobs, view gender identity and diversity more positively than previous generations (Pew Research Center, 2019), and are attracted to jobs in less automatable fields like education. This makes them more prepared to meet the challenges of teaching as our country becomes more diverse. To recruit them, we must change the narrative around the teaching profession to reflect empowerment and social impact.

If we can't convince talented youngsters that teaching is a desirable profession, we can't fix the broken teacher recruitment pipeline. By appealing to their desire to be positive change agents, starting the recruitment process with GYO programs, and flipping the system to reverse policies that have eroded teacher morale, we can reverse trends that have caused the current teacher crisis.

Changing the Perception of the Teaching Profession

A quick experiment shaped my mission soon after the first Educators Rising class began. I showed slides depicting professionals and had students identify skills and expertise each role might require. Airline pilot? A doctor? A business owner? A lawyer? An architect?

A cacophony of student voices exploded with a stream of attributes: quick thinker, creative, problem solver, decisive, levelheaded, educated, composed, persuasive, personable. Students went on, having no problem imagining the qualities needed for success in these fields.

I asked the class for their attention as I dramatically revealed a new picture: a teacher. I asked again, "What skills or expertise might a teacher need in order to be successful?"

There was silence. Then one student cautiously answered, "You have to be patient."

Another mused, "Um … you should probably be good with kids. And, like to talk a lot?"

A final student suggested, "You should know something about whatever you teach."

This led to some snickering. Students gave knowing glances and muttered thinly veiled comments about teachers they believed did not possess that last attribute.

The perception problem was clear. According to these students, all one needs to be a successful teacher is patience, tolerance for children, chattiness, and marginal content knowledge.

Our new teacher pipeline is marred by gaping holes because most members of this generation have no interest in aspiring to become chatty babysitters. This might be why promising students considering teaching are often chastised by peers and adults in their lives: Don't waste your talent. You could be so much more.

Universities have reported surges in person-centered fields of study: social work, counseling, psychology, and sociology. Teaching incorporates all of these disciplines. A relationship driven field like teaching is exactly what so many students are looking for! Since much of teachers' work is done removed from the public eye, however, few relate these fields to teaching.

Without elevating the teaching profession by changing the lens through which people view it, we cannot hope to flip the system.

My Efforts to Expand GYO Program Access

While first exploring GYO programs, I was shocked at the limited access high school students have to this coursework. Unless there were incentives to the school, it was unlikely schools would schedule GYO program classes. If programs were available, students who meet criteria to be excellent teaching candidates rarely got to participate. I became determined to expand access to these programs across my state.

When I brought these issues with my state department of education, I was met with fierce resistance and outright dismissal at suggestions of a pre-educator pathway. I was advised to stick to dual-enrollment or find an "equivalent" College Level Examination Program exam.

I knew all students with potential to be excellent teachers were not going to fit the "traditional" profile. Some might have already been tracked out of college-prep classes, disenfranchised by their school experience, or have discipline records. Others might feel that school has been an unengaging, negative experience. We can't be surprised when, as adults, they're not willing to return.

Most daunting, I realized that if we had any hope of diversifying the pipeline through GYO programs, it could not happen solely through dual-enrollment coursework. Students of color are severely underrepresented in advanced courses. Even in an initial side-by-side pilot of Educators Rising and a dual-enrollment program in my high school, only one student of color qualified for dual- enrollment.

Further obstacles arose when examining a dual-enrollment only approach. Due to rigid ACT requirements, sophomores and juniors who had not yet taken the test were excluded. This prevented many students with attributes likely to make them successful teachers from taking needed courses.

Students far from college campuses in rural areas and without stable inter-net in under-resourced schools lacked access to needed in-person or online classes. Without equitable access, it was impossible to recruit a teaching force that represented and understood the needs of all students.

Further research showed that a few other states had begun working to create pre-educator pathways and develop dual-credit partnerships with universities. Partnering universities, recognizing some of the issues described above, began offering an alternative option to dual enrollment. If students passed coursework, met a few non-academic requirements, and got accepted into the university credit would be retroactively awarded for their pre-edu-cator courses. Willingness to find creative policy solutions and to innovate approaches like this will assist GYO programs in solving our teacher crisis.

Will They Reflect the Students Looking Back at Them?

The lack of diversity in the teaching profession is a problem large enough to warrant a book of its own. The inability of GYO programs to produce more students of color into the pipeline has been a common criticism, although there is currently more focus on reversing this trend. We cannot discuss the power of a flipped system to strengthen democracy without acknowledging the importance of recruiting teachers of color. There is "widespread agreement that our elementary and secondary teaching force should 'look like America'" (Ingersoll & May, 2016). Despite this sweeping realization, America's public schools have become more racially and ethni-cally diverse while the teaching profession has grown less so.

The U.S. Department of Education (2016) recognizes that teachers and leaders of color "will play a critical role in ensuring equity in our education system." The agency has expressed concern that, while over half the student population are students of color, 82% of public-school teachers identify as white, with little change in more than 15 years. Ingersol and May (2016) bring forward the well documented argument that the minority teacher shortage is a substantial reason for the achievement gap and inequitable career outcomes for students of color. These students, particularly in dis-advantaged settings, benefit from seeing themselves reflected in school lea-dership. Since teachers of color are more likely to have high expectations for students of color, there are tangible gains in test scores and substantial decreases in risk of dropping out (Goldhaber, Theobald, & Tien, 2019).

In a significant, large-scale study echoing decades of prior research, it was shown that there is exponential increase in test scores, decrease in dropout rates, and an increase in college attendance for students of color when they had at least one teacher who looked like them in their formative years in education (Gershenson, Hart, Hyman, Lindsay, & Papageorge, 2018). Find-ings were particularly positive when examining outcomes for students from families who are economically disadvantaged. The same study found similar effects when male students were exposed to male teachers—showing that recruitment of men into the profession is also vital.

Though there seems to be no discernable difference in test scores and college admission for white students who have experienced teachers from diverse backgrounds, we can't forget social and global implications of this experience. As we become progressively globally connected by technology, the ability to interact and collaborate with people from divergent backgrounds is crucial. We must ensure that white students see that leadership, competence, and expertise is found in people that don't look like them. I can speak from personal experience of the need to normalize the presence of educated teachers and leaders of colors in our schools. As a teacher of color, I have been met with far too much surprise from students and parents that I am, in fact, qualified to teach, have multiple degrees, and am capable of inspiring student excellence. With the reality that schools and cities in America are becoming increasingly segregated, school might be one of the few places left where this lesson CAN occur. If white students complete their schooling with the implicit belief that only teachers who look like them add value, then we have done them a great disservice and have provided them a woefully deficient education.

For these reasons, it is critical to ensure that we intentionally recruit students of color into meaningful, culturally responsive, engaging GYO coursework at every possible opportunity, regardless of the community. This will not be easy. Students find it difficult to be what they can't see, and given the current lack of diversity in our teaching force, we may have to work even harder to help students of color realize that their consideration of the teaching profession is the only way to ensure future generations have a different educational experience.

Moving Forward

Targeted recruitment, elevating the status of the teaching profession, and pre-educator programs are important aspects of addressing the teacher shortage. My limited experience shows how effective these models can be, but more research and clear, tangible examples of success will allow successful programs to scale. The only way we can study the effectiveness of these programs is to first build them.

If we create the desire and means for talented youngsters to choose teaching as a profession, celebrate its complexity, and then use evidence to continue improving these programs we can improve our education system and build the foundation of a stronger democracy. If we do this, I believe that there will come a time when a future Louisiana Teacher of the Year driving up to a group of students in a brand-new Mercedes Benz will not be met with incredulity. Instead, students might reply, "It's about time you got what teachers deserve."

References

Broadbent, E., Gougoulis, J., Lui, N., Pota, V., & Simons, J. (2017). *Generation Z: Global citizenship survey*. London: Varkey Foundation.

Gallup (2014). State of American schools. Retrieved from http://www.gallup.com/services/178709/state-america-schools-report.aspx.

Gershenson, S., Hart, C. M., Hyman, J., Lindsay, C., & Papageorge, N. (2018). The long-run impacts of same-race teachers. Retrieved from www.nber.org/papers/w25254.

Goldhaber, D., Theobald, R., & Tien, C. (2019). Why we need a diverse teacher workforce. *Phi Delta Kappan*, 100(5), 25–30.

Ingersoll, R., & May, H. (2016). Minority teacher recruitment, employment, and retention: 1987 to 2013. Retrieved from https://learningpolicyinstitute.org/product/minority-teacher-recruitment-brief.

NCES. (2018). Teaching and Learning International Survey (TALIS)—Welcome to TALIS 2018 Results. Retrieved from https://nces.ed.gov/surveys/talis/talis2018/.

PDK Poll. (2018). The 50th annual PDK poll of the public's attitudes toward the public schools: Teaching: great respect, dwindling appeal. *Phi Delta Kappan*, 100 (1), NP1–NP24. https://doi.org/10.1177/0031721718797117.

PDK Poll. (2019). The 51st annual PDK poll of the public's attitudes toward the public schools: Frustration in the schools: Teachers speak out on pay funding and being valued. Retrieved from https://pdkpoll.org/assets/downloads/2019pdkpoll51.pdf.

Pew Research Center. (2019). Generation z looks a lot like millennials on key social and political issues. Retrieved from www.pewsocialtrends.org/2019/01/17/generation-z-looks-a-lot-like-millennials-on-key-social-and-political-issues.

Sutcher, L., Darling-Hammond, L., & Carver-Thomas, D. (2016). A coming crisis in teaching? Teacher supply, demand, and shortages in the U.S. Retrieved from https://learningpolicyinstitute.org/product/coming-crisis-teaching.

Taie, S., & Goldring, R. (2019). *Characteristics of public and private elementary and secondary school principals in the United States: Results from the 2017–18 National Teacher and Principal Survey*. Washington, DC: National Center for Education Statistics.

U.S. Department of Education. (2016). The state of racial diversity in the educator workforce. Retrieved from www2.ed.gov/rschstat/eval/highered/racial-diversity/state-racial-diversity-workforce.pdf

Chapter 20

Supporting Teachers from Marginalized Communities

Michael Peña, Winter Marshall-Allen, Carlos Avila, Melissa Collins, Alhassan Susso, and Jill Davidson

Introduction

Michael Peña

In this chapter, we ask educators that represent a myriad of intersectional identities "What can we do to support all teachers in our education system?" Their stories and experiences can help us design a system that begins with equity rather than setting it as a goal. Their voices begin to bring clarity to the issue of retaining educators that do not fit within the dominant cultural structures that permeate our schools. While no one voice can represent the complexity of any identity, the narrative that runs through their words is clear: as the diversity of our students increases across the country, we need to support educators that are reflective of our communities. By doing this, we can build the strongest education system possible for our students and our democratic society.

Through My Eyes

Winter Marshall-Allen

When I think about the students for which I advocate, I see tomorrow's teachers. I see computer programmers, artists, and environmental scientists. If we want our students to achieve great things, we need to see them for who they are. Diversity and acceptance are the keys to reaching every learner.

How do I know this will work? Because I lived it.

As a bi-racial child with a vision impairment, my experience in public schools wasn't smooth. My mom is Mexican, blind, and a first generation American. My dad is African American and partially sighted; we both have glaucoma. The abuse and neglect they experienced in school molded their expectations for my teachers and school settings. My eyesight and visual presentation of a lazy eye led to social exclusion and a view that I was "less capable." With vision being a prevalent issue in my life, I was unaware of racial biases until middle school, when my parents had an IEP meeting and their ability to advocate for my right to learn became impeded. I remember the judgment they faced because they chose to get married and have a child—as if they caused my visual disability. Bi-racial marriages come with plenty of challenges.

It took a wonderful teacher who saw past my disability and recognized my intelligence before things changed. When I rebelled against my parent's divorce, it took the relationships to bring me back. It was the relationship with my Dad, our school's resource officer and a compassionate intervention from a school principal and counselor, before I believed I was important. Having educators support my needs in the classroom and as a person changed everything. It is that compassion and love which changed my life, and it's what directs my work as an educator.

Educators need opportunities to see all the ways learning can happen, especially for students with different backgrounds, ethnicity, and abilities. For example, a visual learner can have their vision obstructed and learn kinesthetically with auditory instructions. Educators today need training on not just the best practices for cultural sensitivity and social-emotional learning but training in applied behavior analysis. With this, educators can thoughtfully understand, shape, and redirect our own behaviors and student learning. In my twelve years as a special education teacher, I have learned that to truly reach my students, I must also reach out to my community. Teacher preparation programs can and should do more to prepare educators to understand policy and federal education law. Educators today need to connect to their communities, and the only way this will happen is with political action. This must include advocacy for funding and the fundamental value of all people.

Schools reflect our larger communities, and they must lead through acceptance and diversity. When schools hurt, the community hurts, and all of us must collectively act to fix it. I am a living example of what can happen if we get it right. If we embrace diversity and lead with acceptance, the students in our schools today will become tomorrow's great leaders.

Teachers Are an Investment

Carlos Avila

As an early career Latinx educator in New Mexico, I see that our students are not receiving equitable opportunities. To change this, teachers should be provided resources through meaningful, applicable professional development. The education system must treat educators as the professionals we are—and that includes paying all teachers as professionals, regardless of the community where they teach. When all schools are well funded, teachers have the resources needed to create transformative, innovative, and engaging lessons and environments where children can learn and thrive.

By providing opportunities for teachers to network and grow professionally schools can foster a community of learning with fresh insights and perspectives. Investment in our teachers is an investment in our education system and an investment in our communities. In order to revitalize and flip the system, teachers must be allowed to drive it. Each day we see the different needs of our students and do our best to meet them. Often, as we do this, we are struggling against uninformed mandates and policies created by those who never visit our classrooms. Teachers must be given autonomy, respect, trust, and flexibility if we want policy and practice to align.

My teacher certification program left me unprepared to face the challenges of my first classroom. I quickly realized that "inclusion" was little more than a word embedded in children's individualized education programs. Many of those children were not receiving the education they needed and deserved. The current system expects teachers to meet the needs of all children at all levels without providing the proper support to allow teachers to fulfill those needs. If children are at a 1st grade reading level yet are placed in a 6th grade inclusion setting with no support, we are setting these students up for failure. We cannot include students in the classroom without fully integrating them into the classroom and curriculum. If students cannot read or write, we must provide them the support needed to gain those skills. A love for reading is embedded by providing children with access to books—books that reflect their lives, their communities and their identity. Teaching should be authentic and driven by the needs of individual students and classrooms. We must collaborate and advocate for the prosperity of our profession and the quality education our students deserve.

The system needs to start valuing the work teachers do. This includes providing educators with time, respect, influence over education decisions, and support. We are expected to sacrifice more and more of our personal time to meet the needs of our students and our schools. When we focus too much on work, we lose opportunities to focus on ourselves: our wellbeing, our families, and our identities. Schools need to be culturally responsive to both students and staff. As a Latinx educator I represent marginalized voices and share the truth of historic events by moving away from the narratives of white privilege that permeate our textbooks. The autonomy and flexibility to teach to the heart should not be measured or emphasized by a test score when we want to make true and authentic connections.

Supporting Teachers of Color

Melissa Collins

The racial make-up of the teacher workforce has been stagnant over the past decade. According to *The State of Racial Diversity in the Educator Workforce*, Caucasian women make-up more than 80% of the educators in classrooms across America (U.S. Department of Education, 2016). Students of color have limited opportunities to learn in a school where teachers look like them. Racial diversity is essential to any workforce, including education. When students of color have a teacher of color, they are more likely to experience a culturally responsive classroom and an environment conducive to their learning.

Building a diverse teacher workforce requires a commitment from school systems to both recruit and retain teachers of color. When these teachers enter the profession, school systems must explicitly support them. They must be treated as professionals and valued for their important perspectives. Often, teachers of color are not recognized for their hard work and creativity when compared to their Caucasian counterparts. This lack of acknowledgment causes teachers of color to feel inadequate or marginalized. All teachers deserve to know their hard work is valued and appreciated.

Systems tend to reflect the values of majority cultures unless there is explicit attention paid to respecting all. To flip the system, those in power must be willing to intentionally focus on providing leadership opportunities to educators of color. Providing avenues for career advancement and pathways to share exceptional teaching practices leads to stronger collegial relationships and improved student academic achievement.

For the teaching profession to assume a leadership role in the education system, all teachers, including our teachers of color, must be trusted, respected, and supported. Right now, this isn't happening. There is a common misconception that teachers of color leave the profession because of the heavy workload, but my experience tells me they are leaving because they lack support. Ongoing mentorship programs, like those being instituted by the Center for Black Educator Development in Philadelphia, aid teachers in navigating through the curriculum, classroom management, parent communications, and being culturally responsive (Harris, 2019). These programs are essential, but district leaders need to ensure the culture and climate are favorable to learning and producing mentors that act as positive change agents. Instituted with purpose and focus on the needs of teachers of color, mentorship programs can have a positive impact on both new and veteran teachers, leading to highly effective instruction that allows students to excel academically.

To increase teacher diversity, school systems must seek to understand the experiences of our teachers of color and their motivation to enter and remain in the profession.

Support Teachers by Providing Inspiration and Collaboration Opportunities

Alhassan Susso

I became a better, wiser and a more effective teacher during my tenure as the 2019 New York State Teacher of the Year. By traveling to different schools and classrooms, learning different strategies and pedagogical approaches, participating in workshops, and conversing with educators that have diverse experiences and backgrounds from across the nation, I have grown as a teacher and a person. My experiences as a Muslim, African-American male teacher in the country's largest city helped inform and enlighten other teachers with whom I had the opportunity to collaborate, just as their narratives from rural and suburban areas, diverse cultures, and a host of other teaching environments helped me broaden my worldview.

But it should not have taken an award to get these rich experiences. All teachers should be afforded opportunities to cross-pollinate with other brilliant teachers. Avenues should be created in the profession for teachers to more actively explore innovative ideas sprouting up in classrooms across the nation. By harnessing the collective intelligence of teachers, we have the opportunity to improve the overall success of the profession. Teachers are often the best resource for other teachers.

An example of an effective program designed by teachers for teachers is *Elevating and Celebrating Effective Teachers and Teaching* (ECET2). This program was created for exceptional teachers to learn from each other and celebrate the teaching profession. Attending an ECET2 event was one of the most meaningful experiences I have had as a teacher because of how well the program was designed. American Federation of Teachers President Randi Weingarten said it best, "teaching is a profession in which capacity building should occur at every stage of the career—novices working with accomplished colleagues, skillful teachers sharing their craft, and opportunities for teacher leadership" (Strauss, 2016).

A crucial aspect of teaching that is discussed too infrequently is the social and emotional wellbeing of teachers. While discussions of the socio-emotional health of students abound, we often ignore the toll that the job of teaching takes on our educators. More teachers than ever are reporting anxiety and depression. By developing a culture that supports teachers' mental health we can mitigate some of the immense stress that the system pushes onto them, especially in high poverty areas.

I teach in one of the most impoverished areas of New York City, which experiences higher teacher turnover than wealthier neighborhoods (Independent Budget Office, 2014). These turnovers are perhaps the largest obstacle to creating the stable learning environments students like mine need. It should not come as a surprise that the biggest factor for the large turnover in impoverished areas, is teacher exhaustion. I see first-hand the emotional toll of teaching in poor school districts. In addition to being content teachers, we are expected to be language developers and social-emotional coaches. While we devote our full energy to our students, there are no structures in place for our own emotional wellbeing.

Finally, the best way to support teachers is to give them autonomy to experience and explore different opportunities in the teaching profession. Not every teacher wants to leave the profession to become a principal, but all teachers want the respect and agency that professionals deserve. Giving them these opportunities is an important step in providing the support they need to be excellent in their classrooms and in providing the feedback policy makers need to create a more equitable, flipped system.

Supporting Teachers in a Flipped System: A Transgender Perspective

Jill Davidson

I began my career as a school psychologist serving 10,000 students in 28 rural school districts in Oklahoma. Forty years later, I am serving 1,100 students in one comprehensive high school. I am also transgender, still employed 10 years after gender transition.

Being "transgender" means identifying as a gender different than assigned at birth. Each of us has a deep feeling of who we are. As an adult, my identity includes many aspects—I may describe myself as a psychologist, a Jew, a fiddle player, or a decent cook. These are all part of my identity, and these aspects appear at different times in our development. Gender, the sense of being a girl/woman, boy/man, both, or neither, develops very early. For most, this gender matches what they were assigned at birth based on appearance of genitalia. For some, there is a mismatch, with a strong feeling that they are a gender different than they were assigned. While many youths can socially transition at young ages, before they are in a profession, people in my generation did not become aware of options until well into adulthood, often choosing to postpone transitions until families were raised. This meant "coming out" and transitioning later, while employed. Many people would become well established in a career, only to move away, cutting all ties to family and profession and start life over.

After my transition, my previous privilege became visible to me. Before transition, there were occasions when a female speaker would be interrupted by someone to directly ask my opinion. Now, in staff meetings, when I express a contrary opinion, I sometimes notice a male team leader rolling their eyes and being dismissive of my comment. I have to work harder to establish my credibility on some topics, although I think relationships are easier to establish.

In an equitable "flipped system" where all teacher voices are respected and valued, I would be equally able to establish trusting relationships with students, staff, and parents regardless of gender, race, social class, or language status. The current reality is that we are all embedded in systems that need to be flipped, where certain privileges elevate some perspectives over others. Those privileges perpetuate inequity and can be difficult for each of us to see (especially if they benefit us personally) unless we are intentional about looking for them.

What do transgender staff, students, and family members need? Primarily, an infrastructure which protects us—state and local laws and school district policies that prohibit discrimination and harassment based on gender status. A person who transitions is still the same person they were before transition, and communication from colleagues and administrators that they will still be supportive post transition is helpful. It's important for students to see staff who look like them, including in leadership roles. This includes gender diversity more broadly, including equal numbers of women and men, cisgender and transgender, in visible positions of leadership.

Conclusion

Michael Peña

I am an antiracist educator.

Perhaps what I should say is that I am continually in the process of becoming one. That is my goal. I want to decolonize and deconstruct our education system; to rebuild it in such a way that students and educators from oppressed communities can begin to find healing. I want to see Ethnic Studies become not only a required course for every student but also as a pedagogical lens through which teaching and learning occurs. I want to see culturally relevant and sustaining practices as the foundation for today's students and tomorrow's societies. We are the products of the system, and yet we have power to change it.

In educational journalism, across social media platforms, and at conferences we hear the same query: "how do we recruit and retain educators of color?" In the previous chapter Kimberly Eckert showed that the recruitment issue requires comprehensive solutions rather than tweaks around the edges. The same is true, and reflected in the narratives above, when considering how we can retain teachers from historically marginalized communities. On a deep level we must consider how to create a system where students of color and other oppressed identities feel included in our schools. Flipping the system can only happen if we address this issue with the aim of undoing historic supremacist—White, Christian, male, straight, ableist, cis/heteronormative (the ideology that there are only two heterosexual genders)—cultures, upon which American public education has been built.

The contributors to this chapter show retaining educators from our marginalized and oppressed communities demands examining the conditions in which teachers work. Those conditions extend beyond our classrooms and schools. They include all places where education decisions are made, including districts and school boards that represent the community and hire teachers. They include our state superintendents' offices and state boards of education, where diversity is too often seen as a box to be checked. They include the political spaces where our education system is shaped, and curriculum decisions are made. They include our local, state, and national unions, where leaders must acknowledge and act on the rising wave of members focused on a new brand of racial and social justice-minded unionism.

Democracy can only serve society well if all have equal opportunity and influence. An education system in which each teacher is valued and supported because of their unique background and frame of reference is instrumental. If we learn from each of the perspectives above and others like them, we can begin to break systems of oppression and build a foundation for a flipped system.

References

Harris, R. (2019). Profiles in education equity—Sharif El-Mekki: Leading with equity and justice. Retrieved from https://edtrust.org/profiles-in-education-equity-sharif-el-mekki-leading-with-equity-and-justice.

Independent Budget Office. (2014). *Demographics and work experience: A statistical portrait of New York City's public school teachers*. New York: Independent Budget Office.

Strauss, V. (2016, September 9). What if Randi Weingarten were U.S. education secretary?. Retrieved from www.washingtonpost.com/news/answer-sheet/wp/2016/09/09/what-if-randi-weingarten-were-u-s-education-secretary-part-2-in-a-series/.

U.S. Department of Education. (2016). *The state of racial diversity in the educator workforce*. Washington, DC: U.S. Department of Education.

Chapter 21

Democratized Professional Learning

The Edcamp Model

Dan Callahan

In most school districts, professional development looks a lot like the top-down hierarchical education system that needs to be flipped: too much management and not enough leadership. One person, or maybe a small committee, decides what will be learned. Teachers are generally not involved in this decision-making process and are the recipients of mass-delivered, non-differentiated instruction—the exact opposite of what we expect them to facilitate in their own classrooms.

But it doesn't have to be this way. What if we designed professional learning around democratic leadership principles instead?

In 2010, I worked together with a fantastic group of educators from public, charter, and independent schools in the Philadelphia area to find out. Having previously attended an unconference[1] called Barcamp, we worked together to create an event based on the principles of Open Space Technology.[2]

We called it Edcamp. Edcamps are completely free to attend, participant-driven professional development events for educators and anybody with an interest in education. After a volunteer organizing team secures a space to hold the event and some funding, they advertise the event through their networks and work to make sure the day is well planned.

On the day of the Edcamp, participants arrive and check out the schedule that's been placed on the wall. It's a blank grid. It has some rooms and some times on its top and left axes, but everything else is empty. Over the course of the first hour, usually over breakfast, people meet with each other and talk about the things they're interested in. They make connections with new people and catch up with old friends.

There's no keynote at the beginning like you might have at a traditional conference or district professional development day, just a quick gathering where event organizers talk about how the day is going to work, and explain the Rule of Two Feet: you should always be learning or contributing, and if you're not, you should leave a room and find someplace else where you can be learning or contributing.

Then all in attendance collaborate to fill in the grid with sticky notes that have topics they would like to discuss and learn. One person who may want to talk about racial justice in schools puts that on a sticky note and puts it in a blank spot on the grid. They might meet in room 2 at 9:30 with anyone else who wants to explore that topic. Someone else may want to discuss pedagogy with technology. They might meet in room 4 at 10:30.

In a short period of time, the grid fills up, and then people go off to the rooms that interest them the most. The person who posted the sticky note in the grid is the room's host, facilitating the conversation or activity. They are not there to run a PowerPoint or lecture, but to have rich discussions with their peers, try out a new activity, or share resources. There's no one expert in the room; the room itself is filled with people sharing their collective knowledge from a wide range of expertise. Leadership in the room and across the entire event is fluid, with people stepping up when they have something worth sharing and stepping back when somebody else has something of value to add. It is truly a democratic event.

After the first Edcamp, we were intentional about further propagating the underlying democratic principles by creating a wiki with as much information as possible related to how we created Edcamp and what the structure of the day should look like. We actively encouraged other people to create their own Edcamps without asking for permission, only asking that they run a free event that followed the Edcamp format and the general principles of democratically designed professional development.

In 2010, seven more teams created their own Edcamps, from New Hampshire to Florida to Ohio. In 2011, educators across the United States organized 50 Edcamps. Hundreds of Edcamps are now hosted all over the world each year. They are supported in part by the non-profit Edcamp Foundation, which provides some centralized support, resources, and funding to teams getting started with their own Edcamps. (You can learn how to organize an event in your area or find an Edcamp near you on their website: www.edcamp.org.)

Even more important than the events themselves, though, is how the principles behind Edcamp have filtered into schools and districts as Edcamp participants go back to their workplaces. They leave empowered, inspired, and wanting more of their professional development to be democratically designed. I've had the privilege to work with dozens of schools to experiment with the Edcamp model as one aspect of a rich, fully developed professional learning program for its educators. Edcamp is a great tool to use to help teachers investigate their passions and interests, to explore progress on district and individual initiatives, or any other situation where there's no preconceived notion of what the outcome has to be.

Teachers are hungry for professional learning that is engaging and meets their needs. When opportunities are participatory and democratically designed, teachers grow, and students benefit. When participating in an Edcamp teachers form deeper connections around shared principles, discover areas of confusion and disagreement that need to be further addressed, learn about new tools and techniques to explore, and rediscover the value of having the time and space to talk about the things that matter most to them. They grow as professionals and practitioners and develop capacity as educational leaders. Edcamps and democratized professional learning experiences are critical aspects of flipping the system.

Notes

1 An unconference is a participant-driven meeting that eschews traditional top-down structure and sponsored sessions.
2 Open Space Technology is a self-organizing practice that releases the inherent creativity and leadership in people. More information can be found at openspace world.org.

Chapter 22

Pockets of Innovation

Transformational Professional Learning and Development

Trista Hollweck and Dyane Smokorowski

There has been an increased global focus on the importance of developing teachers to support student learning and achievement (Campbell et al., 2017). Teachers report that the business of teacher professional learning is a competitive space with a range of glitzy offerings jostling for their money. Whereas some provisions are focused on teacher growth, others are more aligned with school and system improvement agendas and commodifying educational theory and practice (Andrews & Munro, 2019). With no "one size fits all" model for teacher professional learning and development (PLD), there is value to be found in a variety of different approaches. There is also a robust international scholarship base that highlights successful and unsuccessful models (CUREE, 2012). For Campbell et al (2017), effective PLD components are:

- quality content, support and sustainability;
- a research-informed learning design; and
- an implementation process that is job-embedded, collaborative, and includes active and variable learning experiences.

PLD initiatives must challenge teachers into critical interrogation of practice and meet their needs at different stages in their careers (Hobson et al., 2009; Smith & Ingersoll, 2004). The aim of this chapter is to add to the conversation and highlight three well-established and bespoke transformational PLD initiatives in two disparate school districts that are successfully supporting experienced teachers.

As teacher leaders responsible for the design and development of PLD initiatives, the authors of this chapter know there are "pockets of innovation" worth celebrating in many jurisdictions around the world. Although these following initiatives seem quite different and occur in varied contexts, they share many similarities. Specifically, they were designed, developed and coordinated at a grassroots level by teachers for teachers and aim to offer participants choice, agency, and a robust community for collaborative professionalism (Hargreaves & O'Connor, 2018). Flipping the system includes honoring the professionalism of teachers through well-designed and structured PLD that values individual needs and responds to feedback.

We believe learning from one another about what incites growth, change, and improvement in experienced educators' practice unleashes the potential of transformational PLD and enables teachers to flourish in creating the schools our students deserve (Netolicky, 2020).

Defining the Terms

Professional Learning and Development

The terms *professional learning* and *professional development* are often ill-defined, conflicting, and conflated in the research and practice literature (Campbell, 2019). Because of these varied connotations, Fullan and Hargreaves's (2016) combined term of *professional learning and development* (PLD) is used in this chapter to describe how educators learn and grow as people and professionals. In this conceptualization, professional learning and professional development do not eclipse one another, but instead have mutual interaction and overlap: "In the end, there should be no development without learning, and learning can and often should entail development" (p. 4).

We believe outstanding PLD has potential to not only transform classroom practice, but also individuals, communities, and societies. It can enable educator relationships to thrive while challenging and disrupting established practices. Effective PLD is relevant, addresses individual teacher needs, is experiential and context-specific, leads to a significant change in teacher knowledge and understanding, influences professional practice, and ultimately improves student learning. It supports teachers in reflecting on, questioning and consciously improving their practice, and makes a positive difference in the lives of students and their communities.

Transformational PLD

All teachers need access to varied and personalized opportunities to build content knowledge, gain insights, and apply new understandings to their daily practices (Timperley, 2008). In this chapter, we are interested in the types of PLD that can actively shift cognition, emotion, and capacity. Netolicky (2020) sees *transformational PLD* as "experiences and processes that have an impact on what teachers and school leaders think, believe, feel, and do" (p. 18).

For us, transformational PLD explores real world connections to content, provides teachers with meaningful opportunities to engage intellectually, creatively, emotionally, socially, and/or physically through experiential learning, and embeds discussion and reflection. Through these design features, teachers can capture excitement for rigorous content that leads to exceptional classroom experiences for their students and increased learning.

Teacher Leadership

Teachers need to have agency in their own PLD for it to have relevance. The more they feel able to influence positive change, the more they develop teacher leadership. *Teacher leadership* refers to the set of skills demonstrated by teachers who continue to teach students but also have an influence that extends beyond the classroom (Danielson, 2006).

In the realm of PLD design, teacher leaders understand the evolving nature of teaching and learning, the evolution of established and emerging technologies, and the importance of the entire school community. Additionally, teacher leaders use information about adult learning theory to respond to the diverse learning needs of colleagues by identifying, promoting, and facilitating varied and differentiated PLD experiences (Teacher Leadership Exploratory Consortium, 2008).

Collaborative Professionalism

Collaboration, or collective participation, has been highlighted as one of the best ways to grow and develop teachers and improve teaching, learning and leading (Campbell et al., 2017; Drago-Severson & Blum-DeStefano, 2018). However, it is important to note that there is a body of literature showing collaboration can oftentimes be forced, performative, contrived, inauthentic, and thus, ineffective (Datnow & Park, 2018). Rather than facilitate groupthink, coerced compliance or "contrived collegiality," professional relationships should empower and inspire teachers (Hargreaves, 1994). For Hargreaves and O'Connor (2018), it is when the solidarity of safe, supportive, and trusting relationships is combined with the solidity of robust and rigorous content, focus, and structure, that *"collaborative professionalism"* is established. Specifically, collaborative professionalism needs to be deliberately designed and structured around effective practice, such as student learning, curriculum design, content knowledge and classroom pedagogy. Best stated by Carol Campbell (2019), "collaborative professionalism needs intentional work; it does not just happen" (p. 81). Teachers must have the autonomy to choose to work together and have the time to build respectful and trusting relationships that enable real issues to be raised, discussed and worked through.

Collaborative professionalism is not about being conflict-free or simply building teacher camaraderie. It is about creating powerful learning environments where teams can have courageous conversations, establish peer accountability, and cultivate a sense of collective teacher efficacy (Donohoo et al., 2018).

A Mentoring and Coaching Fellowship

Relatively unknown to most of Canada and even within the province of Quebec, the Western Quebec School Board (WQSB) provides English language education to 6655 students in a geographic area roughly the size of Ireland. Whilst most WQSB schools are situated in the urban core, the district also has a number of rural and northern schools. Historically, the WQSB has struggled to attract and retain teachers new to the district, especially in its rural locales. As such, in 2008, the WQSB introduced its homegrown and self-funded Teacher Induction Program (TIP), developed by a volunteer committee of teachers, administrators, and district leaders. In the WQSB, the TIP is conceived as a comprehensive and sustained PLD process that supports teachers new to the district (called teaching fellows) and seamlessly progresses them into a learning organization (Wong, 2004). As an established and mandatory district-wide initiative, the TIP has three clear aims:

1 Retain effective teachers new to the district;
2 Provide leadership and professional growth opportunities for veteran staff;
3 Improve teaching and learning.

Trista designed, developed and has co-coordinated this program since 2008. In addition, it was the topic of her doctoral work (Hollweck, 2017, 2019a, 2019b). Whereas research shows that beginning teachers benefit from effective induction programs, Trista's qualitative case study examined the impact of the mentor–coach role on experienced teachers' professional learning, practice and well-being.

Within the program all teaching fellows are paired with an administrator-selected mentor–coach as part of the TIP's Mentoring and Coaching Fellowship pillar. Mentor–coaches are most often a veteran teacher from the same school and content area as their fellows. Each mentor–coach and fellow pair is expected to observe the other's practice, meet regularly to set goals anchored in student learning, and reflect on professional growth. Each is also provided with two district-funded release days for self-directed PLD, often used to collaborate and observe other WQSB teachers.

Trista's study found that the success of the Fellowship hinges on mentor–coach effectiveness and that being an experienced teacher does not directly equate with effective mentoring and coaching. Study participants reported that it took three years to better understand the difference between mentoring and coaching and how to implement each approach well. In line with the research on effective PLD, mentor–coaches noted that they needed ongoing and differentiated support, training, and resources to guide the process. In response, the district established a Professional Learning Network (PLN) that met two to three times a year in order to build community and foster collaborative professionalism.

Collaborative professionalism is at the heart of the PLN. Mentor–coaches work together to examine and challenge each other about what it means to be effective. As one participant noted, this critical inquiry process "forces me to question myself. I go back to reflection and how I can better question myself and push myself through."

The PLN was found to improve mentoring and coaching in the district, help mentor–coaches grow as classroom practitioners, and develop teacher leadership. The PLN process also shaped experienced teachers' internal capacities for knowing, doing and being. Best explained by one study participant, "I have opened myself up to more possibilities. I have learned more about things, and had I not been a mentor–coach I probably would still be interested in learning—but not as keen to learn. I now have a much bigger toolkit to work with as a teacher."

According to another participant, the mentor–coach role not only enhanced their own professional practice but helped them better support and grow their colleagues: "my biggest learning experience is learning how to make a space for someone else to shine."

Ultimately, the power of teachers leading teachers within the mentoring and coaching fellowship of TIP was found to positively shift the professional culture of a school district.

Teacher Leader Cohorts

Andover Public Schools is a small, high performing district of 8,964 students spread across 11 campuses in south-central Kansas. Since 2005, the district has seen continuous growth in student population, staff, and technology purchases, which created challenges in supporting teachers. Dyane has served in a leadership role for the instructional technology and academic coaches in the district since 2014.

In an effort to design transformational PLD, a partnership between district administration, the technology department, and instructional technology coaches was formed in 2014 to design teacher leader cohorts with representatives from each of the district's 11 schools. Teachers were given five days of classroom release to participate in the initiative that explored new initiatives in educational technology, expanded professional learning networks through videoconferencing, and investigated school reform possibilities. In support, each had access to individual coaching sessions, book studies, and online technology skill challenges. Requirements were to share learning with colleagues, post classroom stories and teaching ideas on social media, agree to be a destination classroom for district tours and media visits, and participate in global collaboration opportunities. In exchange, each received a classroom set of either Chromebooks or iPads, priority access to both the district IT team and the instructional technology coaches for classroom support, post-graduate credits, and opportunities to beta-test any new technology for the district.

During the original one-year execution, teacher participants struggled to redefine their practice. In response, cohorts expanded to two-years allowing participants to integrate technology seamlessly into rigorous units of study and embrace global connections for student research. Interestingly, the biggest shift occurred when participants discovered the power of their own leadership capabilities. Instead of keeping new knowledge and skills inside the walls of their classrooms, participants gained a district and global mindset. They facilitated national Twitter chats, designed project-based learning units, inspired student activism in community issues, presented at national conferences, authored articles for national media outlets, partnered with community organizations, led district initiatives, and designed PLD for colleagues. After three rounds of teacher leader cohorts, many participants are drivers of district innovation and credit the experience for their professional growth:

> I always left feeling renewed and excited to implement different ideas into my classroom. I cared about it. It was valuable. It was created with me in mind, and I didn't want to nap during it. It was relevant. It gave me ideas for my classroom that I actually used. Your passion was evident. You kept us engaged and involved and learning. You let us move. You gave us a voice. You listened. You cared. I can't articulate how much I appreciate everything you did for us to provide valuable information and made it fun.

Teacher Field Trips

Teacher field trips that took participants off-campus evolved as transformational PLD from the teacher cohorts. The field trips provided teachers learning opportunities that were not readily available at school. Each experience was designed to align with participants' curriculum content and included a hands-on technology skills component. Teachers visited museums, explored underwater ecosystems at an aquarium, and worked alongside research scientists in a cancer laboratory. This type of PLD allows teachers to engage through different media and modalities to gain confidence in designing personalized, and experiential learning for their own students. For example, one cohort group was brought to a local comedy store for an improvisational theater workshop. There, they explored improvisational games that promote creativity, quick thinking, and communication skills. The experience also built community. Teachers engaged in purposeful play and discussed the social-emotional benefits of this type of learning. Another field trip took participants to the Kansas African American Museum where

they experienced cultural awareness training and discussed how local primary artifacts would strengthen classroom conversations.

In 2015, Dyane expanded the concept of teacher field trips into 3–4-day
excursions with the goals of:

1 increasing understanding of learning theory;
2 expanding teacher leadership;
3 rekindling passion for teaching; and
4 inspiring pedagogical innovation.

In these self-funded experiences beyond the local community, participants
toured schools of innovation and held educational roundtables with innovative teachers. Additionally, there were field trips to museums, research
centers, and zoos. Teachers reported these excursions and the accompanying
discussion and reflection ignited new thinking, sparked classroom project
ideas, and positively challenged their educational philosophies.

Conclusion

Captured above are three examples of transformational PLD inspired by
teacher leadership. Each district faces difficult decisions regarding resource
allocation, and funding often remains an ongoing challenge. However, teachers remain untapped professional experts. They also have a comprehensive understanding of their own needs and established relationships with
colleagues that should be harnessed. To flip the system, teachers need to be
trusted as professionals with autonomy and financial support for PLD. This
will allow them to collaboratively design the transformational PLD that will
expand the potential of our schools. We are thankful for the confidence
shown us by our respective districts and hope sharing these pockets of
innovation will start conversations in other districts enabling other teacher
leaders the opportunity to design locally relevant PLD experiences.

References

Andrews, J., & Munro, C. (2019). Coaching for agency: The power of professionally
respectful dialogue. In D. M. Netolicky, J. Andrews, & C. Paterson (Eds.), *Flip the
system Australia: What matters in education.*(pp.163–171). Abingdon: Routledge.
Campbell, C. (2019). Developing teacher leadership and collaborative professionalism to flip the system: Reflections from Canada. In Netolicky, D. M., Andrews, J.,
& Paterson, C. (Eds.), *Flip the system Australia: What matters in education*
(pp. 74–84). Abingdon: Routledge.
Campbell, C., Osmond-Johnson, P., Faubert, B., Zeichner, K., & Hobbs-Johnson, A.
(with Brown, S., DaCosta, P., Hales, A., Kuehn, L., Sohn, J., & Steffensen, K.).
(2017). *The state of educators' professional learning in Canada*: Final research
report. Oxford, OH: Learning Forward.

CUREE. (2012). *Understanding what enables high quality professional learning: A report on the research evidence.* Coventry: Centre for the Use of Research Evidence in Education.

Danielson, C. (2006). *Teacher leadership that strengthens professional practice.* Alexandria, VA: Association for Supervision & Curriculum Development.

Datnow, A., & Park, V. (2018). *Professional collaboration with purpose: Teacher learning towards equitable and excellent schools.* Abingdon: Routledge.

Donohoo, J., Hattie, J., & Eells, R. (2018). The power of collective efficacy. *Educational Leadership*, 75 (6), 40–44.

Drago-Severson, E., & Blum-DeStefano, J. (2018). *Leading change together: Developing educator capacity within schools and systems.* Alexandria: ASCD.

Fullan, M. & Hargreaves, A. (2016). *Bringing the profession back in: Call to action.* Oxford, OH: Learning Forward.

Hargreaves, A. (1994). *Changing teachers, changing times: Teachers' work and culture in the postmodern age.* New York: Teachers College Press.

Hargreaves, A., & O'Connor, M. (2018). *Collaborative professionalism: When teaching together means learning for all.* Thousand Oaks, CA: Corwin.

Hobson, A. J., Ashby, P., Malderez, A., & Tomlinson, P. D. (2009). Mentoring beginning teachers: What we know and what we don't. *Teaching & Teacher Education*, 25 (1), 207–216.

Hollweck, T. (2017). Threading the needle: Examining the Teacher Induction Program (TIP) in the Western Québec School Board. In Kutsyuruba, B, & Walker, K. (Eds.), *The bliss and blisters of early career teaching: A pan-Canadian perspective,* (pp. 205–226). Burlington, Ontario: Word & Deed Publishing.

Hollweck, T. (2019a). "I love this stuff!": A Canadian case study of mentor-coach well-being. *International Journal for Mentoring and Coaching in Education (IJMCE)*, 8 (4), 325–344.

Hollweck, T. (2019b). A patchwork quilt: A qualitative case study examining mentoring, coaching, and teacher induction in the Western Québec School Board. PhD dissertation. Retrieved from https://ruor.uottawa.ca/handle/10393/39919.

Netolicky, D. (2020). *Transformational professional learning: Making a difference in schools.* London: Routledge.

Smith, T. M., & Ingersoll, R. M. (2004). What are the effects of induction and mentoring on beginning teacher turnover? *American Educational Research Journal*, 41 (3), 681–714.

Teacher Leadership Exploratory Consortium. (2008, May). Teacher leader model standards. Retrieved from www.nnstoy.org/teacher-leader-model-standards.

Timperley, H. (2008). *Teacher professional learning and development: Educational practices series 18.* Brussels: International Academy of Education, International Bureau of Education & UNESCO.

Wong, H. K. (2004). Induction programs that keep new teachers teaching and improving. *NASSP Bulletin*, 88 (638), 41–58. Retrieved from http://newteacher.com/pdf/Bulletin0304Wong.pdf.

Epilogue
The Death and Life of the Teacher

Jelmer Evers

I envisioned writing a different epilogue to this wonderful book. As I'm writing this I've been quarantined at home for two weeks now due to the COVID-19 pandemic. Looking out over quiet streets in the medieval canals of Utrecht I am seeing the world grind to a halt. We're living through a global crisis, one which we have only read about in the history books. This is a crisis that has had educators worldwide scrambling to teach children online as 1.4 billion students are now out of school and at home.

When I started teaching seventeen years ago the world was in a completely different, more innocent place. Right from the start I loved teaching, but I was also struggling to survive. After gradually becoming better after five years I finally felt some room in my mind to take a look at the wider educational world around me. This was partially due to taking a new position at a place that exemplified to me what a school should be: a community based on trust, respect, collaboration and a true sense of agency. But when I examined our broader education system, I didn't like what I found. Decentralization, market incentives, new public management and top-down reforms—high stakes testing—had been remaking public education into a commodity and schools into would-be businesses.

These reforms had also profoundly reshaped our profession. Neoliberalism had led to the death of the teacher. Not literally, but "the death of the very idea that a teacher has something to contribute, the very idea that the teacher has a meaningful voice in regard to his work, to what he wants to achieve through his work and by which means he achieves it" (Evers & Kneyber, 2016, p. 3). My colleagues and I were no longer viewed as professionals, but as trained monkeys who simply had to follow "evidence"-based methods. The slow grind of this system had robbed too many colleagues of their moral core and agency, falling into what Étienne de La Boétie called *voluntary slavery*.

For a while I thought that, if only we could strive for democratic professionalism we could reclaim our professional autonomy. If we upheld our standards, engaged in continued professional development, expanded our networks, improved our practice and a deep professional dialogue we could convince politicians and society to trust us, invest in us so we could reclaim our collective autonomy and start building school communities and educational systems based on the principles of trust and collaboration.

I still believe that this flipped system is the foundation for educational quality and equity. But what we underestimated was how far our societies and politics had already been undermined by an economic-political system that benefits the 1% at the expense of the rest of us. After the 2008 crash, austerity and privatization gutted our schools and other public services even more. And after forty years of being constantly bombarded with the virtues of individualism and consumerism we lacked the knowledge, language, ideas and ultimately power to stop the slide into a darker time.

Societies can only take so much. Brexit was a wakeup call and the subsequent United States election of Donald Trump hammered home the fact that history had not ended in 1989 (Fukuyama, 1992). As the Cold War came to a close, we were supposedly entering an era where democracy and capitalism were the sole ideological victors of the 20th Century. Markets would prevail. We were lulled into a false sense of security whilst the foundations were steadily crumbling beneath us. The COVID-19 pandemic is showing us the extent of the damage. Inequality has returned to 19th Century levels. In the United States—the richest country in the history of the world—many people don't have access to healthcare and/or quality education. Right wing extremist political movements are on the rise globally and the pandemic is offering authoritarians a pretense to suspend the rule of law. And whilst teachers are engaging in a herculean effort to move to online education, Big Tech companies are already moving to profit from this disruption by pushing personalized and privatized learning—ruthless disaster capitalism veiled in progressive jargon.

But the pandemic is also opening up another future. Suddenly those who have borne the brunt of the neoliberal assault on our societies for the last forty years, like teachers and nurses, are being hailed as vital professionals. And many underpaid and undervalued key workers are the ones keeping our society functioning whilst the managerial class sits at home. And suddenly there is much money available as needed to save the economy, whereas before we were told there was none. In the past few years we've seen teachers have to go on massive strikes just to defend the status quo.

A better, more democratic and more equitable future won't come about by itself. We have to relearn the language of solidarity and relearn how to organize ourselves. We need to escape the confines of the present moment and our immediate surroundings. Looking back at our history opens up a world of possibilities for our future. John Dewey not only theorized about and practiced education and democracy. He came to the logical conclusion that education by itself is not enough. He also acted on that belief; he was one of the co-founders of the American Federation of Teachers (AFT):

> If teachers are workers who are bound in common ties with all other workers, what action do they need to take? … Ally themselves with their friends against their common foe, the privileged class, and in the alliance develop the character, skill and intelligence that are necessary to make a democratic social order a fact.
>
> (Dewey, 2010, p. 158)

There have been so many teacher activists across the globe who came to the same conclusion: engaging only in the classroom is not enough. Their resolve against all odds offers hope. They helped eliminate child labor, organized for universal suffrage, built free public education for all. In more recent history West-Virginia educators led by example, lighting a flame that inspired teachers around the globe when they went on strike in 2018.

Yes, in a lot of ways the dream of 1989 has turned into a nightmare, but these examples and this book show that it is up to us to reclaim that future. When we breathe life into the teaching profession and our schools, we breathe life into our societies. Public schools are the bedrocks of our communities and democracy. It is there, in our schools and communities—with our students, who are the future—that we will find hope. We will be the role models that show our children the way forward.

This is why this book matters. It is why all the contributions within it matter. Collectively their voices show a world of possibilities for our colleagues. They give hope and direction where before, for many, there was none. Look into the past, beyond the confines of our classrooms and schools, across borders at our fellow educators. There we will see that collectively we can and will rise to the moment that has been thrust upon us.

And just like the other Flip the System books I'd like to finish with this counsel from Hilel the Elder:

> If I am not for myself, who will be for me? And if I am only for myself, what am "I"? And if not now, when?

References

Dewey, J. (2010). *Teachers, leaders, and schools: Essays by John Dewey* (edited by S. F. Stack & D. J. Simpson). Carbondale, IL: Southern Illinois University Press.

Evers, J., & Kneyber, R. (2016). *Flip the system: Changing education from the ground up*. Abingdon: Routledge.

Fukuyama, F. (1992). *The end of history and the last man*. New York: Free Press.

Contributors

Carlos Avila is a second-year educator in Southern New Mexico. As a Latinx and Gay educator he strives to make education inclusive and culturally responsive. With the support of local partnerships and the National Educators Association he has led initiatives that expand support for students, schools, and communities.

Gert Biesta, author of *The Beautiful Risk of Education* (2014), *The Rediscovery of Teaching* (2017), and other books, is professor of public education at Maynooth University, Ireland, professorial fellow in educational theory and pedagogy at the University of Edinburgh, UK, and visiting professor at the University of Agder, Norway.

T. Jameson Brewer, Ph.D. is an assistant professor of social foundations of education at the University of North Georgia. He is co-editor of *Teach For America Counter-Narratives: Alumni Speak Up and Speak Out* (2015). His work has been published in numerous peer-reviewed journals, the National Education Policy Center, *Progressive Magazine*, *Huffington Post*, *Washington Post*, and *Education Week*.

Dan Callahan is an award-winning educator in technology and professional development and is a co-founder of the Edcamp movement. He taught students with special needs in Upper Darby, PA, and technology in Burlington, MA. Dan now works as a Training & Professional Learning Specialist for the Massachusetts Teachers Association.

Melissa Collins, National Board Certified and a Global Teacher Prize Finalist, teaches elementary school in Memphis, TN. She is a recipient of the NEA Horace Mann Award for Teaching Excellence, Presidential Award for Excellence in Mathematics and Science Teaching, National Science Teaching Association Sylvia Shurgrue Award, and West Tennessee Teacher of the Year.

Mairi Cooper, the orchestra director at Fox Chapel Area High School and President of the Pennsylvania Teachers Advisory Committee, believes it is imperative to offer quality public education to every child. Mairi is the 2015–2016 Pennsylvania Teacher of the Year, a Carson Scholars' Power of Excellence recipient, and a Yale University Distinguished Music Educator.

Beth Davey, the 2018 Missouri State Teacher of the Year, is a music teacher at Iveland Elementary School in the Ritenour School District.

Jill Davidson, a school psychologist in Poulsbo, WA, is interested in children's learning strategies, the management of aggressive behavior in children, and gender identity issues. She is the author of *Undercover Girl: Growing up Transgender.*

Kimberly Eckert, a 2020 Global Teacher Prize Finalist and 2018 Louisiana Teacher of the Year, is an Educators Rising Teacher and Innovative Programs Coordinator at West Baton Rouge Parish Schools. She was a NEA Social Justice Activist of the Year finalist in 2019 and the 2018 Louisiana Public Interest Fellow.

Jelmer Evers, a history teacher and union activist in Utrecht, Netherlands, is co-editor of *Het Alternatief* and *Flip the System: Changing Education from the Ground Up,* which launched the international Flip the System movement. He is a two-time Global Teacher Prize Finalist and active transformer of the Dutch education system.

Jinni Forcucci is the 2018 Delaware Teacher of the year, a member of the state's Diverse and Learner Ready Teacher Team, co-leader of Sussex Technical High School's Equity Team and has given a TED-Ed Talk on self-awareness, implicit bias and truth-telling.

Tracey Fritch, a seventh grade ELA teacher in the Rose Tree Media School District, has worked as a classroom teacher, reading specialist, K-8 literacy coach, and consultant in public and private schools. She is a member of the Pennsylvania Teachers Advisory Committee and 2014 Pennsylvania Teacher of the Year Finalist.

Andy Hargreaves was the Thomas More Brennan Chair in Education at the Lynch School of Education at Boston College until 2018. He has consulted with the OECD, the World Bank, governments, universities and teacher unions worldwide. His 30+ books have attracted multiple outstanding writing awards, and he is ranked by *Education Week* in the top 20 scholars with most influence on US education policy.

Trista Hollweck is a *pracademic*, straddling the worlds of research, policy and practice. She is a former teacher, vice-principal, and district consultant. She now serves as a Part-Time Professor (University of Ottawa) and Director for the ARC Education, a global educational movement advancing equity, broad excellence, inclusion, wellbeing, democracy, sustainability, and human rights in professionally run systems.

Kelly D. Holstine is the Director of Educational Equity at OutFront Minnesota and the 2018/2019 MN State Teacher of the Year (the first out LGBTQ+ teacher and second alternative educator to be named). She taught English for twelve years and is a founding member of Tokata Learning Center.

Lindsey Jensen is the 2018 Illinois Teacher of the Year and a 2020 California Casualty Awardee. She is Vice-President of the Illinois State Teachers of the Year Chapter, Vice-President of the Dwight Education Association, and she serves on the Illinois State Board of Education State Preparation and Licensure Board.

Noah Karvelis is a PhD student at the University of Wisconsin-Madison. Previously, he worked in Phoenix, Arizona as an elementary school teacher, union president, and co-founder of Arizona Educators United.

Mandy Manning, the 2018 United States National Teacher of the Year, taught English and math to newly arrived refugee and immigrant students. She is currently digital content specialist for the Washington Education Association.

Winter Marshall-Allen is a Special Education Teacher of 12 years. She is passionate about Native and ethnic student needs, cultural preservation, and the inclusion of students with special education needs in public school settings. She has worked actively with her unions to amplify these issues and address student needs.

Kristen Nichols is in nursing school with hopes of focusing on equity in healthcare. She was a speaker at the 2019 Delaware Department of Education Equity Summit. Since encouragement from her 10th grade English teacher, she has written about her experiences as one of few students of color in her accelerated classes.

Estella Owoimaha-Church, a Global Teacher Prize Finalist, is founder and executive director of Education Ensemble—a nonprofit cultivating inclusive, creative spaces for youth by fostering community and utilizing art as a form of direct-action. A first-generation American of Nigerian and Samoan descent, Estella's passions lie at the intersections of racial justice and arts education. She is committed to ensuring marginalized youth have equitable access to education.

Josh Parker, 2012 Maryland Teacher of the Year, Lowell Milken Unsung Hero Fellow, and NEA Global Fellow, has served within the Baltimore/Washington D.C. corridor as an ELA Instructional Coach, Language Arts Department Chair, Secondary Language Arts teacher, professor and compliance specialist. He is currently Director of Engagement and Programs at Unbound Ed.

Michael Peña, a Biology teacher who administers the social media presence for *Ethnic Studies Now! Washington*. An advocate for racial and social justice, he is currently working to reimagine educator's unions as member-driven antiracist organizations.

Amanda U. Potterton, Ph.D. is an Assistant Professor in the Department of Educational Leadership Studies in the College of Education at the University of Kentucky. Prior to pursuing her Ph.D. she was a special education teacher and New York City Teaching Fellow, and has taught in the United Kingdom.

Pasi Sahlberg, a professor of education policy at the Gonski Institute for Education at University of New South Wales, has worked as schoolteacher, teacher educator, researcher, policy advisor, and has studied education systems and advised education reforms around the world. His book, *Finnish Lessons 2.0: What Can the World Learn from Educational Change in Finland,* won the Grawemeyer Award.

Dennis Shirley is Professor of Education at the Lynch School of Education and Human Development at Boston College. His most recent book is entitled *The New Imperatives of Educational Change: Achievement with Integrity.* He is Editor-in-Chief of the *Journal of Educational Change.* A former English and history high school teacher, he holds a doctorate from Harvard University.

Sean Slade, Senior Director of Global Outreach at ASCD, has written for the *Washington Post* and the *Huffington Post*, and published with ASCD, Routledge and Human Kinetics. He is vice president for advocacy at the International Union for Health Promotion and Education (North America), on the OECD 2030 Future of Education Task Force and UNESCO Chair on Health and Education.

Dyane Smokorowski is a 2019 National Teacher Hall of Fame Inductee, the 2013 Kansas Teacher of the Year, and is currently serving as an Innovation and Technology Lead Teacher in the Andover Public Schools in Kansas.

Michael Soskil, co-author of *Teaching in the Fourth Industrial Revolution: Standing at the Precipice*, was 2017–2018 Pennsylvania Teacher of the Year. In 2016, Dr. Stephen Hawking announced him as one of the top 10 teachers in the world and a finalist for the Global Teacher Prize. In addition to fighting for teacher agency, he helps students take action for social good as an elementary STEM teacher.

Howard Stevenson is Professor of Educational Leadership and Policy Studies in the School of Education, University of Nottingham. He has researched and written extensively on teacher trades unionism, including several international studies for organizations such as Educational International and the European Trade Union Committee for Education. He has worked in both K-12 and higher education sectors and has been a union activist while working in schools and universities.

Karli Sunnergren was the Sussex Technical HS valedictorian in 2019. She studies biological sciences at the University of Delaware. Her passion for equity, developed while realizing her position of privilege in a system in high school, led her to speak at the 2019 Delaware Department of Education Equity Summit.

Alhassan Susso is the 2019 New York State Teacher of the Year, a 2017 Global Teacher Prize Finalist and recipient of the 2020 NEA Award for Teaching Excellence. He teaches Government, Economics and Personal Development at the International Community High School in New York City and is author of *The Light of Darkness: The Story of the Griots' Son.*

Melissa Tomlinson, a special education teacher in New Jersey, found her passion for being a public education advocate when she joined the Badass Teachers Association (BATs). Fighting for educational equity for all students, Melissa currently serves as the Executive Director of BATs and is an active member of the New Jersey Education Association.

Index

Note: page references in bold indicate tables; italics indicate figures.